Oscar Wilde: the aftermath

by the same author

ROOM 3603

THE RISE OF CASTLEREAGH

THE EMPRESS CATHERINE AND PRINCESS DASHKOV

LONDONDERRY HOUSE AND ITS PICTURES

PRINCESS LIEVEN

JUDGE JEFFREYS

MEXICAN EMPIRE

JOHN LAW

A VICTORIAN HISTORIAN: LETTERS OF W. E. H. LECKY

PRIVACY AND THE PRESS

TRIALS OF OSCAR WILDE

MR AND MRS BEETON

CASES THAT CHANGED THE LAW

CARSON

TRIAL OF CRAIG AND BENTLEY

UNITED IN CRIME

THE STRANGE DEATH OF LORD CASTLEREAGH

SIR PATRICK HASTINGS: HIS LIFE AND CASES

TRIAL OF SIR ROGER CASEMENT

With the Marchioness of Londonderry, D.B.E.

THE RUSSIAN JOURNALS OF MARTHA AND CATHERINE WILMOT

MORE LETTERS FROM MARTHA WILMOT: IMPRESSIONS OF VIENNA

With G. R. Falkiner Nuttall

AIR DEFENCE AND THE CIVIL POPULATION

With John Kisch

AN INTERNATIONAL CASE BOOK OF CRIME

OSCAR WILDE: THE AFTERMATH

by

H. Montgomery Hyde

FARRAR, STRAUS & COMPANY
NEW YORK

Library of Congress catalog card number 63-20020
First printing, 1963
Manufactured in the United States of America

TO THE MEMORY

OF THOSE WHO HAVE TOILED

IN THE CAUSE OF

PENAL REFORM

'The prison style is absolutely and entirely wrong. I would give anything to be able to alter it when I go out. I intend to try.'

De Profundis

'It is not the prisoners who need reformation. It is the prisons.'

Letter to the *Daily Chronicle*, May 28, 1897

'I know not whether Laws be right,
  Or whether Laws be wrong;
All that we know who lie in gaol
  Is that the wall is strong:
And that each day is like a year,
  A year whose days are long.'

The Ballad of Reading Gaol

Contents

Acknowledgements

THE author wishes to express his sincere thanks to the following, who have assisted him in the preparation of this book, by kindly permitting quotation from copyright material, by readily supplying information in their possession and by usefully helping in other ways: the former Home Secretary, Major G. Lloyd George, M.P. (now Lord Tenby), and the staff of the Home Office and Her Majesty's Prison Commission; Mr W. J. Harvey, Governor of H.M. Prison, Pentonville; Mr F. C. Ransley, Governor of H.M. Prison, Wandsworth; Mr E. E. Gregory and the Rev L. C. Harman, Governor and Chaplain of H.M. Borstal Institution, Reading; Mr Rupert Hart-Davis; the Controller, H.M. Stationery Office; the Office of Information; the Director, Dr L. C. Powell, and staff of the William Andrews Clark Memorial Library, University of California, Los Angeles; Mr Hugh Klare and Miss D. H. Reekie, Secretary and Assistant Secretary of the Howard League for Penal Reform; the late Sir Max Beerbohm; Lord Burnham; Mr E. W. Colman, executor and trustee in the estate of the late Lord Alfred Douglas; Lady Alistair Graham; William Heinemann Ltd; Mr and Mrs Donald Hyde; Mr Laurence Irving; Sir Shane Leslie, Bt; Mr C. E. May, photographer, of Reading; Mr G. W. Nash, Curator of the Gabrielle Enthoven Collection, Victoria and Albert Museum; Mr Hesketh Pearson; Radio Times Hulton Picture Library; the late Mrs Margery Ross; Sir John Rothenstein; M. Guillot de Saix; Mr Martin Secker; Mrs A. M. Sherard; Mr G. R. Sims; Sotheby and Co.; the late Mr Allan Wade; and Mr J. Alan White, Chairman of Methuen and Co., Ltd.

Note on Authorities

THE following are the principal abbreviations used in the footnote references:

Adey MSS=Papers of More Adey. In the possession of H. Montgomery Hyde.

After Reading=*After Reading. Letters of Oscar Wilde to Robert Ross.* [Edited by Stuart Mason]. London, 1921.

After Berneval=*After Berneval. Letters of Oscar Wilde to Robert Ross.* Edited by More Adey. London, 1922.

Clark MSS=Letters of Oscar Wilde to Robert Ross, More Adey, Lord Alfred Douglas and others. In the William Andrews Clark Memorial Library, University of California, Los Angeles.

Dulau Sale Catalogue=*A Collection of Original Manuscripts, Letters and Books of Oscar Wilde, including his Letters written to Robert Ross from Reading Gaol.* Dulau and Co. Ltd. London [1928].

Glaenzer Sale Catalogue=*The Library of Richard Butler Glaenzer. A Remarkable Assemblage of Manuscripts, Autograph Letters, Presentation Copies and Rare Editions of Oscar Wilde.* New York, 1911

H–D=*The Letters of Oscar Wilde.* Edited by Rupert Hart-Davis. London, 1962.

Harris=Frank Harris. *Oscar Wilde. His Life and Confessions*, 2 vols. New York, 1916.

Home Office Papers=Files Nos. A.56887/1–25 of the Secretary of State. In the Home Office.

Home Office (Prison Commission) Papers=Files Nos. 13629/1–83 of the Prison Commissioners. In the Home Office.

Kern Sale Catalogue=*The Library of Jerome Kern.* 2 vols. New York, 1929.

Mason=Stuart Mason. (Christopher Millard). *Bibliograpy of Oscar Wilde.* London, 1914.

Stetson Sale Catalogue=*The Oscar Wilde Collection of John B. Stetson, Jr.* New York, 1920.

Turner MSS=Letters of Oscar Wilde to Reginald Turner. In the possession of Mr and Mrs Donald Hyde, Somerville, New Jersey, U.S.A.

Except where otherwise stated, all references to *De Profundis* are to the text, edited by Mr Vyvyan Holland and published in London in 1949.

Foreword

'ALL trials are trials for one's life, just as all sentences are sentences of death and three times have I been tried', wrote Oscar Wilde from Reading Gaol in the concluding passages of *De Profundis*. 'The first time I left the box to be arrested, the second time to be led back to the house of detention, the third time to pass into a prison for two years.' Thus Wilde summarized the catastrophe which befell him at the Old Bailey in 1895, when he was at the height of his powers and reputation as a writer and talker.

Shortly after the last war, I completed an account of these three criminal trials, in which Wilde was the central figure. This appeared as *The Trials of Oscar Wilde* in 1948 and formed a volume in the Notable British Trials Series under the imprint of William Hodge & Co. It was by far the fullest account which had hitherto been published of these remarkable legal proceedings, and it contained a noteworthy foreword by the distinguished judge, Sir Travers Humphreys, who had been engaged as a junior counsel in all three trials. The widespread interest aroused by this book encouraged me to consider a sequel to the court-room story and to give an account of Wilde's prison experiences, and his writings which were the direct outcome of those experiences, based on all the existing documentary and other sources of information. This forms the subject of the present volume.

In the preparation of this work, I encountered a serious initial difficulty, which it took me a little time to overcome. The principal documentary source material consists of the Secretary of State's papers and the Prison Commission papers, both of which continue to be preserved in the Home Office. Early in 1954, I wrote to the then Home Secretary, Sir David Maxwell Fyfe, as he then was, requesting permission to see these particular records. The Minister replied that access to the papers had always been restricted, and that, as they had not yet been made open to public inspection at the Public Record Office, he was sorry he could not help me by lifting the restriction.

About three months later, I again approached the Home Secretary and repeated my request, and once more I met with a refusal. Being a Member of Parliament, I then had recourse to putting down a parliamentary question, or rather two questions, on the subject, for oral answer by the Minister in the House of Commons. The questions duly appeared on the Order Paper for June 24, 1954. In answering them, the Home Secretary declined to depart from the attitude he had previously taken up in correspondence with me. But the occasion enabled several Members from both sides of the House to express their views. The official report is as follows:

IMPRISONMENT OF OSCAR WILDE

(Official Correspondence)

Mr MONTGOMERY HYDE (Belfast, North, U.U.) asked the Secretary of State for the Home Department (1) why access to the official correspondence in his Department relating to the imprisonment of Oscar Wilde continues to be restricted: and whether he will now deposit these papers in the Public Record Office:

(2) why he has refused to allow the hon. and learned Member for Belfast North, to see the papers relating to the imprisonment of Oscar Wilde, which are in his official custody.

Sir D. MAXWELL FYFE (Home Secretary, West Derby, C.): Papers relating to ex-prisoners are withheld from public inspection until sufficient time has elapsed to diminish the possibility of their disclosure giving pain to living persons. I do not think I would be justified in making an exception to this practice in the case of Oscar Wilde.

Mr MONTGOMERY HYDE: Is my right hon. and learned Friend aware that this correspondence is of considerable interest to students of English penal history and prison conditions in the last century? It concerns a matter which occurred almost 60 years ago, and should it not conform to the declared policy of my right hon. and learned Friend's predecessor in office, that departmental papers down to 1900 should be made available for public inspection?

Sir D. MAXWELL FYFE: I cannot think that the aspect mentioned by my hon. and gallant Friend in his first sentence would be the primary motive for the disclosure of these documents. With regard to the rest of his supplementary question, I must maintain the position as I have stated it.

Mr E. SHINWELL (Easington, Lab.): Does not the right hon. and learned Gentleman realise that the hon. and gallant Member who asked this question is a prolific writer of articles and books on this subject and is only anxious to augment his own income?

Sir D. MAXWELL FYFE: I think it goes far beyond the Question to discuss the merits and the interests of my hon. and gallant Friend.

Mr MONTGOMERY HYDE: Is my right hon. and learned Friend aware that my request was made for the purpose of conducting a genuine piece of historical research and, further, that access to such papers much later than the year 1897 has been granted to other applicants? Why should an exception be made in this case?

CAPTAIN L. P. S. ORR (Down, South, U.U.): On a point of order. Is not the imputation made by the right hon. Gentleman against my hon. and learned Friend a thoroughly improper and quite unwarrantable one?

Mr E. SHINWELL: Do you appreciate, Mr Speaker, that I was only anxious to point out that hon. Members are frequently in the position of having to augment their incomes?

Mr F. HARRIS (Croydon, North West, C.): Am I not right in thinking that it is the desire of hon. Members opposite to augment their incomes at the present time?

Mr WOODROW WYATT (Birmingham, Aston, Lab.): Is not the Home Secretary aware that he is creating a precedent in refusing this hon. and gallant Friend or anybody else access to the documents in question? In the ordinary way, would they not already have gone to the Public Record Office? Surely, he must give the House some explanation why he is for ever going to deny people research into this very interesting historical event?

Sir D. MAXWELL FYFE: I give the House what I think is a perfectly reasonable explanation, namely, that I must consider the possibility of disclosure giving pain to living persons. By that I must stand.

Mr RICHARD STOKES (Ipswich, Lab.): How does the right hon. and learned Gentleman reconcile the attitude he is now adopting to the attitude taken in connection with another matter, where the persons are living and were caused great inconvenience?

Sir D. MAXWELL FYFE: That was a different matter. That was concerned with trials that were held in camera for reasons of security. The late Government agreed to relax those conditions when the security requirements disappeared, and I have followed their procedure.

MR MONTGOMERY HYDE: In view of the unsatisfactory nature of my right hon. and learned Friend's reply, I beg to give notice that I shall raise this matter on the Adjournment.

CAPTAIN ORR: On a point of order. I wonder, Mr Speaker, if you would give a Ruling on my point of order in view of the imputation?

MR SPEAKER: It is not proper for an hon. Member to make an imputation against another, or to state that a motive that has not been avowed by a Member has actuated him. It is in order for hon. Members to ask questions about matters in which they are personally interested and, therefore, I do not think that in this case a point of order arises.

MR SHINWELL: You do appreciate, Mr Speaker, that there was no question of an imputation against the hon and gallant Member? In such cases as this, is it not the practice to disclose one's interest?

MR SPEAKER: Not at Question time. I have ruled on this before. I found nothing wrong with putting down the Question, and I found nothing wrong in the remark.[1]

A fortnight later, Wilde's only surviving son, Mr Vyvyan Holland, was good enough to send the Home Secretary a letter, in which he asked that an exception to the general rule should be made in my favour. 'Besides myself and my young son,' wrote Mr Holland, 'there are no descendants of my father or of my grandfather alive today. Nor, indeed, so far as I am aware, are there any close relatives living. My only brother, Cyril, who was killed in action in the first War, was unmarried. My father's only brother, his senior by two years, had one child, a daughter, who also died unmarried, while his only sister, my aunt, died in infancy. Consequently I am the only living person whose feelings might be pained by the disclosure of these documents to the public.' Mr Holland went on to point out that my claim was rather a special one, since I had made a close study of his father's life and writings. In these circumstances he asked that I should be allowed to see the papers, suggesting that we might examine them together, as he himself was also naturally interested to know what they contained. This request likewise met with a refusal.

During the few weeks that remained before the House rose for the summer recess, I had hoped to raise the matter in an adjournment debate. But on each occasion I balloted for the

[1] *Parliamentary Debates, House of Commons,* 5th Series, vol. 529, cols. 586–88 (June 24, 1954); *The Times,* June 25, 1954.

choice of subject, I was unsuccessful. So the matter remained, and I could do nothing further during the recess. However, in the meantime there had been a change in the office of Home Secretary, and on the reassembly of the House in the autumn, I made a point of speaking to the new Minister, Major Gwilym Lloyd George. He promised to have the matter reconsidered. Rather to my surprise, he informed me by letter, on November 26, 1954—for I was becoming reconciled to the policy of official refusals–that he had decided to allow me to see the papers, provided that I submitted any material based on these documents which I wished to publish. 'The position has been somewhat changed by the Report of the Committee on Departmental Records which sat under Sir James Grigg', he added in his letter, 'and I have also taken into account the fact that Mr Vyvyan Holland has expressed the hope that your request may be granted.' The Committee referred to by the Home Secretary, which sat under the chairmanship of a distinguished retired civil servant and former Minister of the Crown, had recently recommended that, save in exceptional circumstances, all departmental records should be opened to public inspection after fifty years.[1]

A preliminary examination of the restricted papers in the Home Office, at which Mr Holland was present as well as myself, revealed the existence of no less than 108 files relating to Oscar Wilde's imprisonment. Many of these concern matters of a more or less routine character, such as applications for visits and periodic reports by the Governors and medical officers in the three prisons in which Wilde served out his sentence. But there is much else of a more personal character, particularly the report of two specialists from Broadmoor on Wilde's mental condition, which resulted in his transfer to Reading, and various petitions from the prisoner himself asking for books and writing materials and for remission of the last months of his sentence. There are also interesting petitions from his solicitors and from his friend, Lord Alfred Douglas, praying for his early release, as well as hitherto unknown details of the composition of the long letter, which he wrote from prison to his friend, and which is known to the world as *De*

[1] *Committee of Departmental Records Report*. Cmd. 9163, presented to Parliament, July, 1954. See also *Parliamentary Debates, House of Commons*, 5th Series, vol. 543, cols. 957–60 (July 5, 1955).

Profundis. This remarkable mass of material forms the main basis of this book.

The other principal sources of information consist of Wilde's prison and post-prison correspondence with various friends. His letters to Robert Ross, More Adey and Lord Alfred Douglas (except the *De Profundis* letter which is in the British Museum), amounting to about 200 in all, are preserved in the William Andrews Clark Library in the University of California, Los Angeles.[1] Those to Reginald Turner are in another American collection, that of Mr and Mrs Donald Hyde, of Somerville, New Jersey. With the exception of a small privately printed edition of the Wilde-Douglas letters by the late Mr William Andrews Clark, nothing beyond a few brief extracts from this correspondence was published until the appearance of the definitive edition of *The Letters of Oscar Wilde* by Rupert Hart-Davis in 1962.[2] All the originals I was fortunately able to see during a visit to the United States in 1953, and again in 1957. An interesting MS letter, also previously unpublished, written from Reading to his friend and future biographer Robert Sherard, is in my own collection and is reproduced in facsimile in the present volume. Besides this, I possess the original correspondence which took place during Wilde's imprisonment between his friend, More Adey, and the solicitors instructed on his and his wife's behalf, in regard to his bankruptcy, marriage settlement, contemplated divorce proceedings, and the custody and guardianship of his children.[3] Finally, there is the interesting exchange of letters about the publication of *The Ballad of Reading Gaol*, which Wilde carried on with his eccentric publisher, Leonard Smithers. These are scattered through various collections, including the Clark Library and the Yale University Library: some of them were disposed of at the Glaenzer, Stetson and Kern sales in New York and are now in private hands. However, it has been possible to have most of these in some form, and they have since been included by Mr Hart-Davis in his work.

It is altogether a large store-house of material. I have supplemented it with the published accounts written by those of

[1] Acquired after auction in Dulau's sale rooms in London in 1928. The prison letters to Ross alone fetched £2,000: see *Dulau Sale Catalogue*, item 161.

[2] By Robert Ross in *De Profundis* (1908), by Stuart Mason in *After Reading* (1921) and by More Adey in *After Berneval* (1922).

[3] Adey MSS. Formerly in the collection of the late A. J. A. Symons.

Wilde's friends who were allowed to visit him in prison, such as Robert Sherard, Frank Harris, Robert Ross, Charles Ricketts and Lord Haldane. Besides the complete text of *De Profundis*, which I was the first member of the public to be allowed to see on its being opened for general inspection on 1 January 1960 in the British Museum where it had been sealed up for fifty years, I have made considerable use of the two long letters on various aspects of prison reform, which Wilde wrote to the *Daily Chronicle* after his release.[1] Together with some short extracts from his letters to Ross, originally published in the first German edition of *De Profundis* in 1905, and first published in English in 1908, these formed the sum of Wilde's published prison writings before Mr Hart-Davis published them in full.

The whole constitutes a sombre and at times terrifying picture of penal conditions in England towards the close of the last century and of their impact on a man of Wilde's personality and acute sensitivity. It is in great part a tragic story of human suffering. There is no doubt in my mind that it should be told, and I have tried to tell it in the following pages. The days of the treadmill and crank and other forms of hard labour on an insufficient diet, as Wilde experienced and described them, are happily over. However, there are still some grounds for supporting Wilde's opinion that it is not the prisoners who need reformation so much as the prisons. But that, as Rudyard Kipling would have put it, is another story. This is the story of Wilde's imprisonment and the effect which his punishment had on him. 'Do not forget', he wrote to Alfred Douglas from his prison cell, 'in what a terrible school I am sitting at my task.' I feel it deserves to be remembered.

Nutley, Sussex. H. MONTGOMERY HYDE
October 1962.

[1] Republished by Robert Ross in his edition of *De Profundis* (1908), which forms part of the Collected Works.

Oscar Wilde: the aftermath

CHAPTER I

From Pentonville to Wandsworth

1

In the late afternoon of Saturday, May 25, 1895, Oscar Wilde was found guilty of having committed a number of offences contrary to the Criminal Law Amendment Act, 1887. It was the sixth day of his second trial at the Old Bailey, the jury having disagreed on the first occasion. At this date Wilde was forty-one years of age. Beside him in the dock was a well-educated young man of thirty-three, named Alfred Taylor, who had been indicted with him. In addressing the two defendants from the Bench, Mr Justice Wills informed them that he would be expected to pass the severest sentence which the law allowed. 'In my judgement,' added the judge, 'it is totally inadequate for such a case as this. The sentence of the Court is that each of you be imprisoned and kept to hard labour for two years.'[1]

Some murmurs of 'Oh' and 'Shame' were heard from spectators who had followed the trial, but they were quickly drowned by a hum of approval. When the news reached the crowds waiting in the street outside the Court building, it was likewise received with marks of approbation. Several people literally danced with joy, and some prostitutes were seen to kick up their skirts with glee. 'E'll 'ave 'is 'air cut reglar *now*!' shouted one of them amid shouts of raucous laughter. Meanwhile, Wilde who had heard the sentence with horrified amazement, tried to utter a few words of protest. 'And I? May I say nothing, my lord?' But Mr Justice Wills made no reply beyond a wave of the hand to the two warders, who were also standing in the dock. One of them touched Wilde on the shoulder and in a few instants he was hurried below to the cells.

[1] Full details of the trial are given in *The Trials of Oscar Wilde* (1948), edited by the present writer, republished, with additions, in 1962.

Those familiar with prison conditions in England at that period realised that the punishment which faced Wilde was one of terrible severity.[1] The deterrent object of imprisonment had been officially laid down as 'hard labour, hard fare, and a hard bed'. Evidence given by a variety of witnesses before a recent Home Office Committee on Prisons had shown that two years imprisonment with hard labour, involving solitary cellular confinement, with its attendant laborious and largely useless work in the shape of the treadwheel, the crank and oakum picking, which had to be performed on a poor and inadequate diet, were calculated to break a man in body and spirit.[2] Indeed, old offenders greatly preferred penal servitude, which could not be imposed for less than three years, in a convict establishment such as Dartmoor or Portland, since the work was largely carried out in the open air and there was always the chance of being released on 'ticket-of-leave'. With a sentence of imprisonment, on the other hand, the various forms of hard labour were mainly conducted indoors, usually in the prisoner's cell, and there was no provision for remitting any portion of the sentence for good conduct.[3] The cell in which he was confined for twenty-three out of the twenty-four hours in the day, was badly ventilated and the sanitary arrangements were primitive. The plank bed, on which he was condemned to lie at night, was an instrument of torture, which inevitably produced insomnia. Visitors (for twenty minutes each), and the writing and receiving of a letter, were only allowed once every three months, save in exceptional circumstances. Letters written by prisoners were censored by prison officials, particu-

[1] See generally on prison life at this period, Sidney and Beatrice Webb, *English Prisons under Local Government* (1922), and George Ives, *A History of Penal Methods* (1914), and authorities there cited.

[2] *Report of the Departmental Committee on Prisons* (1895), *passim*. This Committee is usually known as the Gladstone Committee, from the name of its chairman, Mr Herbert (later Lord) Gladstone, M.P. and son of the Liberal leader. Its recommendations led to the passing of the Prisons Act, 1898.

[3] Cp. evidence of Mr J. B. Manning, Governor of Pentonville, before the Gladstone Committee:

Q. Now considering that the penal servitude man for three years can expiate his offence with two years and three months penal servitude, do you consider it hard that the man who is sentenced to two years [imprisonment with hard labour] should have to serve until the last hour of his sentence?—A. Well, I consider that the two years hard labour is a more severe sentence than the three years penal servitude, because the convict only does nine months in separate cells.

Q. And it is the hardest punishment which a prisoner can undergo?—A. Yes.

Q. A very hard punishment?—A. Yes, a very hard punishment.

Report of the Departmental Committee on Prisons (1895), at p. 38.

larly for complaints, as well as 'slang or improper expressions', and on at least one occasion Wilde was to have a passage from one of his letters excised by the Governor's scissors. According to the regulations current in Wilde's time, 'the permission to write and receive letters is given to prisoners for the purpose of enabling them to keep a connection with their respectable friends, and not that they may be kept informed of public events.[1] Wilde was later to urge strongly that prisoners should be allowed the privilege of both letters and visitors once a month. 'One of the tragedies of prison life is that it turns a man's heart to stone', he wrote afterwards. 'The feelings of natural affection, like all other feelings require to be fed. They die easily of inanition. A brief letter, four times a year, is not enough to keep alive the gentler and more humane affections by which ultimately the nature is kept sensitive to any fine or beautiful influences that may heal a wrecked or ruined life.'

During the first three months of imprisonment the prisoner was allowed no books at all, except a Bible, prayer-book and hymn-book. Thereafter he was allowed one book a week from the prison library. The latter's stock consisted chiefly of third-rate theological works which had been selected by the prison chaplain. As Wilde wrote when he came out, 'the present prison system seems almost to have for its aim the wrecking and destruction of the mental faculties. The production of insanity is, if not its object, certainly its result. . . . Deprived of books, of all human intercourse, isolated from every humane and humanising influence, condemned to eternal silence, robbed of all intercourse with the external world, treated like an unintelligent animal, brutalised below the level of any of the brute creation, the wretched man who is confined in an English prison can hardly escape becoming insane.'[2]

Since his trial had ended late on a Saturday afternoon, it was apparently not possible to make arrangements for Wilde's reception in a regular prison before the weekend. He was therefore kept until the following Monday afternoon in one of the cells in Newgate Gaol, which was adjacent to the Old Bailey. He was then handcuffed and taken out to a prison van which was waiting at the gate. In this vehicle, the old horse-

[1] For the text of these regulations, see below, Appendix A.
[2] Letter to the *Daily Chronicle* on the Prison Bill, March 24, 1898.

drawn type of 'Black Maria', he was taken to Pentonville, which was to be his immediate future home. Situated off the Caledonian Road in North London, Pentonville was the gaol to which prisoners who lived on the north side of the River Thames, or who had committed offences there, were normally sent. This institution had been built by the Government just over half a century previously, and, with its layout of separate cells, it was designed to serve as a model for other local prisons, such as Wandsworth and Reading, in which Wilde was later to be incarcerated. It was approached through a massive gateway constructed in the manner of a portcullis, with an Italian-style clock-tower dominating the main building in the background. Beyond this entrance a smaller gate to the left led to the reception block, where all prisoners were taken on their arrival. Internally the main building consisted of a central hall, from which four wings radiated after the fashion of spokes of a half wheel. Each wing contained 130 cells, arranged in three galleries or storeys one above the other. The gallery floors were of iron work, with iron handrails, and they were reached by iron staircases. Above the well of the hall and along the galleries large sheets of wire netting were stretched so as to prevent suicides.

Wilde's first experience of Pentonville was thoroughly disagreeable, and he always remembered it. After he had gone through the reception office, where his particulars were entered in the prison records (he gave his occupation as 'author'), he was weighed and measured and he handed over his personal belongings.[1] He was taken to the baths and told to strip. After waiting his turn in a small cubicle, he was made to get into a filthy bath, in which other prisoners had preceded him. There followed a medical examination, as a result of which he was certified as 'fit for light labour', which meant that he could be put to such tasks as picking oakum and sewing mail bags. He then put on the coarse prison-dress with its distinguishing broad arrow marks, and followed a warder to the cell where he was locked in for the night. 'At first it was a fiendish nightmare,' he told Frank Harris: 'more horrible than anything I had ever dreamed of: from the first evening when they made me undress before them and get into some filthy water

[1] The Nominal Register, with Wilde's entry, is still preserved in Pentonville. His weight on reception was just under 14 stone and his height 6 feet.

they called a bath and dry myself with a damp brown rag and put on this livery of shame. The cell was appalling: I could hardly breathe in it, and the food turned my stomach; the smell and sight of it were enough: I did not eat anything for days and days and days, I could not even swallow the bread; and the rest of the food was uneatable; I lay on the so-called bed and shivered all night long. . . . After some days I got so hungry I had to eat a little, nibble at the outside of the bread, and drink some of the liquid; whether it was tea, coffee or gruel, I could not tell. As soon as I really ate anything it produced violent diarrhoea and I was ill all day and all night. From the beginning I could not sleep I grew weak and had wild delusions. . . . The hunger made you weak; but the inhumanity was the worst of it. What devilish creatures men are. I had never known anything about them. I had never dreamt of such cruelties.'[1]

Wilde had been in Pentonville for less than a fortnight when disquieting rumours about his mental condition began to reach the outside world. According to an agency report, which appeared in several newspapers, including the *Pall Mall Gazette* and the *Daily Chronicle*, Wilde had actually become insane.[2] His condition, which was stated to have first manifested itself to the prison barber, was said to be causing anxiety to the officials in Pentonville. Among those who read this account in the *Daily Chronicle* was the Home Secretary, Mr Asquith, who had known the prisoner in the heyday of his social success and indeed had been his host on at least one occasion.[3]

He immediately gave directions to inquire whether there was any foundation for the statement. On the same day, June 5, the Medical Officer at Pentonville examined the prisoner. He stated that Wilde had not been in hospital or padded cell and had 'given no anxiety to any of the officials' in Pentonville.

[1] Frank Harris. *Oscar Wilde* (New York, 1916), II, 331–2.

[2] *Pall Mall Gazette*, June 4/5; *Daily Chronicle*, June 5, 1895.

[3] Herbert Henry Asquith (1852–1928), later Liberal Prime Minister and 1st Earl of Oxford and Asquith, was Home Secretary from 1892 to 1895. About a year previously Wilde had been a guest at a luncheon party given by Asquith and his wife at their house in London. 'Of all those present, and they were most of them brilliant talkers, he was without comparison the most brilliant, and in a perverse mood he chose to cross swords with one after another of them, overpowering each in turn with his wit, and making special fun of Asquith, his host that day, who only a few months later, as Home Secretary, was prosecuting him on the notorious criminal charge which sent him to hard labour in prison': Wilfrid Scawen Blunt. *My Diaries* (1919), I, 178-9.

'He was placed under observation on first reception for seven days to be specially watched', the report continued, 'as is frequently done with prisoners owing to depression and mental strain of their trial and sentence. With the exception of a little relaxed throat, for which he has been treated, he is in good health and perfectly sane.'[1] To the prison doctor Wilde may have appeared to be superficially in good health. That this was far from being the case subsequent events were to show only too well.

It may be noted here that Wilde's opinion of medical officers attached to prisons was the reverse of flattering. His father had been a distinguished surgeon, and from earliest youth Wilde had always regarded doctors as by far the most humane profession in the community. But his gaol experiences caused him to make a striking exception in the case of prison doctors. At that time they usually, if not always, had large private practices and held appointments in other institutions. 'The consequence is that the health of the prisoners is entirely neglected,' wrote Wilde, 'and the sanitary conditions entirely overlooked.' As for the doctors themselves, they were 'as far as I came across them, and from what I saw of them in hospital and elsewhere, brutal in manner, coarse in temperament and utterly indifferent to the health of the prisoners or their comfort'.[2]

The cell in which Wilde found himself at Pentonville, and which was copied by most of the other English prisons, was 13 feet long, 7 feet wide and 9 feet high, giving 819 cubic feet of air space. This was intended to provide an adequate size for strictly separate confinement with cellular labour. The stone or brick-wall surface and the ceiling were lime-washed. The door was of solid construction, being lined with sheet iron to prevent tampering by ingenious prisoners, and in the middle was a small glass peep-hole, covered by a movable shutter, to enable the interior of the cell to be observed by patrolling warders. Artificial illumination was provided by flaring gas-jets let into the corridor outside. This cast a pale glare through a glazed opening in the cell wall above the door. In day time only a relatively small amount of natural light penetrated through the cell window, which consisted of fourteen small opaque panes of glass, situated at a height of 6 feet 9

[1] Home Office Papers. [2] Letter to the *Daily Chronicle*, March 24, 1898.

inches above the floor level, and preventing even a glimpse of the sky. Ventilation was provided partly by a ventilator in the window and partly by gratings. But Wilde found that the window ventilator was too small and badly constructed to admit any adequate amount of fresh air, while the gratings were usually choked up. The result, in his experience, was that for most of the day and night prisoners were breathing the foulest possible air. He was later to describe it in *The Ballad of Reading Gaol.*

> Each narrow cell in which we dwell
>   Is a foul and dark latrine,
> And the fetid breath of living Death
>   Chokes up each grated screen,
> And all, but Lust, is turned to Dust
>   In humanity's machine.

The cell was indeed as bare and repellent as it was possible to make it. The only articles of furniture permitted were the plank bed, blanket, hard pillow and a small table for the prisoner's toilet and feeding utensils. Nothing was allowed in the way of personal possessions, not even a photograph of the prisoner's wife and children, which might break the monotony of the cell wall or help to keep alive any feeling of family affection. A daily cell inspection was carried out, at which each prisoner had to exhibit the contents of his cell, such as they were, in the prescribed order. These official visitations became a nightmare for Wilde and in consequence he developed a nervous habit, which his friends noticed when he came out of prison, of always arranging objects in front of him symmetrically. 'I had to keep everything in my cell in its exact place,' he said, 'and if I neglected this even in the slightest, I was punished. The punishment was so horrible to me that I often started up in my sleep to feel if each thing was where the regulations would have it, and not an inch either to the right or to the left.'[1] In time, however, he was to learn to do this correctly. One of the warders, who had him in his charge for a time at Reading, has described how Wilde, when he had arranged all his tins as they should be, 'would step back and view them with an air of child-like complacency'.[2]

[1] Robert Sherard. *Oscar Wilde. The Story of an Unhappy Friendship* (1902), p. 235.

[2] Robert Sherard. *Life of Oscar Wilde* (1906), p. 389.

At one time each cell was equipped with a form of latrine, but the closets were later removed, principally because, it appears, the drainpipes facilitated unauthorised communications with the inmates of adjacent cells. In place of the old latrine the prisoner was supplied with a small tin chamber pot. This he was allowed to empty three times a day. But he was not allowed to have access to the prison lavatories, except during the one hour when he was at exercise. And after locking-up time, between five o'clock in the evening and five the following morning, the prisoner was forbidden to leave his cell under any pretence or for any reason, for the warder on night duty had no key. The prison diet consisting as it did mostly of weak gruel—so-called 'stirabout', of coarse Indian meal—suet, water, and greasy cocoa, was the frequent cause of diarrhoea, and the miseries and tortures which sufferers from this endemic prison complaint underwent, especially at night, can be imagined. It was no uncommon thing for warders, when they came in the mornings out of the fresh air to open and inspect the cells, to be violently sick. Wilde witnessed this himself on a number of occasions and several warders went out of their way to mention it to him 'as one of the disgusting things which their office entails on them'.

At certain times in the day the warders would serve out astringent medicines. But after a comparatively short time, usually about a week, the medicine produced no effect at all. In Wilde's words, 'the wretched prisoner is then left a prey to the most weakening, depressing and humiliating malady that can be conceived: and if, as often happens, he fails, from physical weakness, to complete his required revolutions at the crank or the mill he is reported for idleness, and punished with the greatest severity and brutality'.[1] It is true that prisoners were not as a rule employed beyond the first month of their sentence on these particular forms of hard labour, both of which Wilde seems to have escaped, since experience had shown that their further prolongation made them virtually unendurable. At this time, too, the treadmill was not so popular with the authorities as the crank. This latter diabolical instrument was a cylindrical metal drum fitted with a handle to be turned and resembling the old-fashioned type of patent knife-grinder. On one side was a clock-like face, which recorded the number of

[1] Letter to the *Daily Chronicle*, March 24, 1898.

revolutions made. The requisite amount of resistance was obtained by a metal band applied on the axle inside, which retarded its motion by friction. The ordinary resistance was about 6 lb. Prisoners were expected to perform 10,000 revolutions a day, which occupied them for about six hours. It was a particularly futile operation, since, unlike the treadmill which often pumped water or ground corn, the labour involved was absolutely unproductive.

After a month of the crank or treadmill prisoners were put on to a lighter class of labour, but still irksome and to a large extent also unproductive. This took the form of such tasks as sewing mail bags, making mats and picking oakum, which like the crank had to be performed by the prisoner in the silence of his cell. The most extensive of these occupations was oakum picking, although the industrial demand for oakum had long since fallen away due to the substitution of iron ships for wooden ones. In this stage of his imprisonment the prisoner was allowed to sleep on a hard mattress for five days a week. But in Wilde's case this concession did not relieve his insomnia. 'For sleep, like all wholesome things is a habit,' he said. 'Every prisoner who has been on a plank bed suffers from insomnia. It is a revolting and ignorant punishment.'

> The brackish water that we drink
>   Creeps with a loathsome slime,
> And the bitter bread they weigh in scales
>   Is full of chalk and lime.
> And sleep will not lie down, but walks
>   Wild-eyed, and cries to Time.

Wilde's prison routine was as follows. He got up at 6 a.m. and cleaned out his cell. At seven he had breakfast, consisting of cocoa or porridge and eight ounces of brown unbuttered prison bread. He was then taken out with other prisoners for exercise which lasted an hour. On returning to his cell he picked oakum until midday, when dinner was brought round. This meal consisted of greasy bacon and beans with bread and potatoes and either suet pudding or soup, and on one day a week he had cold meat. At 12.30 oakum picking was resumed and he was expected to continue with this occupation until 6 p.m. He then had tea or gruel and again eight ounces of bread and at seven the lights were turned out and he went to bed. A newspaper report accurately described his life at this time: 'He is compelled to pick a certain quantity of oakum per day, is not allowed to converse with anyone, and with the exception of an hour's exercise is kept in solitary confinement in his cell.'[1]

> With midnight always in one's heart,
> And twilight in one's cell,
> We turn the crank or tear the rope,
> Each in his separate Hell,
> And the silence is more awful far
> Than the sound of a brazen bell.
>
> And never a human voice comes near
> To speak a gentle word:
> And the eye that watches through the door
> Is pitiless and hard:
> And by all forgot, we rot and rot,
> With soul and body marred.

Once a week the daily routine was varied by the ringing of the Sabbath bell. 'Then', in the words of one who had experienced it at Pentonville a few years before Wilde, 'cells give up their dead and corridors are full of the pale, skilly-fed shuffling crowd, and soon each seat is filled, a warder duly placed at each end to see that the worshippers do not engage in speculations as to the nature of the Trinity, but stand and kneel and sit, do everything in fact other congregations do, omitting only the due dumping of the threepenny bit into the plate, and not forgetting that when two or three are gathered thus to pray, their Creator stands amongst them, although they are thieves. And thus assembled in their hundreds, to make their prayer before the God of Prisons, the congregation sits—prisoners and captives, shut within themselves, and each man tortured by the thought that those outside have lost him from their minds.' The great moment was when the chaplain announced the hymn. 'Then like an earthquake the pent-up sound breaks forth, the chapel quivers like a ship from stem to stern, dust flies, and loud from every throat the pious doggerel peals. And in the sounds the prison melts away, the doors are opened, and each man sits in his home surrounded by his friends, his Sunday dinner smokes, his children all

[1] *Morning*, June 6, 1895. See also *Report of Departmental Committee on Prison Dietaries* (1899).

clean-washed and by his side, and so we sing; lift up our hearts and roar vociferously (praising some kind of God), shaken inside and out, yelling, perspiring and shouting each other down'.[1]

What was in store for Wilde, he was to sum up in conversation, after he had experienced 'hard labour' for about twelve months. 'Starvation and purging alone would break down anyone's strength,' he told Frank Harris, who visited him at this time. 'Everyone knows that you are purged and starved to the edge of death. That's what two years' hard labour means. It's not the labour that's hard. It's the conditions of life that make it impossibly hard: they break you down body and soul. And, if you resist, they drive you crazy.'[2]

2

The lesson which Wilde set himself to learn in prison was that of humility. From the outset he found it very hard, since he began each day by going down on his knees and washing the floor of his cell. 'For prison life with its endless privations and restrictions makes one rebellious. The most terrible thing about it is not that it breaks one's heart—hearts are made to be broken—but that it turns one's heart to stone. One sometimes feels that it is only with a front of brass and a lip of scorn that one can get through the day at all.' To succeed he felt that he must overcome this mood of rebellion which 'closes up the channels of the soul and shuts out the airs of heaven'. His achievement he was to epitomise in the composition of the work known as *De Profundis*, which he was to begin and complete in his prison cell eighteen months later. 'The plank bed, the loathesome food, the hard ropes shredded into oakum until one's fingertips grew dull with pain, the menial offices with which each day begins and finishes, the harsh orders that routine seems to necessitate, the dreadful dress that makes sorrow grotesque to look at, the silence, the solitude, the shame—each and all of these things I had to transform into a spiritual experience.'[3]

It might perhaps be expected that Wilde would have derived some spiritual consolation from the ministrations of the prison

[1] R. B. Cunninghame Graham, quoted by A. F. Tschiffely, *Don Roberto* (1937), pp. 227–9.

[2] Harris. II, 339. [3] *De Profundis. The Complete Text* (1949), pp. 81, 91.

chaplain. But about this official Wilde's experiences were as discouraging as those with the prison doctor. 'The prison chaplains are entirely useless, he wrote. 'They are, as a class, well-meaning, but foolish, indeed silly men. They are no help to any prisoner. Once every six weeks or so a key turns in the lock of one's cell door, and the chaplain enters. One stands, of course, to attention. He asks one whether one has been reading the Bible. One answers "Yes" or "No", as the case may be. He then quotes a few texts and goes out and locks the door. Sometimes he leaves a tract.'[1] The chaplain at Pentonville was evidently a typical example as described by Wilde. 'Did you have morning prayers in your house?' he is said to have asked the prisoner on the occasion of their first meeting. 'I am sorry. I fear not,' said Wilde. To which the chaplain replied, 'You see where you are now.'[2]

When Wilde was allowed to have a book from the prison library, the chaplain selected *A Pilgrim's Progress* by John Bunyan, which he evidently considered particularly suitable for the prisoner on account of its high moral tone: incidentally it had been written in prison.

The first person to give Wilde any feeling of hope for the future was his first visitor from the outside world. This was the Liberal lawyer and politician, Mr R. B. Haldane, Q.C., M.P., who had been a member of the Departmental Committee, known as the Gladstone Committee, which had recently reviewed in searching terms the whole range of prison administration.[3] According to Haldane, he used to meet Wilde in the days of his social success, and, although he had not known him well, he was 'haunted by the idea of what this highly sensitive man was probably suffering under ordinary prison treatment'. His visit to Pentonville was probably prompted by the alarming accounts which had appeared in the *Daily Chronicle* and other newspapers about Wilde's mental condition, and he may well have been encouraged to make it by the Liberal Home Secretary, Mr Asquith, to whom no doubt he reported the result of his mission.[4]

[1] Letter to the *Daily Chronicle*, March 24, 1898.

[2] Charles Ricketts. *Recollections of Oscar Wilde* (1932), p. 22.

[3] Richard Burdon Haldane (1856–1928), statesman, lawyer and philosopher. He was subsequently War Minister and twice Lord Chancellor, being created Viscount Haldane in 1911.

[4] R. B. Haldane. *An Autobiography* (1929), at pp. 166–7. Haldane states that his meeting with Wilde took place in Holloway, but this is a mistake for Penton-

Before he saw Wilde, Haldane met the prison chaplain in the Governor's room at Pentonville. This reverend gentlemen said he was glad Haldane had come since with the prisoner Wilde he had 'failed to make any way'. In view of his remarks to Wilde at their first meeting this was hardly surprising. The visitor then saw Wilde himself alone in a special room. 'At first he refused to speak,' noted Haldane afterwards in his account of their interview. 'I put my hand on his prison-dress-clad shoulder and said that I used to know him and that I had come to say something about himself. He had not fully used his great literary gift, and the reason was that he had lived a life of pleasure and had not made any great subject his own. Now misfortune might prove a blessing for his career, for he had got a great subject.' Haldane added that he would try to obtain for him the privileges of books and writing materials, so that in due course he 'would be free to produce'.

Wilde was so overcome by this prospect that he burst into tears. Nevertheless he promised to make the attempt. For books he asked eagerly, saying that all he had to read was *A Pilgrim's Progress* and that 'this did not satisfy him'. He asked among others for Flaubert's works, paticularly *Madame Bovary*. But Haldane replied that the dedication by that author to his advocate, who had successfully defended him on a charge of obscene publication, made such a work as *Madame Bovary* unlikely to be sanctioned. At this remark, according to Haldane, Wilde began to laugh and immediately became cheerful. After some discussion they hit on the works of St Augustine, several books of Cardinal Newman, Mommsen's *History of Rome*, Pascal's *Pensées* and Walter Pater's book on the Renaissance. These Haldane succeeded in procuring for him and they accompanied him to his next prison, when he moved, although the Governor of Pentonville objected to some of them as being 'of a controversial character' and consequently contrary to the Local Prison Code.[1]

One day, about a year after Wilde's release, Haldane received

ville. Wilde was asked by the Deputy Governor in charge at Pentonville on June 12, 1895, whether he was willing to receive a special visit from Haldane, and he replied that he was. Haldane's order stated that 'the visit will take place in a room and be unlimited as to time': Home Office (Prison Commission) Papers.

[1] Governor of Pentonville to Prison Commissioners, July 2, 1895: Home Office (Prison Commission) Papers. Haldane later added ten more volumes of Pater and some other books. At Haldane's request the collection was subsequently presented to the Wandsworth Prison Library.

a small anonymous parcel. When he opened it he found a copy of *The Ballad of Reading Gaol*, which was originally published under the pseudonym C.3.3. It had been sent by the author to the man who had first befriended him in prison, and its recipient had no difficulty in recognizing the author's identity. 'It was the redemption of his promise to me,' wrote Haldane afterwards.

Haldane had promised to get in touch with Wilde's family and give them news of the prisoner. He could not see Mrs Constance Wilde and the two children, as they had gone abroad, but he called at 146, Oakley Street, Chelsea, where Wilde's mother, the widowed Lady Wilde, was living with her other son Willie and her daughter-in-law. Willie Wilde had recently got married for the second time, and his wife, Lily, was expecting a child.[1] This prompted Mrs Lily Wilde after seeing Haldane to write to the Governor of Pentonville and ask him to give 'my unhappy brother-in-law' a message which the Governor seems to have done. 'As I am expecting my confinement shortly and one's life is always more or less in danger,' she wrote, 'perhaps you would relax the rule. If so, would you give him my fondest love and say how often I think of him and long to see him: also, what perhaps will give him the most pleasure, that his Mother is wonderfully well.' She added that she had heard nothing of Mrs Constance Wilde and the children, so that she presumed Wilde's wife was 'thinking of following the advice of Sir George Lewis'[2] and petitioning for a divorce.[3]

Wilde's next outside visitor brought less pleasant news. It was a clerk from the Marquess of Queensberry's solicitors who came down to Pentonville to serve him with a bankruptcy notice. On June 21, 1895, Queensberry filed a petition in the Bankruptcy Court, asking for a receiving order to be made. The sum claimed was £677, being the amount of the petitioning creditor's taxed costs in connexion with the prosecution of Lord Queensbury by Wilde for criminal libel, at which trial Queensberry had been acquitted, Wilde's arrest following im-

[1] She was Sophie (Lily), youngest daughter of William A. Lees of Dublin. She bore her husband a daughter. After Willie Wilde's death, in 1899, she married Alexander Louis Texeira de Mattos. She died in 1921.

[2] The well-known solicitor.

[3] On April 19, 1895, Mrs Wilde had written to a friend: 'As soon as this trial is over, I have to get my judicial separation, or if possible my divorce in order to get the guardianship of the boys.' Communicated by Sir Shane Leslie.

mediately afterwards. This news came as a cruel blow, and it made Wilde feel very bitter for a long while to come. At the time of the original trial, he had received definite assurances from his friend Lord Alfred Douglas, Queensberry's son, that the various members of the Queensberry family who hated its head, particularly the eldest surviving brother, Lord Douglas of Hawick, would be responsible for the costs of the libel prosecution into which Alfred Douglas had been conspicuous in egging Wilde on.[1] This was a subject to which Wilde in *De Profundis*, and in his other prison correspondence, was to revert with bitterness again and again. 'I felt most strongly', he told Douglas, 'that these costs should have been paid by your family. You had taken personally on yourself the responsibility of stating that your family would do so. It was that which made the solicitor take up the case in the way he did. You were absolutely responsible. Even irrespective of your engagement on your family's behalf you should have felt that, as you had brought the whole ruin on me, the least that could have been done was to spare me the additional ignominy of bankruptcy for an absolutely contemptible sum of money, less that half of what I spent on you in three brief summer months at Goring.'[2]

At the request of Wilde and that of his legal advisers, who felt that his continued presence in London could only do him harm, Lord Alfred Douglas had gone to France on the eve of his friend's trial. He had wisely decided to remain there after Wilde's conviction. As he had no money beyond a small allowance from his mother, he was unfortunately unable to help Wilde over the bankruptcy notice. Instead he occupied himself in writing letters to the English Press, which the editors declined to publish, and he also drafted a petition to Queen Victoria praying Her Majesty to pardon the imprisoned poet and dramatist.[3]

[1] Lord Alfred Bruce Douglas (1870–1945) was the third son of the eighth Marquess of Queensberry. In spite of the reputation which he achieved as a poet, his life was incessantly marked by controversy, due largely to his unfortunate friendship with Wilde. See particularly his *Oscar Wilde and Myself* (1914), *Autobiography* (1929), *Without Apology* (1938) and *Oscar Wilde: A Summing Up* (1940), and also, on his relations with Wilde, my edition of *The Trials of Oscar Wilde* (1948) and my foreword to *The Black Douglas* (1949), by Douglas's nephew, Francis, tenth Marquess of Queensberry, and Percy Colson.

[2] *De Profundis*, 58.

[3] For the text of this petition see below, Appendix B. Queen Victoria never saw it, since it was intercepted by her Private Secretary who forwarded it to the Home Office.

In the same month Wilde's solicitors, Messrs Humphreys Son & Kershaw, who had represented him in the various trials, were active on his behalf. They also petitioned the Queen through the Home Secretary on the grounds of the excessive severity of the sentence, that Wilde had been kept in custody illegally for three weeks after his arrest in April, notwithstanding that bail had been tendered on his behalf, that he made no attempt to evade his trial, that the date of all the charges were more than two years prior to his arrest and that he 'still asserts his innocence'. It must be admitted that this document, which was dated June 18, 1895, was not particularly convincing. In the words of a Home Office minute, which accompanied it to the Secretary of State 'the weakness of their case is evident from the nature of this petition'. It was seen by Mr Asquith on June 22, who inevitably declined to advise the Queen to exercise the royal prerogative of pardon.[1] In fact it was one of the Minister's last official acts, since the Rosebery Government fell a few days later and the Conservatives took office. The new Home Secretary was Sir Mathew White Ridley, Bart., member of an old Northumbrian family, who was to show himself rather less sympathetic towards Wilde than his predecessor had been.[2]

One other official act of Asquith's at this time was fortunately destined to exercise a beneficial effect on Wilde's lot and indeed on the lot of all prisoners in Her Majesty's gaols. This was the appointment of Mr (later Sir) Evelyn Ruggles-Brise, an enlightened and humane administrator, to be Chairman of the Prison Commission. Ruggles-Brise, who was a comparatively young man—he was thirty-eight, actually three years younger than Wilde—had previously been a member of the Prison Board, and the evidence which he gave before the recent Departmental Committee on Prisons had determined Asquith to remove the then Chairman, Sir Edward Du Cane, a staunch upholder of the prison system in all its harshness, and put in his place a younger man whom he felt to have the disposition as well as the ability to carry into effect the Committee's recommendations. 'Always remember that a prisoner is still a human being', wrote an ex-convict to the new Chairman on learning of his appointment.

[1] Home Office Papers.

[2] Sir Mathew White Ridley (1842–1904) was Home Secretary from 1895 to 1900, when he was raised to the peerage as Viscount Ridley.

'Act and posterity will, as in the case of the immortal Howard, honour your memory.' Ruggles-Brise did act, and the result of his action was to be seen in the Prisons Act of 1898, which completely revolutionised the old system. Wilde's sentence had, of course, been completed some time before this measure became law, so that he was unable to benefit directly from its provisions. But such alleviations of the system as he did enjoy, particularly in respect of visitors, were largely due to the humanising influence of Evelyn Ruggles-Brise.[1]

Meanwhile, in what seems to have been an attempt to stave off the bankruptcy proceedings, Wilde's solicitors sought permission from the Home Office to see their client 'with reference to the translation and publication of some of his works'. The request was made on June 24, but it was not until three weeks later, on July 15, that permission was granted. The delay was no doubt due to the change of Home Secretaries and possibly also to a misunderstanding of the nature of the publications contemplated. Because Wilde had been convicted of alleged immoral practices, it seems to have been assumed by one senior Home Office official that the publications might also be immoral. 'Let them see him in the ordinary course as his solicitors to take his instructions in regard to property and business matters', wrote this official on the relevant file. 'If they publish anything objectionable it will be their look out and the Law can intervene.'[2]

When the solicitors received the necessary order and were ready to see Wilde, they learned somewhat to their surprise that he had been removed from Pentonville to another prison.

3

Wilde was transferred from Pentonville to Wandsworth Prison on July 4, 1895.[3] What determined the Prison Commissioners on this change to a gaol south of the Thames is not clear, for we know that, when Asquith inquired after the state

[1] Sir Evelyn Ruggles-Brise (1857–1935) was Chairman of the Prison Commission from 1895 until his retirement in 1921. He was the founder of the 'Borstal' system for juvenile offenders. See Shane Leslie, *Sir Evelyn Ruggles-Brise* (1938).

[2] Home Office Papers.

[3] The order for removal was sent by the Prison Commissioners to the Governor of Pentonville on June 25. In the removal form signed by the Acting Governor and Medical Officer Wilde's general conduct and general health in prison were described as 'good'. It was also stated that he had been 'employed at oakum picking': Home Office (Prison Commission) Papers.

of the prisoner's health early in June, it was the intention of the authorities that he should serve out his sentence in Pentonville.[1] Both Ruggles-Brise and Haldane had considerable confidence in the Chaplain at Wandsworth, the Rev W. D. Morrison, and they may have wished to bring Wilde into touch with this clergyman, on whom they could rely to keep a particular eye on him. It may be said that Mr Morrison hardly deserved the severe criticism passed by Wilde on prison chaplains as a whole, which has already been quoted. Indeed, it was largely due to Mr Morrison's outspoken articles in the *Fortnightly Review* on the shortcomings of the prison system that the Gladstone Committee had been appointed in 1894, which was eventually to lead to such drastic changes.[2] Yet even this courageous reformer tended on his own admission to become indifferent to the harshness of the régime. 'The great difficulty with all of us in prisons,' he said in his evidence before the Committee, 'is that we are so accustomed to seeing people under punishment and under suffering that we are apt to get a little hard in the matter unless we take very great care.'[3]

Like Pentonville, Wandsworth was a large establishment —indeed it was larger than the neighbouring establishment north of the river—having an average of over 1,100 prisoners in its cells. Although built less than ten years after Pentonville, architecturally it had none of the impressiveness of the 'model prison' with its great portcullis entrance. While its outbuildings exhibited all the bad taste of Cockney-Italian villas, 'the central mass arising behind the stunted gateway' was 'heavy to clumsiness and the whole aspect of the structure uncommanding as a Methodist Chapel'.[4] The Governor, Captain Helby, was a retired naval officer, who appears to have been a firm believer in the efficacy of a strict prison discipline. The Medical Officer, Dr R. F. Quinton, had a reputation for ability; like Wilde, he was an Irishman and, by a coincidence, had been educated at the same school in the north of Ireland.[5]

[1] Home Office Papers: Minute of June 6, 1895.

[2] Rev William Douglas Morrison (1852–1943) was Chaplain in H.M. Prison Service from 1883 to 1898 and Rector of St. Marylebone, London, from 1898 to 1941. He was the author of a number of works on criminology.

[3] *Report of Departmental Committee on Prisons* (1895), at p. 118.

[4] H. Mayhew and J. Bunny, *Criminal Prisons of London* (1862), p. 116.

[5] Dr Richard Frith Quinton (1849–1934) was later Governor of Holloway and wrote several works on criminology. He had been educated at Portora Royal School, Enniskillen, but was some years senior to Wilde there.

But some of the warders seem to have treated the prisoners fairly roughly. Wilde told Frank Harris, when he came to see him later on at Reading that 'some of them at Wandsworth were brutes', and gave a typical illustration of their behaviour. One day a warder came into his cell. 'Take off your boots,' he said. Wilde began to obey. Then he asked: 'What is it? Why must I take off my boots?' The warder did not answer, but took the prisoner's boots and said: 'Come out of your cell.' 'Why?' Wilde asked again. Again no reply. Wilde grew frightened. What had he done? Was he going to be punished? As soon as they were in the corridor, the warder ordered him to stand with his face to the wall, and then went away. Wilde stood there in his stockinged feet waiting. The cold chilled him through. He began first standing on one foot, and then on the other, wondering what they were going to do to him. Then after what seemed an eternity he heard the warder coming back. He did not dare to move or look round. The warder paused beside him for a moment and threw down a pair of boots. 'Go to your cell and put those on,' he commanded. Wilde went back to his cell shaking in every limb. 'That's the way they give you a new pair of boots in prison, Frank,' he said. 'That's the way they are kind to you.'[1]

However the Prison Commissioners may have thought that Wilde would benefit from these new surroundings, he found them far less easy to bear than those he had left. 'At Wandsworth I thought I should go mad,' he admitted afterwards. The food was worse than at Pentonville. 'It even smelt bad. It was not fit for dogs.'[2] He became more and more mentally depressed and longed to die. 'It was my one desire.' Time and again his thoughts turned to suicide. 'During the first six months I was dreadfully unhappy, so utterly miserable that I wanted to kill myself,' he told the French writer André Gide afterwards. 'But what kept me from doing so was looking at the others, and seeing that they were as unhappy as I was and feeling sorry for them.'[3] From one fellow-prisoner he received a touching expression of sympathy, which landed him in trouble. One day

[1] For doubts cast on this story, see below, Appendix E, p. 214.
[2] Harris. II, 332–3.
[3] André Gide. *Oscar Wilde. A Study*. Translated by Stuart Mason (1905), p. 63.

at exercise in the prison yard, a prisoner whispered to him in the hoarse voice men get from long and compulsory silence: 'I am sorry for you; it is harder for the likes of you than it is for the likes of us.'[1] This kindness brought tears to the unhappy Wilde's eyes. 'No my friend,' he cried, 'we all suffer alike.' He had not yet learned to speak like the other prisoners, without moving his lips. In the result he was punished for talking, and, as he told the Governor that it was he who had begun the talking, he received double punishment.[2]

The deterioration in Wilde's condition gradually increased, although it was scarcely noticeable to the casual observer. One of several French journalists, M. Gaston Routier, who obtained permission to visit the prison, saw Wilde there during the first half of August and reported the fact to his newspaper. 'In traversing the gallery', he wrote, 'I met Oscar Wilde and three or four other prisoners; at my approach the warder, who accompanied them, made them turn with their faces to the wall, and Oscar Wilde, after throwing me two or three sidelong glances, philosophically contemplated the wall with his hands behind his back. . . . He seemed to be slightly thinner, but otherwise well enough; he had the resigned air of a man waiting for the end of an irksome task.'[3] On the other hand, the chaplain realised that mentally as well as physically Wilde was far from well. 'For a time he bore the change with remarkable fortitude,' noted the Rev W. D. Morrison, 'accepting with apparent resignation the plank bed, the coarse fare, the ill-fitting garments, the rigid silence, the oakum picking, the monotonous

[1] *De Profundis*, 122.

[2] Gide, *op. cit.*, 66–8. Gide attributes this incident to Reading, but Wilde states in *De Profundis* that it took place in Wandsworth. The punishment for this breach of regulations was confinement in a dark cell for up to three days on a diet of bread and water.

[3] Communicated by M. Guillot de Saix. Lord Alfred Douglas wrote at this time to the Home Secretary from France, asking whether it was a fact that 'permission was given to a gang of filthy journalists to go and gape at Mr Oscar Wilde in his prison dress' in Wandsworth Gaol. 'If it is true that such permission was granted,' Douglas continued, 'allow me to express the opinion that whoever was responsible for granting the permission was guilty of an outrage against humanity and common decency, the outrage of exhibiting to a gang of sightseers the spectacle of a great poet and man of incomparable genius in shameful dress and under the revolting conditions to which a nation of cowards and hypocrites has condemned him. If you, sir, are the person responsible for this disgusting outrage, pray have no hesitation in accepting these remarks as addressed to yourself, or in requiring from me any satisfaction or explanation you may deem due to you.' In the circumstances it is hardly surprising that the official who read this letter, before passing it to Sir Mathew Ridley, should have minuted it for the Secretary of State's guidance: 'Nothing this man says seems to require any attention.' Home Office Papers.

isolation and all the daily humiliations of a prisoner's lot. But at the end of a few weeks it was easy to see that this man would break down long before his sentence came to an end. He was losing flesh, he was refusing food, his face was assuming a deathly pallor; he was presenting all the physical symptoms of an approaching crisis. The great silent machine into whose clutches he had fallen was slowly but inevitably undermining his reserves of strength. One of the most painful experiences of prison life is to watch the process of exhaustion in operation to know it can be stopped, and yet to be quite unable to interfere with it, until the fatal collapse is close at hand.'[1]

[1] *Fortnightly Review*, vol. 61, at p. 781 (May, 1898): 'Prisons and Prisoners'. Morrison does not mention Wilde by name in this article, but it is clear from the context that he is referring to him.

CHAPTER II

Bankruptcy and Breakdown

1

AT this time Wilde was subjected to the additional strain of the long drawn out bankruptcy proceedings. On Queensberry's petition a receiving order had been made on July 25. Four days later the Official Receiver sent an officer of the court to Wandsworth Prison to take a statement of his affairs from the debtor. This statement, which the Official Receiver duly reported at the first meeting of Wilde's creditors on August 26, revealed that his assets consisted almost entirely of royalties from his books and plays. According to Wilde, his income had averaged not less than £2,000 a year from this source: he attributed his apparent insolvency to the failure of his prosecution of Lord Queensberry and his subsequent arrest and conviction, which had resulted in the complete cessation of his income, since his plays were immediately taken off and there was no sale for his books. Apart from an interest under his father's will in a small property in Ireland, which produced between £100 and £150 a year and which he shared with his brother Willie, his only other asset was a reversionary life interest in his wife's marriage settlement. This settlement produced an income of about £800 a year for Mrs Constance Wilde; and, since the trust deed contained no provision that in the event of his becoming bankrupt his interest should vest in the children of the marriage, the creditors claimed to have the life interest sold for their benefit. At the moment, however, the interest had little actuarial value, since Wilde was several years older than his wife, and her life from every other point of view was a better one than his. Nevertheless, it was entitled to rank as an asset in the bankruptcy. In fact it was to assume considerable importance for reasons which appear presently.

A week or so later, Wilde's solicitors obtained a special visiting order enabling them to take the necessary depositions from their client so as to file his Statement of Affairs in connexion with the bankruptcy. The occasion was also memorable for the first message which Wilde received, since his imprisonment began, from Alfred Douglas. The solicitors had been in touch with Douglas in the forlorn hope of receiving some financial aid from him. The firm had sent down one of their clerks and a Commissioner of Oaths to Wandsworth and the interview took place in the presence of the customary warder. Suddenly the clerk leaned across the table and, having consulted a piece of paper, which he pulled from his pocket, said to Wilde in a low voice: 'Prince Fleur de Lys wishes to be remembered to you.' Wilde stared at him. He repeated the message, adding mysteriously: 'The gentleman is abroad at present.' Suddenly the meaning flashed on Wilde and he laughed bitterly. 'In that laugh was all the scorn of all the world.' He later wrote to Douglas in a letter which Douglas never read: 'You were, no doubt, quite right to communicate with me under an assumed name. I myself, at that time, had no name at all. In the great prison where I was then incarcerated, I was merely the figure and letter of a little cell in a long gallery, one of a thousand lifeless numbers as of a thousand lifeless lives. But surely there were many real names in real history which would have suited you much better, and by which I would have had no difficulty in recognising you at once? I did not look for you behind the spangles of a tinsel vizard suitable only for an amusing masquerade.'[1]

The first general meeting of Wilde's creditors took place in Bankruptcy Buildings in Carey Street before the Official Receiver, Mr A. H. Wildy. Mr Travers Humphreys, who had appeared as Wilde's junior counsel in all three trials and also at the preliminary police court proceedings, represented the debtor. He stated that, although every effort had been made, Wilde was not in a position to submit an offer to his creditors. For this reason it was not considered necessary for him to attend the meeting. In these circumstances it only remained to pass a resolution that he be adjudged bankrupt and to appoint a trustee. This was accordingly done on the motion of Lord Queensberry. The Official Receiver was appointed trustee.

[1] *De Profundis*, 59–60.

At the same time, the date of the debtor's public examination was fixed for four weeks later.[1]

Wilde had now completed nearly three months of his sentence, when under the prison regulations he would be entitled to receive and send a letter and also to receive a visit of twenty minutes' duration from a friend. It appears that Lord Alfred Douglas applied to the Governor for permission to write to him, but that Wilde felt obliged to reserve this privilege for the first time for 'family business'. According to his own account, the first letter he was allowed to read came from his brother-in-law, Otho Holland Lloyd, who informed him that if he 'would only write once' to his wife she would in all probability for his sake, and for the sake of their children, take no action for divorce, as she was being pressed by Sir George Lewis and other family advisers to do. Wilde not unnaturally regarded it as his duty to write to her. Surprising as it might seem to some of his friends, he was really very fond of his wife and felt sorry for her, although he was aware that she could not understand him and he had been 'bored to death with married life'. Also, he could not bear the idea of being separated from his two small boys, especially Cyril, the elder, 'one single hair of whose little golden head', he told Alfred Douglas, 'should have been dearer and more valuable to me than, I will not say, you from top to toe, but the entire crysolite of the whole world: was so indeed to me always, though I failed to understand it till too late'.[2]

The text of Wilde's letter to his wife has not survived. But whatever he wrote to her must have touched her deeply. At this time Constance Wilde was staying with friends on the Continent, and she accordingly wrote to the Governor for a visiting order, as she had an opportunity of travelling to England with a friend, who had agreed to look after her on the journey. The Governor replied that her husband had just received a visit and was not due for another 'for a considerable time'. However, he advised her to apply to the Prison Commissioners, since the circumstances seemed exceptional. This Constance Wilde did, and soon afterwards left for England in

[1] *The Times*, August 27, 1895. According to the Official Receiver, the accounts showed unsecured liabilities of £2,676 and partly secured debts of £915, a total deficiency of £3,591 being disclosed. The adjudication order was made on August 31.

[2] *De Profundis*, 57–8.

the expectation that her request would be granted. 'My husband, I have reason to know, is apprehensive of my obtaining a divorce from him within a short time', she wrote. 'As my mind is not however definitely made up to this step, but is dependent on questions which can only properly be discussed between him and me personally, I am most anxious to be allowed to talk over matters with him and discuss the arrangements, business and others of an intimate nature, by which so extreme a step might be avoided.'[1]

The visit to which the Governor had referred was the first which Wilde received from any of his friends. It came from Robert Sherard, his future biographer and 'that bravest and most chivalrous of all brilliant beings', as Wilde described him in *De Profundis*.[2] It took place on August 26, 1895, almost exactly three months to the day after the prisoner's conviction. The visiting order was for two, but though he wrote to other friends, he could find no one to accompany him. It was, of course, the holiday season, which may have accounted for the fact that, in Sherard's words, 'everybody was unfortunately engaged'.

When he came to write about it, Sherard had no distinct recollection of that painful meeting, except the shock to his nerves caused by the rattle of the warders' keys and the clang of iron doors. The interview took place in a vaulted room, which appeared to Sherard like a prison chamber in some old-fashioned melodrama. Prisoner and visitor were separated by a double row of iron bars, and in the passageway between stood a warder, who kept his eyes fixed on a noisy clock, which ticked

[1] Mrs Constance Wilde to Prison Commissioners, September 13, 1895: Home Office (Prison Commission) Papers.

[2] Robert Harborough Sherard (1861–1943), journalist and great-grandson of the poet Wordsworth. His father was a clergyman, the Rev B. Sherard Kennedy, of Stapleford Park, Melton Mowbray. Soon after leaving Oxford he dropped his surname of Kennedy in favour of his family name of Sherard, under which he wrote and by which he was always known. His first literary work, a volume of poems entitled *Whispers*, appeared in 1884 and was dedicated to Wilde. He subsequently wrote five books and numerous articles on Wilde, which are valuable for their personal reminiscences but deficient as an objective account. In his application to the Prison Commissioners, dated August 15, Sherard wrote: 'I am one of O. W. Wilde's oldest friends, and it would be a great kindness both to him and to me if you would accord me leave to see him under the conditions prescribed by the prison regulations.' For twenty years Sherard was a newspaper correspondent in Paris, and he later lived in Corsica, where he started a publishing business. His personal account of his association with Wilde, *Oscar Wilde. The Story of an Unhappy Friendship*, was first published in a privately printed edition in 1902 and republished in 1906.

away the brief allowance of twenty minutes. Both Sherard and Wilde clung to the iron bars for support, while Sherard noticed that his friend's hands were disfigured and his nails broken and bleeding from picking oakum, also that his head and face were untidy with growth of hair. They talked mostly of literature. Wilde was now allowed one book a week from the prison library, which included the volumes which Haldane had provided. What he complained of most, according to Sherard, was that this ration was quite insufficient for an omnivorous reader. To the visitor Wilde appeared greatly depressed and at one moment there were tears in his eyes. Sherard affected a cheerfulness which he was far from feeling, but just as their time together was up, Sherard won a laugh from him. As he left the gaol, the visitor was accosted by a reporter from an evening newspaper. 'I was much struck by his courage and resignation', Sherard was later reported as saying, 'though his punishment weighs terribly upon him.'[1] Shortly after this Sherard informed the *Daily Chronicle* that the prisoner was 'insufficiently fed' and was 'suffering greatly from sheer want of nourishment'.[2]

Prompted probably by Press statements about Wilde's state of health, the Prison Commissioners asked the Governor of Wandsworth at this time for a medical report, what he was employed on and whether the Governor had any suggestions to make regarding his treatment. On September 18 the Medical Officer, Dr Quinton, reported as follows:

> Reg. No. 13090 Oscar Wilde is in good general health at present. Although he is on extra diet, he has lost a good deal of weight (22 lbs) since reception. He was then very fat. His reception weight was 190 lbs and today it is 168. He makes no complaint of his health or treatment, says he sleeps better lately than at first, but complains of feeling hungry, especially in the evening. I am recommending a further increase in diet for him in consequence of his loss of weight.

To this report the Governor, Captain Helby, added the following remarks:

> Oscar Wilde is employed in his cell on the pouch-making industry (bags for letter-carriers for the Post Office). I have previously

[1] R. H. Sherard. *The Story of an Unhappy Friendship* (1902), pp. 196 *et seq.*; *Life of Oscar Wilde* (1906), p. 373; *The Real Oscar Wilde* (1915), p. 386.
[2] *Daily Chronicle*, September 28, 1895.

intimated to him that if suffering from *special* mental depression, any application from him to work out of his cell would be considered. His reply was that if he found it so he would apply (through the Medical Officer).

I have no suggestion to make regarding his treatment. I have reason to think that a more helpful prospect about his family arrangements and future, which has recently been opened to him, has relieved his mind of one great cause of despondency, and will probably enable him to bear his imprisonment better.

I may observe that he lost weight principally during the earlier part of his sentence (which accords with general experience)—since his transfer here (4th July) he has only lost 8 lbs. The Medical Officer has taken cognizance of this circumstance and has ordered him some additional diet.

When they had read these reports, Ruggles-Brise and the other Prison Commissioners decided to send down Dr R. M. Gover, the Superintending Medical Officer of Prisons, to Wandsworth to see whether Wilde could not best be employed in labour outside his cell. Dr Gover duly visited Wandsworth on September 20 and reported to the Prison Board on the same day.

I have seen Oscar Wilde in consultation with Dr. Quinton. He was cheerful and comfortable, and had just eaten a hearty dinner. As his appetite is exceedingly good, he thoroughly appreciates the very considerable increase that Dr. Quinton has made in his diet.

I had a long conversation with him and found no evidence of despondency. On the contrary, the prisoner is adjusting himself in a sensible manner to his new environment, and seems to have no difficulty in reconciling himself to the inevitable. He did not manifest any want of nerve or courage, and I could find nothing in his demeanour, appearance or conversation to indicate that he is in the least degree 'crushed' or 'broken'. He does not appear to wish to be placed in association. In point of fact he stated to me that he had a dislike of seeing 'fresh faces'. I should imagine from what dropped from him that he would like to be left a little more to himself.

In cases of this kind it is sometimes advisable not to manifest great solicitude, and I think it would be desirable, for the present at least, to leave him where he is. At the same time he will be carefully watched, and the able medical officer Dr. Quinton will do whatever is necessary.

The truth is that Wilde was a consummate actor and was in

fact much nearer a breakdown than appeared to the two doctors. Dr Gover proposed to see him again shortly and to consider with the prison doctor the advisability of allowing him to work out of his cell. But, before he could do this, the crisis had occurred.

2

Constance Wilde arrived in London on September 19 to find an order waiting which entitled her to visit Wandsworth. Two days later the meeting took place in the most painful and humiliating conditions. 'It was indeed awful, more so than I had any conception it could be', she told Sherard afterwards. 'I could not see him and I could not touch him and I scarcely spoke. . . . When I go again, I am to get at the Home Secretary through Mr. Haldane and try and get a room to see him in and touch him again. He has been mad these last three years, and he says that if he saw Alfred Douglas he would kill him. So he had better keep away, and be satisfied with having marred a fine life. Few people can boast of so much.'[1]

The circumstances of this visit and other visits which he received in prison were described by Wilde after his release in a letter on prison reform which he sent to the *Daily Chronicle*. He urged that 'the mode at present in vogue of exhibiting a prisoner to his friends' should be changed. 'Under the present system', he wrote, 'the prisoner is either locked up in a large iron cage or in a large wooden box, with a small aperture, covered with a wire netting, through which he is allowed to peer. His friends are placed in a similar cage, some three or four feet distant, and two warders stand between to listen to, and if they wish, stop or interrupt the conversation, such as it may be . . . To be exhibited like an ape in a cage, to people who are fond of one, and of whom one is fond, is a needless and horrible degradation.' Wilde argued that such interviews should take place in the same conditions in which a prisoner was allowed to see his solicitor, that is to say in a room with a glass door, on the other side of which stood the warder.[2] It is significant that a similar opinion had already been expressed

[1] Sherard. *Unhappy Friendship*, 202. There is a facsimile reproduction of Constance Wilde's letter to Sherard in his *The Real Oscar Wilde*, at p. 173.
[2] *Daily Chronicle*, March 24, 1898.

by the chaplain at Wandsworth in his evidence before the Departmental Committee on Prisons.[1]

A day or two after Constance Wilde's visit, Sherard, who claims to have persuaded her to forgive him, was allowed to see Wilde again, a special order being granted on the grounds that he had 'matters of most urgent importance to communicate to the prisoner'. The ostensible grounds were the conditions under which a reconciliation could be effected between Wilde and his wife, but the visit seems to have been prompted mainly by a piece of news about Alfred Douglas which had come to Sherard's knowledge. Sherard said he had heard that Douglas had written an article on Wilde which contained a number of Wilde's letters to Douglas. The article was to be published in a Paris monthly magazine, the *Mercure de France*. Sherard asked Wilde if this really was his wish. Considering that it was due to Douglas's carelessness that two of the more compromising examples of their correspondence had been produced by Lord Queensberry and quoted with deadly effect in Wilde's trials, it was not surprising that the prisoner should have been 'greatly taken aback and much annoyed'. He begged Sherard to use his influence with the editor to have the article stopped. Later he was to write to Douglas: 'You had left my letters lying about for blackmailing companions to steal, for hotel servants to pilfer, for housemaids to sell. That was simply your careless want of appreciation of what I had written to you. But that you should seriously propose to publish selections from the balance was incredible to me. And which of my letters were they? I could get no information.'[2] Indeed Sherard had no knowledge at the time as to which letters Douglas wished to include in his article, but he told Wilde he would do his best to prevent any of them from appearing.

Sherard later recalled that they had a long and pleasant talk together, though a warder sat with his eyes glued on Sherard's hands, lest the visitor should attempt to slip any contraband article to the prisoner. He found Wilde 'greatly cheered by his wife's visit'. The interview lasted for an hour and Sherard

[1] 'In the case of first offenders I should allow an interview between husband and wife, and in the case of first offenders it might take place free from humiliating barriers. Interviews of that character are very heartbreaking. The wife, if she is the innocent person, and the husband, if he is the innocent man, feel it very keenly.' Evidence of the Rev W. D. Morrison, *Report of Departmental Committee on Prisons* (1895), at p. 106.

[2] *De Profundis*, 58.

later passed to other literary topics. But this subject seemed subversive to the warder, who interrupted the conversation by saying that, if they had finished discussing 'business', the interview must be held to be terminated. 'Whereupon to his great horror', noted Sherard afterwards, 'I put my arms round my friend and pressed him to my bosom, and so departed.' For these attentions Mrs Wilde was very grateful. 'I thank you for your kindness to a fallen friend', she wrote to Sherard at the time. 'You are kind and gentle to him, and you are, I think, the only person he can bear to see.'[1]

Wilde's next ordeal was the Bankruptcy Court. On September 24, 1895, he was brought up in the custody of two policemen for his public examination. A considerable crowd had collected in Carey Street in anticipation of an entertaining spectacle. But, though they caught a glimpse of the debtor in handcuffs, they were largely disappointed. Pending an application for an adjournment, which was made by counsel on his behalf, Wilde waited with the policemen in an adjoining room. Incidentally, he was to pay a warm tribute in *De Profundis* to these two members of the Metropolitan police 'who, in their homely, rough way strove to comfort me in my journeys to and from the Bankruptcy Court under conditions of terrible mental distress'. It appeared that several of his friends had subscribed various sums of money, and with others, which were anticipated as forthcoming, there was, said counsel 'every reason to believe' that 'there would be sufficient to pay all the creditors 20s in the pound'. No creditor appeared to oppose the application, and in these circumstances the Registrar adjourned the examination for seven weeks.[2] Meanwhile, one of the friends in question, Robert Ross,[3] was waiting in the long dreary corridor outside, so that, as Wilde put it in a memorable passage in *De Profundis*, 'before the whole crowd, whom an action so sweet and simple hushed into silence, he might gravely raise his hat to me, as, handcuffed and with bowed head, I passed him by. Men have gone to heaven for smaller things than that.[4]'

[1] Sherard. *Unhappy Friendship*, 202–4. [2] *The Times*, September 25, 1895.

[3] Robert Baldwin Ross (1869–1918), author and art connoisseur, was a Canadian. He later became Wilde's literary executor and edited the collected editions of his works. For a time, with two other of Wilde's friends, More Adey and Arthur Clifton, he was a member of a firm of picture dealers in London, the Carfax Co. He was also an Additional Trustee of the National Gallery. An interesting selection from his wide correspondence has been published: see Margery Ross, *Robert Ross, Friend of Friends* (1952). [4] *De Profundis*, 68.

Wilde was now approaching a complete breakdown. What with the strain of the bankruptcy, added to the purgings and the semi-starvation and sleeplessness, he grew noticeably weaker. His clothes seemed literally to hang on him and he could scarcely move. In fact, as has already been seen, he had lost more than a stone and a half in weight. One Sunday morning, about ten days after his visit to Carey Street, and after a particularly bad night, he was unable to get out of bed. A warder entered his cell, and Wilde told him he was ill.

'You had better get up,' said the warder ominously.

'I can't,' murmured the wretched man from the bed. 'You must do what you like with me.'

Half an hour later the prison doctor came and looked in at the cell door. He did not come near the prisoner, but contented himself with calling out: 'Get up. No malingering. You're all right. You'll be punished if you don't get up.' Then he went away.[1]

Somehow Wilde forced himself to get up and struggled into his prison clothes. While dressing, he fell and bruised himself. Then, with the other prisoners he went to chapel where they sang hymns, 'dreadful hymns all out of tune in praise of their pitiless God'. He could hardly stand up. Everything kept disappearing and coming back faintly before his eyes. Finally he collapsed in a heap on the floor of the chapel.

When he recovered consciousness, he was in an infirmary cell. He felt a pain in his ear, where he had fallen. But there was a kind warder beside him who urged him to eat something. There were clean white sheets on the bed, and he kept pushing his toes against them, they were so smooth and cool and clean. The warder gave him some thin white bread and butter. It was the first he had tasted since becoming a prisoner. 'I shall never forget it', he recalled afterwards. 'The warder was so kind. I did not like to tell him I was famished; but when he went away I picked up the crumbs off the sheet and ate them, and when I could find no more I pulled myself to the edge of the bed, and picked up the crumbs from the floor and ate those as well; the white bread was so good and I was so hungry.'

One of the first to visit him in the infirmary cell was the kindly chaplain, the Rev W. D. Morrison. He remembered

[1] Harris. II, 334–6. For doubts cast on this and other stories, for which Frank Harris is the authority, see below, Appendix E, p. 212.

afterwards using the word patience in the course of conversation. 'I could be patient,' said Wilde miserably, 'for patience is a virtue. It is not patience, it is apathy you want here, and apathy is a vice.'[1]

A week or so later, when he had recovered some of his strength, he was removed to the general infirmary ward, where he had the company of several other sick prisoners. He greatly appreciated this change. But he still felt wretchedly ill, and while in this condition he was called out of the ward to see the prison Governor. He found Captain Helby at his desk with a letter in his hand, which the Governor proceeded to read out. It was addressed to the Governor from Lord Alfred Douglas and confirmed what the prisoner had heard from Sherard about the article, 'On the Case of Mr. Oscar Wilde', which Douglas had written for the *Mercure de France*. This communication also enlightened Wilde as to which of his letters Douglas wished to include in the article, and which Sherard had been unable to tell him. They were the letters which Wilde had written while he was on remand in Holloway prison awaiting his first trial, and later, after the jury had disagreed and he had been let out on bail before coming up at the next Old Bailey sessions; 'the letters', as Wilde subsequently reproached Douglas, 'that should have been to you things sacred and secret beyond anything in the whole world!' Wilde could now only reiterate his refusal to allow the letters to be published. He thought that at least Douglas might have remembered the sonnet, which Wilde had written after he had witnessed the sale at a public auction in London of Keats's love letters to Fanny Brawn.

> . . . I think they love not art
> Who break the crystal of a poet's heart—
> That small and sickly eyes may glare and gloat.[2]

Unfortunately Douglas had acted from the best of intentions. He honestly believed that, if it were published, the article with the letters would have the effect 'of completely rehabilitating Oscar, at any rate in France'. There is no doubt, however, that, contrary to what Douglas himself thought of them, the appearance of these letters in print, even in a French translation, would have done Wilde more harm than the two com-

[1] *Fortnightly Review, loc. cit.*

[2] *De Profundis*, 60–1. The Keats letters were sold at Sotheby's on March 2, 1885. Wilde was present throughout the sale and made several purchases: Stuart Mason, *Bibliography of Oscar Wilde* (1914), p. 60.

promising letters which had been quoted in the trials. Wilde seems to have realised this. But, as events turned out, he had alarmed himself unnecessarily. Sherard was already in touch with the editor of the *Mercure de France*, and, although the article was already in type, the editor wrote to Douglas asking him to omit the letters. This Douglas refused to do, and the whole article was in consequence withdrawn.[1]

3

Almost from the beginning of Wilde's imprisonment, rumours had been current outside the prison that he was suffering from a serious mental breakdown. Consequently when the news leaked out, early in October, that he was in the prison infirmary in Wandsworth, it was thought that he was now in danger of going completely out of his mind, if indeed he had not already done so. Apparently Sherard was allowed to visit Wilde again at this time. He was accompanied by a French journalist named Edouard Conte, and he seems to have been assiduous in drawing attention to his condition, notably in the pages of the *Daily Chronicle*. He wrote to another of Wilde's friends, More Adey, early in October: 'I saw him in the infirmary at Wandsworth on Monday. He is a perfect wreck and says he will be dead before long.'[2] Sir Mathew Ridley seems to have realised that there would be an extensive public outcry in the country, if Wilde was allowed to go mad or to die in prison, since he gave instructions at this time that some official action should be taken. Accordingly, on October 10, Mr Kenelm Digby, the Permanent Under-Secretary at the Home Office,[3]

[1] Sherard. *Unhappy Friendship*, 204–5. Douglas has given his version of the affair in Chapter XXI of his *Autobiography* (1929). At Wilde's request Robert Ross asked Douglas to hand over these and all other letters in Douglas's possession with the object of their being sealed up until Wilde came out of prison (see letter from Wilde to Ross, May 1896: H–D, 400). This Douglas refused to do. He subsequently destroyed the letters and, apart from a few sentences which he quoted from memory in his *Autobiography*, the original English text does not appear to have survived in any copy. But Wilde's bibliographer C. S. Millard ('Stuart Mason') succeeded in getting the text of the French translation of the article and letters and he translated them back into English. From Millard's MS. which was shown to me by courtesy of Mr G. F. Sims, I was able to make a copy of this re-translation, which shows clearly that right up to the time of his conviction Wilde was devoted to Douglas.

[2] Communicated by courtesy of Mr G. F. Sims.

[3] Sir Kenelm Digby (1836–1916) had previously been an Oxford law don and a county court judge. He was Permanent Under-Secretary at the Home Office from 1895 to 1903.

authorised two mental specialists from Broadmoor, Dr David Nicolson and Dr Richard Brayne, to visit Wilde in the infirmary and report on whether there should be any change in his present treatment, 'serious representations having reached the Secretary of State as to the mental condition of the prisoner, Oscar Wilde'.[1]

Before this visit took place, the prisoner received two other visits, which must be mentioned. The first was from Robert Sherard's brother, Mr R. S. Kennedy, who, like Sherard, had been in touch with Mrs Constance Wilde, with a view to preventing the contemplated divorce proceedings; he was allowed to see Wilde as a special visitor to discuss the conditions under which she was willing to abstain from such proceedings. This application was made before Wilde's meeting with his wife some weeks previously, so that when Mr Kennedy arrived at Wandsworth on October 14, this question had already been more or less settled. Mr Kennedy seems to have devoted the interview to questioning Wilde about his treatment in prison, in such a manner that the warder, who was on duty on this occasion, subsequently made a report in writing to the Governor. The visitor, according to the warder, 'in the course of conversation informed the prisoner that it was thought something could be done, by means of the *Daily Chronicle*, to call attention to his case, meaning to me to infer that a correspondence should be started in this paper. The prisoner expressed himself as not being in favour of this course, and the prisoner seemed very averse to any publicity of this kind.' The Governor in turn passed on this information to the Prison Commissioners with the suggestion that it might be advisable to transfer Wilde to a country prison where he might be less accessible to such influences. 'I may also add that the prisoner is at present under medical treatment in the infirmary,' wrote Captain Helby, 'and this makes it more likely that irregular communications may pass (through prisoners on discharge) with outside agitators.' Unfortunately, from the official point of view, Mr Kennedy was already on his way to Madagascar, where he intended to settle, so that there was no means of reproving him. As for the

[1] The 'serious representations' may have been made by the Conservative M.P. and philanthropist, Ernest Flower, with whom More Adey had been in touch. Some articles in the *Daily Chronicle* and again in the French Press condemning Wilde's treatment, which appeared about this time, may also have contributed to the Home Secretary's action.

Governor's proposal, Ruggles-Brise gave directions that it must await the result of the inquiry by the two specialists.

The other visit, also specially allowed, brought Wilde bad news. It was from his sister-in-law, Lily Wilde, who told him that his mother was not expected to live long and was making her will. The fact is that she had never really got over the shock of Oscar's trial and imprisonment and she had now come to feel that she had nothing to live for.[1]

The medical inquiry took place on October 22, and the two specialists reported to the Home Secretary a week later. They stated they could discover no evidence of mental disease in the prisoner, whom they were first able to observe through a spy-hole in one of the doors leading to the infirmary. They saw Wilde, apparently in excellent spirits, the centre of a group of other prisoners, whom he was holding entranced by his talk. Subsequent conversation with him confirmed the doctors in their initial impression that his mental faculties were unimpaired and furthermore that he was no longer suffering from any physical complaint. On the score of future treatment, they made a number of recommendations, which appear from their report. The principal one was to confirm the Governor's proposal that he should be transferred to some other prison outside London, where there were better opportunities than at Wandsworth for open-air activities such as gardening, for the doctors seem to have taken an unfavourable view of Wilde's expressed dislike of all forms of outdoor exercise.

Broadmoor Criminal Lunatic Asylum.
29th October, 1895.

. . . After spending some portion of his imprisonment in Pentonville prison where he lost weight to some extent, he was transferred to Wandsworth, where in spite of being put on extra diet he continued to lose weight, the maximum recorded loss being 22 lbs. As he was a man of bulky and flabby physique and weighed originally 195 lbs this loss under the circumstances is not surprising: nor is it necessarily an unmixed evil, especially as there was no corresponding loss of 'condition', the prisoner himself informing us that he had never accustomed himself to walking or physical exercise of any sort and found no pleasure in either.

In the early part of the present month he appears to have deve-

[1] Home Office (Prison Commission) Papers. The visit from Mrs Lily Wilde took place on October 17, 1895.

loped a tendency to diarrhoea due possibly to the proportion of oatmeal and brown bread in the dietary. For this he was removed for treatment to an infirmary cell and afterwards placed in association in the infirmary upon hospital diet with white bread and extras. Up to this time he had been employed making canvas bags for the post office in the ordinary prison cell.

With regard to the prisoner's present condition, when we first saw him he was unaware of our presence and he was smiling and conversing apparently in a friendly and cheerful way with the other inmates of the ward. During our interview with him he entered freely into the circumstances of his past history, more especially as they had relation to his present position which he appeared to feel acutely, and upon which he dilated with great fervour and some amount of emotional depression, occasionally accompanied by tears. This display of feeling was no doubt referable, as he himself gave us to understand, to remorseful and bitter thoughts of the blasting of his future by the abominable follies of the past, and we do not regard it as being either unnatural or as indicating mental derangement. The display was possibly accentuated by the sympathetic nature of our inquiries, and by the knowledge that friends were agitating on his behalf, a fact which he is quite capable of taking advantage of.

He expressed himself as being quite satisfied with his present treatment and as being comparatively happy in his associated infirmary ward, signifying his intense dislike of the thought of having to return to the ordinary prison cell. He has gained 6 lbs in weight during the past week or two, and says he has much improved during that time. He struck us as being a man of indolent and lethargic temperament: and the medical officer informed us that he is very careless and slovenly in his habits and unwilling to take exercise. He does not appear to sleep very well at night, but in other respects his present bodily condition is satisfactory, and he complains of no bodily illness. He has a most excellent appetite and enjoys all the food he now gets and says he 'could do with more'. This we regard as being a valuable and healthy sign.

So far as his mental condition is concerned we found no indications of disease or derangement and we have explained that any tokens of mental depression which have manifested themselves were, up to the present at least, due to the natural and not unhealthy operation of circumstances and to the existence of a limited circle of thoughts which are unusually active in their character. He answered all our questions rationally and sensibly and if at times he responded slowly the reply always showed that careful consideration had been given to it.

It is our opinion that, taking imprisonment for what it is and what it is intended to be, its operation upon the mind of prisoner Oscar Wilde has not been such as to give rise to anxiety or alarm.

As to what may happen in a mind constituted as his is during the remainder of his imprisonment, we can only hazard an opinion: but so far as our inquiry has enabled us to judge, we have no reason to think that with the consideration which has, and will be, given to the circumstances of his case, any untoward or undesired result of a detrimental kind is likely to occur.

Further treatment.

(a) As some difficulty will be found in again locating him in an ordinary cell at Wandsworth after his stay in the associated infirmary, it would be well, under all the circumstances, to select a suitable prison in the country or away from London to which he should be transferred in the course of a week or two when his further associated treatment is uncalled for and his health still further improves.

(b) Location in a cell larger than the usual size.

(c) To be allowed such association with other prisoners as may be deemed advisable or desirable or convenient. It would not however be right to allow a man with his proclivities and with his avowed love for the society of males to be in association *except under the continuous supervision of a warder.*

(d) Variation of employment by giving him some bookbinding or other work which would be the means of enabling the time to pass in a less uninteresting way than a man brooding on the past.

(e) the continuation of such minor relaxations of the full rigour and discipline of prison life as have already been sanctioned, especially should a freer range of books be allowed and a larger supply.

(f) a country prison would suit well for insisting on the prisoner taking outdoor exercise *with some garden work,* with a view of a more wholesome state of his tissues being induced and his mind being thereby roused to more healthy action so far as the subjects of his thoughts are concerned.

(g) Points referring to the maintenance of his physical health.

He appears to require additional food: and an increase in this and an allowance of the Admiralty cocoa would be advantageous if thought to be necessary.

In conclusion we desire to bear testimony to the judicious care and treatment with which the Medical Officer of Wandsworth Prison has managed this difficult case.

DAV. NICOLSON
RICH. BRAYNE

On receipt of this report in the Home Office, a copy was forwarded to the Prison Commissioners and they were asked to what prison they thought Wilde should be sent. At the same time their attention was drawn to the passage in the report describing Wilde's conduct in conversing with the other prisoners in the infirmary ward, since talking between prisoners was expressly forbidden by prison rules. This prompted an immediate request to the Governor for information as to the nature of the supervision carried on in the infirmary. Captain Helby replied that the wards were constantly and necessarily left without any immediate supervision by a prison officer owing to the construction of the present old building and the limited staff. This in turn brought a curtly worded order from the Secretary to the Prison Board: 'Be so good as to make arrangements at once to ensure one officer being present at all times both by day and by night in the room in which the prisoner Oscar Wilde is located. Officers in whom you have complete confidence should be selected for this duty and they should be instructed to put a stop to all conversation in the ward.' The order was carried into effect on the same day, extra staff being sent to Wandsworth to take the place of the officers detailed for this special duty.

Meanwhile, the prisoner's health continued to improve and he put on some weight. On November 12, he was considered well enough to attend his adjourned public examination in the Bankruptcy Court. Up to the last moment his solicitors hoped that the need for this additional trial would be obviated by the subscription of a sufficient sum of money by Wilde's friends to enable his creditors to be paid in full. A certain amount had already been subscribed, but the balance was not forthcoming and the public examination duly took place. It was conducted in open court by the Official Receiver, Mr A. H. Wildy.

'Step by step with the Bankruptcy Receiver', wrote Wilde afterwards in *De Profundis*, 'I had to go over every item of my life. It was horrible.' He had never kept any books or accounts, he told the Official Receiver, but he estimated that his expenditure 'during the two or three years preceding the receiving order was at the rate of £2,900 a year'. Much of this went in the entertainment of Lord Alfred Douglas, as he was subsequently to remind that young man in several stinging passages in *De Profundis*. Between the autumn of 1892 and the date of his imprisonment, he reckoned he spent over £5,000 on Douglas, irrespective of bills outstanding at the time of his arrest—for instance, a number of these proved in the bankruptcy showed together £233 'in respect of tobacco, wines and jewellery supplied to the debtor'. An average day's expenses in London—'for luncheon, dinner, supper, amusements, hansoms and the rest of it'—ranged from £12 to £20. In a single week in Paris he spent £150 which besides their two selves included the expenses of Douglas's Italian servant. In the summer of 1893 he took a house for three months at Goring on the Thames at a total cost of £1,340. 'Though it may seem strange to you that one in the terrible position in which I am situated should find a difference between one disgrace and another,' he told Douglas, 'still I frankly admit that the folly of throwing away all this money on you, and letting you squander my fortune to your own hurt as well as mine, gives to me and in my eyes a note of common profligacy to my bankruptcy and makes me doubly ashamed of it.'[1]

Exactly a week later the Chairman of the Prison Commissioners informed the Home Secretary that, since the bankruptcy proceedings had now come to an end, Wilde would be removed to Reading Prison, where 'suitable occupation in the way of gardening and bookbinding and library work will be found for him'.[2] The transfer took place on the following day.

[1] *De Profundis*, 19–20.
[2] Minute of E. Ruggles-Brise, November 19, 1895: Home Office Papers.

CHAPTER III

Reading under Major Isaacson

1

THE passage in *De Profundis* which caught the attention of the critics and the public perhaps more than any other, when the book first appeared in a severely expurgated version in 1905, was that in which Wilde described his journey from Wandsworth to Reading. It has become, owing to frequent quotation, one of the best known passages in this work which Wilde composed in prison.[1]

> On November 13th, 1895, I was brought down here from London.[2] From two o'clock till half-past two on that day I had to stand on the centre platform at Clapham Junction in convict dress, and handcuffed, for the world to look at. I had been taken out of the hospital ward without a moment's notice being given to me. Of all possible objects I was the most grotesque. When people saw me they laughed. Each train as it came in swelled the audience. Nothing could exceed their amusement. That was, of course, before they knew who I was. As soon as they had been informed they laughed still more. For half-an-hour I stood there in the grey November rain surrounded by a jeering mob.

No wonder that for a year afterwards Wilde was to weep 'every day at the same hour and for the same space of time'. According to Sherard, Wilde's initial recognition on the station platform was accompanied by a particularly revolting exhibition of British philistinism and cruelty. A man, who had been staring at the handcuffed figure explained, for the benefit of the other onlookers: 'By God, that's Oscar Wilde.' He then stepped up to him and spat in his face.[3]

[1] *De Profundis*, 115–16.

[2] According to an official statement by the Deputy Governor in charge of Wandsworth, the transfer to Reading took place on November 20, 1895: Home Office (Prison Commission) Papers.

[3] Sherard. *Unhappy Friendship*, 212.

Situated at a short distance from the centre of the town, Reading prison was one of the smaller county prisons, which had been built on the Pentonville model. In this fortress-like battlemented building of red brick, a maximum of 192 men, each occupying a single cell, could be accommodated at any one time. There was also separate cellular accommodation for 29 women. The main building, which was reached through an iron-barred gate, across a courtyard and up a flight of steps, was designed in the form of a cross. The wing, through which both prisoners and visitors entered for the first time, consisted of the administrative block, including the Governor's office and Visiting Justices' room, and two condemned cells. This led to a large central hall, where the three ordinary cell blocks or galleries met. These galleries, which were designated 'A', 'B' and 'C', comprised four floors or landings. Wilde was allocated Cell 3 on the third landing of Gallery 'C', so that his prison number, by which he was officially known, was 'C.3.3'. (It was under this number that *The Ballad of Reading Gaol* was originally published.) The cell faced south, with a view across the exercise yard, so that on bright days a few rays of sunlight did penetrate through the small window set high up in the wall. By standing on his table and peering out, the prisoner could just catch a glimpse, beyond the yard, of 'some poor black soot-besmirched trees', as he described them. Twice before his release Wilde was destined to see these trees break into bud.

The average number of male prisoners at Reading in Wilde's time was 150, including about 45 soldiers, and these were under the direct charge of a chief warder, six warders and eight assistant warders. There were in addition the chaplain, medical officer and schoolmaster, who was employed on a part-time basis.[1] Finally, there was the Governor, Major Henry B. Isaacson, a military despot, under whose harsh rule Wilde was to suffer for the next eight months. He was a Jew, 'tall and not unlike the headmaster of a public school', according to Robert Ross, who was not unfavourably impressed by him on the occasion of their first meeting.[2] But to Frank Harris, a fairly acute observer, to whom he boasted that he was 'knocking the nonsense out of Wilde', the Governor

[1] *Report of Prison Commissioners* (1896).
[2] See below, p. 59.

seemed 'almost inhuman'.[1] Wilde has himself put it on record that under Major Isaacson 'the [prison] system was carried out with the greatest harshness and stupidity'.[2] He was 'very harsh,' Wilde later told André Gide, 'because he was entirely lacking in imagination'.[3] This testimony would seem to be borne out by official facts and figures, notably in the number of punishments awarded by him for breaches of prison regulations: it is significant that under his successor the number immediately fell by nearly two-thirds.[4] In his evidence before the Departmental Committee on Prisoners' Education, which reported about this period, Major Isaacson proclaimed his firm belief that any instruction should be given to a prisoner by the schoolmaster in his cell 'on account of the separation' rather than in a class. He was strongly opposed to the idea of allowing any prisoner to have a library book until he had served at least two months of his sentence. Nor was he in favour of making any relaxation of this rule, even on Sunday, when first- and second-stage prisoners were frequently shut up in their cells for the whole day with absolutely nothing to do except pick the oakum which was usually left there. Asked if he did not think Sunday was rather a dull day, the Governor of Reading gaol replied: 'Yes, it is a dull day for those who cannot read.' When it was put to him that it was a little hard on a prisoner to have to wait for two months for a library book, Major Isaacson's answer was characteristic: 'He values it a great deal more when he gets it.'[5]

> The Governor was strong upon
>   The Regulations Act:
> The Doctor said that death was but
>   A scientific fact:
> And twice a day the Chaplain called.
>   And left a little tract.

In this oft-quoted stanza from *The Ballad of Reading Gaol*, Wilde described the three principal prison figures as he remem-

[1] Harris. II, 606. [2] Letter to the *Daily Chronicle*, May 28, 1897.

[3] A. Gide. *Oscar Wilde*, trans. Stuart Mason (1905), p. 65.

[4] *Report of Prison Commissioners* (1896). During the year ended March 31, 1896, there were over 700 punishment awards in Reading prison, of which more than half took the form of reductions in diet. During the following year there were 360.

[5] *Report of Departmental Committee on the Education and Moral Instruction of Prisoners in Local and Convict Prisons, 1896.*

bered them, when a fellow prisoner was lying in the condemned cell. The chaplain, the Rev Martin Friend, struck Robert Ross, when he visited Reading, as being 'a nice, kind fellow'. But whatever his duties in connexion with those under sentence of death, the chaplain only saw the ordinary prisoner for a few minutes once a month in his cell. He was in charge of the small and inadequate prison library.[1] As for Dr Oliver Maurice, who, according to Ross, 'resembled a bullying director of a sham city company and had a greasy white beard', he saw Wilde on his admission and examined him again two months later, at the express request of the Home Office, when he pronounced the prisoner to be 'in good health both bodily and mentally', adding that 'the only complaint he makes is that he has restless nights'.[2] Wilde later told Ross that the doctor was 'very unkind to him'. Wilde had complained of increasing deafness in his right ear, which had been injured when he fainted and fell in the prison chapel at Wandsworth. An abscess had formed causing a perforation of the drum, but the doctor would appear to have made no serious attempt to effect a cure. His eyesight also began to cause trouble, and when his friend, More Adey, was eventually able, in the early part of 1896, to secure for him an edition of the Latin poets, he found it gave him a headache to read them for any length of time.[3] Otherwise, with the lighter work in the shape of bookbinding and gardening, together with rather a better diet, 'his physical condition to some extent improved'.

Meanwhile, a group of Wilde's friends, headed by More

[1] In an interview on his retirement after forty-one years in the prison service, the Rev Martin Friend spoke of Wilde as he remembered him: 'The prison routine was naturally trying to such a temperament, but sometimes in conversation in his cell his eye would light up, his body would straighten and he would pull himself together and seem, as it were, almost to project himself physically back into his old intellectual life.' Asked how Wilde's bearing and conversation in prison threw light on the sincerity or otherwise of his religious professions in *De Profundis*, the chaplain replied: 'That, of course, touches the great question about Wilde's whole life. There is no doubt that he wrote for effect, but at the same time I should say from my acquaintance with him that the spiritual side of his nature was thoroughly real. He was certainly not an atheist, though he never when I knew him came within reasonable distance of anything that could be described as orthodox religion.' *Daily News*, December 11, 1913.

[2] Report of Dr O. C. Maurice, January 20, 1896: Home Office Papers.

[3] On January 23, 1896, the Secretary to the Prison Commissioners wrote to the Governor of Reading, informing him that More Adey had received permission to send the following books for Wilde's use: Liddell and Scott's *Greek-English Lexicon*, *Corpus Poetarum Latinorum*, a Latin Dictionary, Dante's *Divina Comedia* and an Italian Dictionary and Grammar. The books were received at Reading on February 3, 1896: Home Office (Prison Commission) Papers.

Adey,[1] had prepared a petition for presentation to the Home Secretary praying the Queen for Wilde's early release. The petition was drawn up in writing, but it was not printed for general circulation, the object being to obtain the signatures of a few well-known individuals in the learned professions, literature, the arts and the Church, whose calling and character would place them beyond the suspicion of having any prejudice in favour of the prisoner or of any laxity of view with regard to offences of the kind of which he had been convicted. The first draft seems to have been the work of George Bernard Shaw, who knew Adey through their common interest in Scandinavian literature. Shaw had never been particularly friendly with Wilde, although they were fellow Irishmen; but he felt that his continued confinement under harsh prison regulations would incapacitate him from resuming his literary and dramatic work, if he were to serve the full term of his sentence. Shaw's draft was probably revised and amended by Adey. In its final version the petition set out that the prisoner had 'already suffered a punishment equivalent to any penalty the legislature intended to inflict' under the Criminal Law Amendment Act 'for offences of this class', and further that, if he should survive and complete his sentence, 'it is greatly to be feared he would ultimately be incapacitated from following his profession, and thus would be deprived, in the prime of life, of the means of earning a livelihood'. The petition concluded by praying that 'Your Majesty's merciful consideration may be extended to a Prisoner who must feel the weight of so terrible a punishment in a disproportionate degree to that which would be experienced by one not accustomed to work entirely, as in the Prisoner's case, with his brain'.[2]

Bernard Shaw told Wilde's brother Willie at this time that, although he and the Rev Stewart Headlam, a fellow Fabian

[1] William More Adey (1858–1942), writer and art connoisseur. In 1892 he collaborated with Robert Ross in a biography of Wilde's literary great-uncle, Charles Maturin. As a young man he also helped William Archer to interpret Scandinavian literature to the English public, and published an admirable translation of Ibsen's drama *Brand*, which was successfully produced at the Court Theatre in London in his version. He was later associated with Ross in the direction of the Carfax Picture Gallery, and from 1911 to 1919 was joint editor of the *Burlington Magazine*. As Ross's literary executor he took over the management of the Wilde literary estate, jointly with Wilde's surviving son Mr Vyvyan Holland, and in this capacity edited the second of the two short volumes of Wilde's post-prison letters to Ross, *After Reading* (1921) and *After Berneval* (1922). His later years were clouded by a long mental illness.

[2] *Oscar Wilde: Three Times Tried* (1912), p. 468.

Socialist, who had gone bail for Wilde after his first trial, were ready to sign the petition, 'that would be no use, as we were two notorious cranks, and our names would by themselves reduce the petition to absurdity and do Oscar more harm than good'.[1] Willie Wilde remarked that he did not think signatures would be obtainable. Events soon proved him right. The only prominent individual, whom Adey could persuade actually to sign, was Professor York Powell, Regius Professor of History at Oxford.[2] Several other signatures of influential men were promised; but, when the time came, they were not forthcoming. Most people were afraid to sign. Some refused on moral or conscientious grounds. Among the latter was Holman Hunt, the Pre-Raphaelite artist and painter of religious pictures, of which the best known is 'The Light of the World'. 'I must repeat my opinion that the law treated him with exceeding leniency,' Hunt wrote to Adey in his letter of refusal, 'and state that further consideration of the facts convinces me that in justice to criminals belonging to other classes of society, I should have to join in the cry for doing away with all personal responsibility, if I took any part in appealing for his liberation before the completion of his term of imprisonment. While such a course might seem benevolent to malefactors, it would scarcely be so to the self-restrained and orderly members of society.' As Wilde's younger son was later to put it in his autobiography, it is only fair to suppose that Holman Hunt, when he wrote this letter, had forgotten the quotation which inspired his celebrated painting.[3] In these circumstances the petition project had to be dropped for the time being.

2

It was about this time that Lady Wilde's condition took a decided turn for the worse. Early in the New Year she caught a chill, which developed into an acute attack of bronchitis, and complications followed. When she realised that she was

[1] Harris. II (supplement by G. B. Shaw), 5.

[2] Frederick York Powell (1850–1904), an authority on early English history, occupied the Regius Chair of History at Oxford from 1894 until his death.

[3] 'I expect to pass through this world but once. Any good, therefore, that I can do, or any kindness that I can show to any fellow creature, let me do it now. Let me not defer or neglect it, for I shall not pass this way again.' Cited with the letter from Hunt dated November 30, 1895, in Vyvyan Holland's *Son of Oscar Wilde* (1954), at p. 204.

seriously ill, she asked that her son Oscar should be allowed to come and see her. Naturally enough this request was refused as being contrary to prison regulations. 'May the prison help him,' she said, when they brought her the news in bed, turning her face to the wall. These were her last recorded words. She died on February 3, 1896.[1]

Oscar Wilde was always superstitious and he liked to think too that he possessed certain psychic qualities. After he came out of prison, he told the American writer, Vincent O'Sullivan, quite seriously, that on the night of his mother's death she appeared to him in his cell. She was dressed in outdoor clothes, and he asked her to take off her hat and cloak and sit down. But she shook her head sadly and vanished. It was then, he said, that he knew she was dead.[2]

He had always been deeply devoted to his mother, of whose achievements he was very proud. Even his profligate elder brother Willie, between whom and Oscar there was not much love lost, had to admit that, 'despite all his faults and follies, he was always a good son to her'.[3] The tribute which he paid to her memory along with that of his father, forms one of the most striking passages in *De Profundis*. 'Her death was terrible to me,' he wrote, 'but I, once a lord of language, have no words in which to express my anguish and my shame . . . she and my father had bequeathed me a name they had made noble and honoured, not merely in literature, art, archaeology and science, but in the public history of our country and its evolution as a nation. I had disgraced that name eternally. I had made it a low byword among low people. I had dragged it through the very mire. I had given it to brutes that they might make it brutal, and to fools that they might turn it into a synonym for folly. What I suffered then, and still suffer, is not for pen to write or paper to record.'

It was from his wife, 'always kind and gentle to me', that Wilde learned the news of his mother's death. Rather than that he should hear it from 'indifferent lips', his wife, who was now known as Mrs Holland—she was herself far from well at this time—travelled from Genoa to Reading to break to Wilde 'the tidings of so irreparable, so irredeemable a loss'.[4]

[1] Harris. II, 539. [2] V. O'Sullivan. *Aspects of Wilde* (1938), p. 63.
[3] Communicated by Mr G. F. Sims.
[4] *De Profundis*, 65–6. This visit took place on February 19, 1896. It was treated by the Prison Commissioners as a special visit.

They also discussed together the future of their two children, and he told her that 'if she was frightened of facing the responsibility of the life of another, though her own child, she should get a guardian to help her'. He begged her not to spoil Cyril, as Lady Queensberry had done with her son, Alfred Douglas. Wilde later told his friend and literary executor, Robert Ross, how kind his wife had been to him during this visit. It was to be the last time that Wilde ever saw his wife, although, unknown to him, she is believed to have caught a glimpse of him on one other occasion in prison. Owing to various difficulties, they were never able to meet after his release.

That his wife certainly hoped to see him again is clear from the fact that, on leaving the prison, she told the Governor that she would apply again for a visiting order in three months' time, when her husband was due for another visit in the ordinary way. However, the reconciliation which had been completed by the stress of Lady Wilde's death, was unfortunately destined to be frustrated through the well-meant but ill-judged action of Wilde's friends over his interest in his wife's marriage settlement. It will be remembered that the creditors in the bankruptcy had claimed to have Wilde's contingent interest in the marriage settlement sold for their benefit, although it had little actuarial value. Several of Wilde's friends, notably Robert Ross and More Adey, had approached Constance Wilde's solicitors, Messrs Hargrove & Co., with a view to coming to some amicable arrangement by which the life interest could be purchased in their joint names for the purpose of resettlement on Wilde and the two children of the marriage, Cyril and Vyvyan. Acting on the advice which they had apparently given their client and which she had accepted, her solicitors replied that Mrs Wilde would be a party to no arrangement which did not give her the entire legal as well as the actual control of the children. To this Wilde's friends would not agree and the negotiations for a friendly arrangement fell through.

Mrs Wilde's solicitors now put in a bid with the Official Receiver of £25, while Mr Martin Holman, the solicitor instructed by More Adey, countered with an offer of £30. The Official Receiver, whose duty it was to obtain the best possible price for the creditors, found his task made increasingly difficult when he received a petition signed by a large number of them urging him to accept the lower offer. (Constance Wilde's visit to Reading took place while this business was going on.) As a result Mr Hargrove informed Wilde that, if he withdrew his opposition to the purchase of the whole life interest of his wife, she would settle on him one-third of the income from the settlement, amounting to about £200 a year, should her death occur before his, and in addition she was agreeable to pay him an equivalent sum during her lifetime, provided she had full control of the children. In the light of this offer, Wilde wrote to Ross, asking him to let Hargrove know at once that Constance could have the interest on these terms. 'I feel that I have brought so much unhappiness on her and such ruin on the children', he wrote, 'that I have no right to go against her wishes in anything. She was gentle and good to me here, when she came to see me. I have full trust in her. Please have this done *at once*, and thank my friends for their kindness. I feel I am acting rightly in leaving this to my wife.'[1]

Unfortunately these instructions were not followed. On the contrary, Wilde's friends persisted in their attempts to secure the life interest, or rather a half-share of it, for which they offered the Official Receiver £50, in the expectation that Constance Wilde would buy the other half, and a resettlement could take place by mutual arrangement for the benefit of the children. No doubt More Adey and Robert Ross acted with the best intentions, but, as events turned out, the results had disastrous results on the relations between husband and wife. Complete estrangement followed, since Constance naturally thought that the opposition was due to her husband's action. And, sad to relate, the estrangement was destined to become permanent.

3

Encouraging news now reached Wilde from France. Little sympathy had been shown for him in that country when he was convicted. But, when details of the effect, which the severe prison régime was having on Wilde's constitution, became known in Paris, perfidious Albion was denounced in various quarters for subjecting such a distinguished man of letters to the iniquities of '*le har' laboore*', as the French referred in conversation to his additional punishment. Several sympathetic

[1] Wilde to Ross, March 10, 1896: Clark MSS.: *Dulau Sale Catalogue*, 20; *De Profundis* (1908 ed.), 1–2; H–D, 399.

articles appeared in the French Press, the writers including literary figures like Octave Mirbeau, Henry Bauer, Paul Adam and Hugues Rebell. This development prompted the American-born poet, Stuart Merrill, who had made France his adopted country and habitually wrote in French, to draft a petition to Queen Victoria, praying 'in the name of humanity and Art' for Wilde's release.[1] Unfortunately, like Adey's in England, the project had to be abandoned through lack of signatures. Potential subscribers may have been unwilling to compromise themselves in the eyes of the public, particularly as Merrill had published the text of the petition in an advanced literary journal, *La Plume*, which was suspected of anarchist leanings. Still it was an encouraging gesture, and it was reinforced by a powerful article in *Le Journal* from the pen of Edouard Conte, the journalist who had accompanied Sherard on the occasion of his last visit, in which the writer drew attention to the possibility of Wilde becoming insane, if his imprisonment was much further prolonged.[2]

Soon after this another event occurred across the Channel, which was to be of considerable consequence to Wilde. Indeed, he always attributed the amelioration in his treatment which occurred at this time, particularly in the shape of a more generous supply of books, to this event. On February 10, 1896, his *Salomé* received its first performance at the Theatre de l'Œuvre in Paris. It was produced by M. Lugné-Poë, who also played the part of Herod.[3] The title role was taken by Mlle Lina

[1] Stuart Fitzrandolph Merrill (1863–1915), American poet, identified with the symbolist movement in French literature. He helped to revise and correct Wilde's original French text of *Salomé*. His interesting recollections of Wilde, whom he first met while on a visit to London in 1898, were written in French in 1912 in a MS. which is in my possession. A translation with an introduction and explanatory notes by me was published in the international review *Adam*, Nos. 241–3 (1954).

[2] Leon Lemonnier. *La Vie d'Oscar Wilde* (1931), pp. 196–200.

[3] Aurelien Marie Lugné-Poë (1869–1940), French actor-manager. In 1893 he founded the Theatre de l'Œuvre in Paris with the object of making known the dramatic works of foreign writers to French audiences. He remained the theatre's manager and chief actor until his retirement in 1929. Among other writers besides Wilde whom he introduced to the French stage were Ibsen and Maeterlinck. Wilde did not know him personally at this period, and only met him for the first time when he came out of prison. 'Of Lugné-Poë, of course, I know nothing', wrote Wilde on June 1, 1897, just after his release, when he was staying at Berneval, 'except that he is singularly handsome, and seems to me to have the personality of a good actor, for personality does not require intellect to help it: it is a dynamic force of its own, and is often as superbly unintelligent as the great forces of nature, like the lightning that shook at sudden moments last night over the sea that slept before my window': see below, p. 50, note 2.

Muntz. Originally written four years previously for the great tragic actress Sarah Bernhardt, the Lord Chamberlain had refused to license its public performance in England, since it infringed the rule forbidding the introduction of Biblical characters on the stage. The news that it should have been decided to produce it in France while he was still in prison may have first reached him through his wife, when she came to tell him of Lady Wilde's death. It was certainly confirmed soon afterwards by Robert Ross, who also seems to have told Wilde something of the mixed reception of the play at the hands of the critics, although Henri Bauer gave it an enthusiastic notice in the *Echo de Paris*. 'Please write to Stuart Merrill in Paris, or Robert Sherard, to say how gratified I was at the performance of my play', he wrote to Ross on March 10, 'and have my thanks conveyed to Lugné-Poë. It is something that at a time of disgrace and shame I should still be regarded as an artist. I wish I could feel more pleasure but I seem dead to all emotions except those of anguish and despair. However, please let Lugné-Poë know that I am sensible of the honour he has done me. He is a poet himself.'[1]

As Wilde wrote to Alfred Douglas shortly after his release, 'the production of *Salomé* was the thing that turned the scale in my favour, as far as my treatment in prison by the Government was concerned, and I am deeply grateful to all concerned in it'.[2] The immediate result was that Wilde was asked to submit a list of books which he wished to have sent to him in prison. The list was returned to him with many of the requests deleted, but in spite of these erasures, a considerable number of others was permitted. Some of the distinctions are interesting. For instance, he was allowed to have a copy of *Salomé*, but not the Press notices of the French production. Flaubert's *Salammbô* was allowed, but the same author's *La Tentation de St. Antoine* was forbidden. Strindberg was passed, but Ibsen was proscribed, likewise the current issue of the *Quarterly Review* and Sienkiewicz's classic *Quo Vadis?* Three books by John Addington Symonds and the contributions of the Rev W. D. Morrison, the Wandsworth prison chaplain, to the Criminology Series, were also struck out. Among the books

[1] *De Profundis* (1908 ed.), 2; *Dulau Sale Catalogue*, 20; H–D, 399.

[2] Wilde to Douglas, June 1, 1897: A. C. Dennison and Harrison Post. *Some Letters from Oscar Wilde to Lord Alfred Douglas* (San Francisco, 1924), at p. xxvii; H–D, 588.

and authors for whose works he asked were Prosper Merimée, Anatole France, Pierre Loüys, Montaigne, a French Bible, a French-English dictionary, 'some mystical books', W. B. Yeats's *The Secret Rose*, two novels by A. E. W. Mason and translations of two of Calderon's plays. He asked too for manuscript notebooks, pencils and foolscap paper, but these items were heavily scored through, as being against prison regulations. Nevertheless, what he was allowed in the way of additional reading matter was a great step forward in comparison with what he had previously been permitted.[1]

When Frank Harris came to see him later in the year, Wilde complained he was always being punished and that the Governor's favourite punishment was to take away his books. But his breaches of the prison rules seem to have been minor ones—late rising, not having his cell and its contents in order, talking to another prisoner at exercise and so on—since Major Isaacson in an official report at the end of his term of office at Reading described Wilde's conduct as 'Good'. It was virtually impossible for any prisoner, no matter how efficient and well-behaved, to avoid breaking some of the rules, which to one warder at the time in Reading seemed to have been made 'with no other object than to be broken, so that an excuse may be found for inflicting additional punishment'. A warder could easily find fault, real or imaginary, with a prisoner, just as a non-commissioned officer could catch out a private soldier in an alleged infringement of Queen's Regulations. Wilde was unquestionably bullied by a few of the warders at Reading. On the other hand, it is known that others went out of their way to treat him kindly. Two of these latter have recorded brief recollection of their unusual charge, which throw some light on Wilde's reactions to them and their duties.[2]

His hair, which had been close cropped during the earlier stages of his imprisonment, had grown long again while he was in the infirmary at Wandsworth. The warder, whose duty it was to reduce Wilde to the same condition as the other bullet-headed prisoners, remembers how it fell to him to carry out the order that Wilde's locks must be shorn at once. 'Must it be cut?' Wilde cried piteously, as the warder produced the

[1] The list, which was described in the *Catalogue of Wilde MSS.* at Dulau's Sale in London in 1928 (p. 18), is now in the William Andrews Clark Library in the University of California, Los Angeles. See also H–D, 399.

[2] *Evening News*, March 1–2, 1905; Sherard, *Life*, 386–402.

clippers. 'You don't know what it means to me.' And the tears rolled down his cheeks. Prisoners were naturally not allowed razors but were from time to time shaved by the prison barber. This regulation was an especial hardship for Wilde. 'If I could but feel clean, I should not feel so utterably miserable,' he told one of the friendly warders, touching his chin. 'These awful bristles are horrid.' When he left his cell to see a visitor, he would be careful to take his handkerchief to conceal his chin as much as possible. This same warder had sometimes to come to his cell with the news that a visitor was waiting for him and the summons often threw the prisoner into a state of nervous agitation. 'I never knew what fresh sorrow may not have entered my life,' he told the warder, 'and is in this manner broken to me so that I may carry it to my cell, and place it in my already overstocked storehouse which is my heart. My heart is my storehouse of sorrow!'

This same warder remembered how 'the Poet', as he called Wilde, seemed to suffer from boredom during service in the prison chapel. He would sit listlessly with his elbow resting on the back of the chair, his legs crossed, and would gaze dreamily around him. Sometimes a friendly nudge would be needed to remind him that a hymn had been given out and that he must rise and sing, or at least appear to sing. He was not inspired by the sermons he heard from the chaplain. He particularly objected to the line of argument which represented that society did not wish to punish the congregation, although they had erred and sinned against society, 'that they were undergoing a process of purification, that their prison was their purgatory, from which they could emerge as pure and spotless as though they had never sinned at all, and that, if they did so, society would meet and welcome them with open arms'. According to this warder, Wilde would smile a cynical, disbelieving smile, which often shadowed despair. 'I long to rise in my place and cry out', he told the warder, 'and tell the poor, disinherited wretches around me that it is not so, to tell them that they are society's victims, and that society has nothing to offer them but starvation in the streets, or starvation and cruelty in prison.'

Wilde has recalled, in *De Profundis*, that for a while after his transfer to Reading, he was filled with a sense of rage and determined to commit suicide on the very day on which he left prison. After a time this evil mood passed and was replaced by a feeling of utter despair, so that 'I made up my mind to live, but to wear gloom as a king wears purple: never to smile again'. Gradually he began to feel differently and he realised that it would be both ungrateful and mean of him 'to pull so long a face that when my friends came to see me they would have to make their faces still longer in order to show their sympathy'. And so he would make great efforts to appear cheerful.[1]

He naturally responded to the advances of the friendly warders. One of them, aware that Wilde had a distinguished literary reputation, was constantly trying to improve his own mind with the prisoner's help.

'Excuse me, sir, but Charles Dickens, sir,' asked the warder on one occasion, 'would he be considered a great writer now, sir?'

'Oh, yes. A great writer indeed. You see he is no longer alive.'

'Yes, I understand, sir. Being dead he would be a great writer, sir.'

On another occasion, John Strange Winter was mentioned.

'Would you tell me what you think of him, sir?'

'A charming person,' Wilde replied, 'but a lady, you know, not a man. Not a great stylist, perhaps, but a good simple story-teller.'

'Thank you, sir, I did not know he was a lady, sir.'

On a third occasion the warder asked about another woman novelist.

'Excuse me, sir, but Marie Corelli. Would she be considered a great writer, sir?'

This, admitted Wilde, in recounting the incident to the artist, Will Rothenstein, was more than he could bear. Putting his hand on the man's shoulder, he said to him gravely, 'Now don't think I've anything against her moral character, but from the way she writes she ought to be here.'

'You say so, sir, you say so,' replied the amazed warder in wide-eyed belief.[2]

Another warder had recently got married. A certain weekly journal was offering a silver tea-service to the young couple who could give the best reason why this service should be given

[1] *De Profundis*, 86.
[2] Sir William Rothenstein. *Men and Memories* (1931), I, 311.

to them. The warder told Wilde about this, and Wilde wrote out five reasons, which certainly should have secured the service.

> (1) Because evidently spoons are required, and my girl and I are two.
> (2) Because it would suit us to a T (tea).
> (3) Because we have good 'grounds' for wanting a coffee pot.
> (4) Because marriage is a game that should begin with a love set.
> (5) Because we cannot get legally married without a proper wedding service.

Wilde's skill at newspaper competitions quickly spread through the prison, and he helped other warders with their contributions. Later the story went that, thanks to him, one of them had won a grand piano.[1]

The same warder, who had got married, later told Wilde that he was expecting a child to be born in the next year, which was the year of Queen Victoria's Diamond Jubilee. The warder asked the prisoner to suggest a suitable name for a child born in this year. In a few minutes, Wilde who had by this time been provided with writing materials, wrote out the following short essay, which he gave the warder and which the latter carefully preserved.

> Every baby born in the course of this great and historic year should have a name representative in some way of what this year signifies to the British Empire. That is clear. The only question is what is it to be.
>
> St. George would be a capital name—it is a real christian name, and is borne by Mr. St. George Mivart, a well-known writer—the only objection to it is that it refers too specially to England, and leaves out St. Patrick, St. Andrew and St. David.
>
> Victor, the masculine equivalent of Victoria, would be good, but not the best possible.
>
> People are sometimes christened Tertius and Decimus, as being the third and tenth sons. Why not call the boy Sexagesimus? Thus the sixtieth year of Her Majesty's reign would be commemorated. Still that is an awkward name, and would not make the youthful owner popular at school.
>
> Well, we call girls Ruby, Pearl and other names of precious

[1] Sherard. *Unhappy Friendship*, 226. 'You don't know that since I have been here,' he told Ross on one of his visits, 'I have won a silver tea-service and a grand piano.' T. Sturge Moore and Cecil Lewis. *Letters and Journals of Charles Ricketts* (1939), p. 112.

jewels, and the Irish call their babies 'My jewel' and the French 'Trés bijoux'. Mr. Walter Pater, whose prose we all admire for its noble qualities, called one of his characters Emerald.

Jacinth, which is a precious stone, is also a christian name, the same as Hyacinth and Amethyst. Garnet is a christian name and the name of a jewel. Lord Wolseley was Sir Garnet Wolseley.

There is also a name Royal. It is a very good name, but not sufficiently distinguishing.

Diamond must be made a popular name, so I hope to hear it has been given to our baby boy.

As for his fellow-prisoners, Wilde was gradually able to get to talk to each of them, as they did not go in the same order each day at exercise. Eventually he knew each one's name and history and the date of his release. In a number of instances he was able to arrange, through Robert Ross, for a small sum to be waiting for the prisoner to collect at the post office. 'The only really humanising influence is the influence of the prisoners,' was his considered opinion when he himself regained his liberty. 'Their cheerfulness under terrible circumstances, their sympathy for each other, their humility, their gentleness, their pleasant smiles of greeting when they meet each other, their complete acquiescence in their punishments, are all quite wonderful, and I myself learned many sound lessons from them.'[1]

4

Except for the visit from his wife, which was a special one allowed on compassionate grounds, Wilde was strictly kept to the quarterly visits from two friends, as prescribed by prison rules. The first of such visits which he received at Reading appears to have been made by Robert Sherard about a fortnight after his arrival, and the second by Robert Ross and Ernest Leverson[2] together towards the end of February, 1896. More Adey also saw him about the same time as Sherard. Only Sherard has recalled the details of his visit, which differed in some particulars from the conditions at Wandsworth with its iron bars. 'It was a painful interview in a degrading kind of rabbit hutch,

[1] Letter to the *Daily Chronicle*, May 28, 1897.

[2] Ernest Leverson was the son of a diamond merchant, while his wife Ada ('the Sphinx') had a considerable success as a novelist and was a particular friend of Wilde's (see below, p. 141). Wilde stayed in their house while he was out on bail between the trials.

over which wire netting was nailed, as though for the caging of an animal . . . The hutch was almost in complete darkness, and of my friends presence I perceived little beyond his hesitating and husky voice . . . I am sure that Wilde was glad of it, for, further to hide his face from my eyes, he put a blue handkerchief over his mouth and cheeks. No doubt disfiguring growths of hair were thus masked.'

Somewhat to his surprise, Sherard found the prisoner well informed of current events. The author of *La Dame aux Camelias*, the younger Alexander Dumas, whom they both knew personally, had died a couple of days before. Wilde had already heard of it.[1] 'I told him that I should look to him for the world's news,' noted Sherard, 'and I heard a laugh in the dark depths of the wire cage.' At this interview Sherard had a particularly private piece of news to tell Wilde, which was the name that his wife and the two children had adopted in place of Wilde. For this purpose Sherard began to speak in French, but was brusquely interrupted by the warder on duty, who exclaimed: 'Stop that now! No foreign tongues allowed here.' However, Sherard succeeded in achieving his object before he was stopped. 'It interested me, as a point of psychology,' wrote Sherard afterwards, 'to observe with what anxiety he asked what the new name was. In his prisoner's dress, in a shameful cage, his pride remained such that he was keenly desirous to be assured that his people had not assumed a name plebeian or ill-sounding. He approved, when I had conveyed to him what the name was.' The name which Wilde heard for the first time in this curious manner was Holland. It belonged to fairly distant ancestors of his wife's on her father's side. And well might Wilde have approved, since the Hollands were an ancient Lancashire family, which included Sir Otho Holland, one of the original Knights of the Garter.[2]

When the next quarterly visit was due, Robert Ross applied to the Governor to have his name put on the list of those who wished to see the prisoner. He was informed by return of post that 'Prisoner Oscar Wilde desires that Mr. Sherard and yourself will visit him at your convenience', and that 'both visitors must make their visit together'.[3] The visit duly took place on

[1] Sherard. *Unhappy Friendship*, 213–14. Dumas died on November 27, 1895.
[2] Vyvyan Holland. *Son of Oscar Wilde* (1954), p. 76.
[3] Sherard. *The Real Oscar Wilde*, 141–2.

a very hot day towards the end of May. It is of particular interest, since on the way back to London Ross made detailed notes of the meeting and next day he wrote a long account of it, in the form of a letter to their mutual friend More Adey, which has fortunately been preserved.[1]

On their arrival at the prison, Ross and Sherard were escorted to 'the usual hutch' by a polite warder who locked them in. They had to wait a considerable time. The reason for the delay was that Wilde did not expect them until the following day, and was not prepared for visitors. The result was that he was ill at ease throughout the interview. 'I could not collect my thoughts', he wrote to Ross next day. 'When you are good enough to come and see me, will you always fix the day? Anything sudden upsets me.' When he eventually arrived, Sherard was in the compartment opposite Ross. This seemed to disconcert the prisoner, and he asked Sherard as being the taller to move into Ross's compartment and stand behind him, which Sherard did looking over Ross's shoulder. Sherard did not improve matters by appearing very nervous and breaking down most of the time. 'I do not know why, I am sure,' noted Ross, 'but he was much shocked by the change for the worse.'

This is how the prisoner appeared to Ross, after serving exactly half his sentence:

> He is much thinner, is now clean shaven so that his emaciated condition is more apparent. His face is dull brick colour. (I fancy from working in the sun in the garden). His eyes were horribly vacant, and I noticed that he had lost a great deal of hair (this when he turned to go and stood in the light). He always had great quantities of thick hair, but there is now a bald patch on the crown. It is also streaked with white and grey. . . .
>
> The remarkable part of the interview was that Oscar hardly talked at all except to ask if there was any chance of his being let out, what the attitude of the press and public would be, as to whether any of the present Government would be favourably disposed towards him. He cried the whole time and, when we asked *him* to talk more, he said he had nothing to say and wanted to hear *us* talk. That, as you know, is very unlike Oscar.

Slowly and with apparent difficulty Wilde gave his friends

[1] Although undated, this letter was almost certainly written on May 23, 1896. For the complete text, see Margery Ross, *Robert Ross Friend of Friends* (1952), at p. 39. The original is in the William Andrews Clark Library in the University of California, Los Angeles.

particulars about himself in response to their questions. He was still not allowed pencil and paper. He had been sleeping better but suffered from anaemia ('You could easily tell that', commented Ross) and gout. His sight, which had been affected in the winter through reading by gaslight, was better. He then asked his friends, 'did we think his brain seemed all right?' He was afraid that 'confinement would deprive him of his mind. It was a constant dread'. He repeated what he had told Ross in a letter that the 'Greek and Latin poets gave him a headache and that his thoughts wandered'. He could only read a little at a time, but he had read everything in the prison library several times. Pressed by Ross to say the kind of books he would like, he asked for Chaucer, a prose translation of Dante, Walter Pater's latest book, which Ross had mentioned, and 'some large volume of Elizabethan dramatist or dramatists'. Some of his remarks puzzled his visitors. Asked how he felt generally, he said in a low voice half-aside: 'They treat me cruelly.' Ross thought this must have had reference to the prison food, since Wilde added, as if for the benefit of the warder, 'I have only been in the infirmary for two days since I was at Reading'. But Sherard thought he must be referring to his prison chores, since he had seen a number of prisoners scrubbing the courtyard of the gaol when he arrived. Questioned about the prison doctor Wilde said: 'The doctor is unkind to me.' He complained that his sister-in-law, Lily Wilde, who had married his elder brother Willie, had made mischief between him and his wife and between his wife and More Adey. But Ross could not persuade him to say any more on this subject. On the subject of his wife's marriage settlement he said he was 'not interested'. Ross then asked him if he had seen Constance lately. He said no, 'but he believed she was coming soon'. Messages were given to him by Sherard from various French friends and by Ross from various English friends. 'Thank them all for their messages', he said. He asked about several individuals such as Miss Schuster ('the lady of Wimbledon') who had sent him some money for his use, as she had also done to help with his defence at the time of the trials, and Alfred Douglas, whom he learned was living in a villa at Naples and was about to bring out a volume of poems. At the end of the visit Ross remarked, apparently quite casually, that Douglas was dedicating the poems to him and that he had a message for him about it in a letter from Douglas which he showed Wilde through the bars of the cage. Wilde seemed taken aback. 'I would rather not hear about that just now,' he said.

For the visitors it was an unhappy and depressing interview. Wilde seemed to take no interest in any of the literary or artistic news, which they gave him, but appeared to talk to himself while they did so. There were several awkward pauses in the conversation. At other times Wilde would interrupt and ask a question which had no bearing on the subject. 'Where are you going to for the summer?' he asked Ross *à propos* of nothing in particular. By this time Sherard had pulled himself together and like Ross tried to cheer up the prisoner. But their efforts were not a success. 'Our proud cheerfulness did not seem to amuse poor Oscar at all,' Ross noted afterwards, 'and our attempts to talk of cheerful things were a total failure.' As they said good-bye, Sherard asked if he could come next time. 'Yes,' said Wilde, 'do come.' Something seemed to be weighing heavily on his mind. What it was Ross did not discover until he received a letter from Wilde several days later.

As Ross and Sherard came out with the warder into the prison yard, they noticed two men standing in the middle. The warder whispered that they were the Governor and the doctor. Sherard said he wished to see neither, although they had discussed together the advisability of asking to see the doctor. But Ross decided he must approach one or the other, and he had to make up his mind quickly as to which to approach. Remembering what Wilde had said about the doctor and the latter's appearance quite confirming what Wilde had remarked, Ross decided to go for the Governor. He accordingly took out a card and, giving it to the warder, sent him over to Colonel Isaacson with a polite message requesting a few minutes' conversation.

> He at first was haughty and impatient, but became quite polite and amiable after a few minutes. Of course, I got nothing out of him, but he impressed me favourably[1] and even Sherard who stood at a little distance said he was pleasantly surprised. I told him I was anxious about Oscar's mental condition and general health, admitted that physically he was better since he came to Reading, but feared for his capability when released.

[1] Ross revised this opinion when he learned the details of this Governor's harshness. 'Isaacson was a perfect monster', he later told Frank Harris: see Harris. *Oscar Wilde*, II, 606.

Isaacson replied that every man over forty was something of a doctor and that he being over forty he considered Oscar was doing as well as could be expected. Mentioned that the Home Secretary had sent books for Oscar with instructions about them: that naturally Oscar felt the imprisonment more than another man who had not had his education and way of life; that, if Oscar was ill, we should be told of it; that he could see the Doctor every day if he liked; that every care was taken of him, etc.

While we were talking, the Doctor was snuffling and shuffling about, making impatient gestures. About 30 wretched convicts were scraping the walls of the courtyard and scrubbing the stone, and through an open door I saw the cause of the revolting stench I noticed when Leverson and I went to the Prison and that was worse on this occasion—great coils of tarred rope for making into oakum.

The polite warder, who had acted as their escort, then disappeared, and the two visitors were let out of the prison by a rude warder, whom Sherard recognised as having admitted him on the occasion of his previous visit. 'We both of us were very nearly violently sick afterwards', wrote Ross in concluding his description of the visit.

I will now tell you my own impression of Oscar's condition. I do not think they treat him badly. Of course, he does not get enough food for a person of his build, and I firmly and honestly believe apart from all prejudice that he is simply wasting and pining away; to use the old cliché, he is sinking under a broken heart. I believe that anyone who knew him at all in former days, but who was without any *parti pris* for his release or imprisonment, and visited him for an hour as a purely scientific subject as the result of Hard Labour on certain constitutions, would arrive at the same conclusion. Of course, he would have to conceal from Oscar that his visit was actuated by anything save friendly interest, otherwise Oscar would hastily assume one of his hundred artificial manners, which he has for every person and every occasion, even when broken as he is now.

Each person has his view as to what constitutes a decayed mind. But if I were asked about Oscar before a commission, I should say that confinement, apart from all labour or treatment, had made him temporarily *silly*. That is the mildest word that will describe my meaning. If asked whether he was going to die, [I should say that] it seems quite possible within the next few months, even if his constitution remained unimpaired, but for the causes that wives and husbands die shortly after each other, for no particular cause, or men who have lost all their money or their '10 o'clock business' or young girls whose engagements have gone wrong. I should be less surprised to hear of dear Oscar's death than of Aubrey Beardsley's, and you know what he looks like.

5

What had particularly disturbed Wilde, during the visit from Ross and Sherard, was explained in the letter which Ross received on prison notepaper shortly afterwards. 'You said that Douglas was going to dedicate a volume of poems to me. Will you write to him at once and say he must not do anything of the kind? I could not accept or allow such a dedication. The proposal is revolting and grotesque.' At the same time he asked Ross to get from Douglas a number of his letters which were in his possession, as well as books and jewellery, which he had given him. 'All these are to be sealed up and left with you. The idea that he is wearing or in possession of anything I gave him is peculiarly repugnant to me.' In this letter Wilde wrote in withering terms of his former friend, begging Ross to copy out what he had written and send it to Douglas 'so that he should have no loophole of escape'.[1] Later, in *De Profundis*, he was to recall for Douglas's benefit, the effect which the news had on him when he first heard it. 'The tidings seemed to give me a sort of nausea for life. I saw nothing, but silently went back to my cell with contempt and scorn in my heart. How could you dream of dedicating a volume of poems to me without first asking my permission? Dream, do I say? How could you dare to do such a thing? . . . The first volume of Poems that in the very springtide of his manhood a young man sends forth to the world should be like a blossom or flower of spring, like the white thorn in the meadow at Magdalen or the cowslips in the Cumnor fields. It should not be burdened by the weight of a terrible and revolting tragedy, a terrible revolting scandal.'[2]

The letter, sent by Ross at Wilde's bidding, seems to have come on Douglas like a thunderbolt. In his reply Douglas described himself as being 'deprived of all power of thought and expression'. Nevertheless, he refused to surrender any of the

[1] Wilde to Ross, May 23, 1896. Clark MSS; H-D, 400.
[2] *De Profundis*, 66, 68.

articles which Ross demanded from him. As for his poems, which were already in the press, it was too late to cancel the dedication.[1] Unfortunately too he had made matters worse by writing an article for a French literary magazine, *La Revue Blanche*, which had already published several of his poems, ostensibly to introduce the collected edition to the French public, but really to offer his comments on '*l'affaire Wilde*' and the conduct of Mr Asquith's Government over the Wilde trials. Sherard who had heard about it tried to have the article stopped. On this occasion he was unsuccessful, and its publication, with its thinly veiled defence of homosexuality, further damaged Wilde's cause.[2] To crown everything, Douglas wrote to his mother, complaining of the expressions which Wilde had used about him in his letter to Ross, and Lady Queensberry, who said she was 'greatly annoyed', let it be known to sundry of Wilde's friends, and to others not so friendly as well, that he had turned against her son. The result was that Wilde lost some of the sympathy which had gradually been growing up for him on account of his sufferings in prison.

About this time, Frank Harris, who was then editing the *Saturday Review*, returned from a trip abroad to learn from Ross and others of Wilde's friends what effect prison was having on him. Harris decided to seek an interview with Ruggles-Brise with the object of securing some improvement in his conditions. Somewhat to his surprise, he found the Chairman of the Prison Commission most accommodating. According to Harris, Ruggles-Brise admitted that 'an exceptional man ought to have exceptional treatment' and went so far as to say that Wilde 'should be treated with all possible consideration, that certain prison rules which pressed very hardly upon him should be interpreted as mildly as possible'. He admitted that the punishment was much more severe on him than the ordinary criminal and he seemed to have nothing but admiration for his brilliant gifts. 'It is a great pity that Wilde ever got into prison,' he added, 'a great pity.'

Ruggles-Brise asked Harris if he would be willing to go down to Reading and let him know what he thought of Wilde's

[1] The poems were published by *Mercure de France* with a page by page French prose translation by Eugene Tardieu. Douglas subsequently refused the French publishers permission to reprint them: see his *Autobiography* (1931), at p. 130.

[2] *La Plume*, June 1, 1896. For further details see the present writer's *Trials of Oscar Wilde*, pp. 362–5.

condition, with any suggestions that might occur to him, provided the Home Secretary approved. Harris replied that he would be glad to do so. A few days later Ruggles-Brise told Harris that Sir Mathew Ridley was quite agreeable to the proposed visit, and provided him with a note of introduction to the Governor, requesting Major Isaacson to give the visitor all the information he needed about the prisoner. Harris was also allowed to see Wilde out of hearing though within sight of a warder. 'The Home Secretary thinks it would be a great loss to English literature', said Ruggles-Brise, 'if he were really injured by prison discipline.'

The visit took place as arranged on June 16, 1896, and the interview was held in a private room in the prison. The same friendly warder, who met Ross and Sherard, had already brought Wilde in before Harris arrived. He then withdrew and remained outside the door while the two men conversed. First of all, they shook hands and then sat down opposite to each other at a plain deal table. Harris's initial impressions were similar to those of Ross. To Harris it seemed that Wilde had changed greatly since they had last met a year previously. He looked thinner and much older. His dark brown hair was streaked with grey, particularly in front and over the ears. On the other hand, Harris thought that physically he appeared better than he had been for several years before his imprisonment, when he had tended to become bloated and flabby, although in repose his face now wore a nervous, depressed and harassed air.

At first Wilde was reluctant to talk. But gradually Harris coaxed him to unburden himself of his troubles. 'The list of grievances would be without end', Wilde said. 'The worst of it is I am perpetually being punished for nothing. The Governor loves to punish and he punishes by taking my books from me. It is perfectly awful to let the mind grind itself away between the upper and nether millstones of regret and remorse without respite. With books my life would be livable—any life,' he added sadly.

Harris promised to get him more books and also writing materials, which he was confident he could arrange to do. 'Force yourself to write,' he advised Wilde hopefully. 'You are looking better than you used to look. Your eyes are brighter, your face clearer.'

The prisoner summoned up a feeble smile. 'I've had a rest cure, Frank,' he said.

'You should give a record of this life, as far as you can, and of all its influence on you,' Harris went on. 'You have conquered, you know. Write the names of the inhuman brutes on their foreheads in vitriol, as Dante did for all time.'

'No, no, I cannot,' Wilde replied. 'I will not. I want to live and forget. I could not. I dare not. I have not Dante's strength, nor his bitterness. I am a Greek born out of my time.'

When the interview was over and the prisoner had gone back to his cell, the friendly warder returned to escort the visitor out. Harris thanked him for being kind to his friend.

'He has no business here, sir,' said the warder. 'He's no more like one of our reg'lars than a canary is like one of them cocky little spadgers. Prison ain't meant for such as him, and he ain't meant for prison. He's that soft, sir, you see, and affeckshunate. He's more like a woman, he is; you hurt 'em without meaning to. I don't care what they say, I likes him. And he do talk beautiful, sir, don't he?'

'Indeed he does,' Harris agreed, 'the best talker in the world.'

Before leaving Reading, Harris met both the Governor and the prison doctor. It was on this occasion, according to Harris, that Major Isaacson boasted that he was 'knocking the nonsense out of Wilde'. To Harris this Governor seemed 'almost inhuman'. Nor does the doctor appear to have impressed him any better. For the first time in his life Frank Harris, so he has said, realised the full, incredible meaning of 'Man's inhumanity to man'.

On his return to London Harris went to see Ruggles-Brise. 'No one could have shown me warmer sympathy or more discriminating comprehension', Harris noted afterwards. 'I made my report to him and left the matter in his hands with perfect confidence.' At the same time, on his own admission, he took care to tell Ross and other mutual friends of what had happened and to assure them that Wilde's circumstances would soon be bettered. As is known, Harris was never at all shy of blowing his own trumpet. But, even allowing for the exaggerated emphasis, which he placed on his actions, there can be no doubt that the report which he gave Ruggles-Brise of his visit to Reading did have some positive effect, as will shortly be seen.[1]

6

At their interview at Reading Harris had urged Wilde when he could to write about his prison experiences or, at least, to utilise them for a future literary work. Although Wilde had demurred to this suggestion, it is significant that it was during the earlier part of this summer of 1896 that the incident occurred, which inspired Wilde to the composition of his best known poetic work. This, at Robert Ross's suggestion, he was to call *The Ballad of Reading Gaol.* The idea of the ballad originated on a day in May when Wilde noticed a newcomer of about thirty years of age among the remand prisoners during exercise in the prison yard. Like the other remand prisoners he wore his ordinary clothes, in which he had been arrested.

He walked amongst the Trial Men
  In a suit of shabby grey;
A cricket cap was on his head,
  And his step seemed light and gay;
But I never saw a man who looked
  So wistfully at the day.

I walked with other souls in pain,
  Within another ring,
And was wondering if the man had done
  A great or little thing,
When a voice behind me whispered low,
  '*That fellow's got to swing.*'

Through the prison grapevine Wilde learned who this young man was and why he had 'got to swing'. He was a trooper in the Royal Horse Guards, by name Charles Thomas Wooldridge, and he had been charged with the murder of his wife, a young woman of twenty-three, who was employed at the time as an assistant in the Eton Post Office. According to an account of the crime given in the local newspaper, Trooper Wooldridge is said 'to have cut his wife's throat in a very determined manner, she having excited his jealousy, and (so far as the evidence went) greatly annoyed him'.[2]

[1] Harris. II, 327 *et seq.*

[2] *Reading Mercury*, July 10, 1896.

So with envious eyes and sick surmise
We watched him day by day
And wondered if each one of us
Would end the self-same way,
For none can tell to what red Hell
His sightless soul may stray.

At last the dead man walked no more
Amongst the Trial Men,
And I knew that he was standing up
In the black dock's dreadful pen,
And that never would I see his face
In God's sweet world again.

Wooldridge was tried before Mr Justice Hawkins at the next Berkshire Assizes, was found guilty on June 17, 1896, and was sentenced to death.

The man in red who reads the Law
Gave him three weeks of life,
Three little weeks in which to heal
His soul of his soul's strife,
And cleanse from every blot of blood
His hand that held the knife.

He was brought back to the prison and placed in the condemned cell, where two warders kept watch over him day and night, lest he should cheat the gallows of its prey. Several public petitions praying for the sentence to be respited were forwarded to the Home Secretary, but Sir Mathew Ridley refused a reprieve.

The man had killed the thing he loved,
And so he had to die.

Meanwhile the prison routine went on in an atmosphere of mounting tension and dread, which can only be fully realised by those who have been in prison when it is known that an execution is to take place.

We tore the tarry rope to shreds
With blunt and bleeding nails
We rubbed the doors, and scrubbed the floors
And cleaned the shining rails:
And rank by rank, we soaped the plank,
And clattered with the pails.

We sewed the sacks, we broke the stones,
We turned the dusty drill:
We banged the tins, and bawled the hymns,
And sweated on the mill:
But in the heart of every man
Terror was lying still.

The unfortunate trooper was due to die on July 7. It was the first time for twenty-three years that an execution had taken place at Reading, so it was naturally quite an event in the prison. No attempt seems to have been made to conceal from the other prisoners the grim nature of the preparations that were being made, since the gallows were erected near the exercise yard in a shed, which had been originally built for the purpose of taking prisoners' photographs. It looked to Wilde like a photographer's studio on the sands at Margate. In fact until the dread preparations began he had always thought it was the studio for photographing prisoners. ('In itself it is a wooden, oblong, narrow shed with a glass roof.'[1]) On the afternoon before the hanging, Billington, the public executioner, arrived in the prison and, having viewed the condemned man from a hidden vantage point so as to assess his height and weight, tested the gallows and arranged for a 'drop' of six feet seven.[2] In the course of the same afternoon Wilde was returning from work with other prisoners to the cells, when they passed an open grave.

With yawning mouth the yellow hole
Gaped for a living thing;
The very mud cried out for blood
To the thirsty asphalte ring
And we knew that ere one dawn grew fair
Some prisoner had to swing.

Right in we went, with soul intent
On Death and Dread and Doom:
The hangman, with his little bag,
Went shuffling through the gloom:
And each man trembled as he crept
Into his numbered tomb.

[1] See *After Berneval. Letters of Oscar Wilde to Robert Ross* (1922), p. 16.

[2] The executioner's attention was drawn to the fact that this was considerably in excess of the scale officially laid down. But Billington insisted that in the circumstances this 'drop' was the correct one. For these details I am indebted to the old Execution Book, which is still preserved in the prison and which I was able to see by courtesy of the late Governor. (Reading is now a Borstal Institution.)

That night the warders, when they looked through the cell peep-holes in making their rounds, were amazed to see men kneeling in prayer, which they had never seen praying before. At 5.30 the prisoners rose as usual and cleaned their cells. But they remained locked in, which was the practice in those days when an execution was taking place. They could do nothing but wait dumbly 'for the stroke of eight'. For a quarter of an hour before that the tenor bell of St Lawrence's Church nearby tolled solemnly. At last came the fatal signal.

> With sudden shock the prison-clock
>   Smote on the shivering air,
> And from all the gaol rose up a wail
>   Of impotent despair,
> Like the sound that frightened marshes hear
>   From some leper in his lair.

At this moment, Wooldridge, whom, we are told, had submitted to the preliminary pinioning 'with marvellous firmness', was being conducted from the condemned cell to the gallows shed both of which were situated only a few steps away from the entrance to the three ordinary cell blocks in the prison. The procession was made up of the Governor, chaplain, doctor and Under-Sheriff, in addition to the executioner and two warders. Arrived in the shed the condemned man was said to have taken his stand on the trapdoor almost as if he were on parade. Billington then fastened his feet, adjusted the white cap and drew the bolt.[1]

> And as one sees most fearful things
>   In the crystal of a dream
> We saw the greasy hempen rope
>   Hooked to the blackened beam,
> And heard the prayer the hangman's snare
>   Strangled into a scream.
>
> And all the woe that moved him so
>   That he gave that bitter cry
> And the wild regrets, and the bloody sweats,
>   None knew so well as I:
> For he who lives more lives than one
>   More deaths than one must die.

[1] Wilde never saw the condemned man after his conviction. But he told one of the prison warders, with whom he had become friendly, that 'those moments when the bell rang out, and his imagination conjured up the execution scene, were the most awful of a time rich in horrors': *Evening News*, March 2, 1905.

In accordance with the law, Wooldridge's body was left hanging in the execution shed for an hour. It was then taken down and an inquest was held by the prison doctor who pronounced, in Wilde's memorable phrase, that 'Death was but a scientific fact'. The remains were then buried in the grave, which Wilde and the other prisoners had seen and which was filled with quicklime. It was thus 'nigh on noon' when the prisoners were at last released from their cells for exercise.

The Warders strutted up and down
And kept their herd of brutes,
Their uniforms were spick and span,
And they wore their Sunday suits,
But we knew the work they had been at,
By the quicklime on their boots.

For where a grave had opened wide
There was no grave at all:
Only a stretch of mud and sand
By the hideous prison-wall,
And a little heap of burning lime,
That the man should have his pall.

The Chaplain does not kneel to pray
Beside his unhallowed grave,
Nor mark it with that blessed cross
That Christ for sinners gave,
Because the man is one of those
Whom Christ came down to save.

When he came to write *The Ballad*, Wilde was to dedicate it to the memory of the executed guardsman, describing him by his initials and similarly veiling his own authorship in the anonymity of his cell number. At the same time, in writing poor Wooldridge's epitaph, he wrote his own, for Robert Ross was to have the words inscribed on Wilde's grave in Père Lachaise Cemetery.

And alien tears will fill for him
Pity's long broken urn,
For his mourners will be outcast men
And outcasts always mourn.

CHAPTER IV

Reading under Major Nelson

1

WILDE had now been in prison for nearly fourteen months. Although he was better physically than he had been at Wandsworth, there had been a marked deterioration in his mental condition, evident from his interviews with Ross and Sherard and Harris. He lived in constant fear of going out of his mind. There was one last resort open to him. It was the right of every prisoner to petition the Home Secretary on any matter, and the Governor was bound to forward the petition to the Minister, unless it was patently frivolous. Wilde accordingly asked for facilities to draw up a petition praying for the termination of his sentence on grounds of health. He was given the customary form printed on blue prison paper, together with pen and ink, and he thereupon set to work. It is possible that he was encouraged in his task by the knowledge that some of his friends outside, notably More Adey and Frank Harris, were engaged in a similar task and were preparing to forward their petitions to the Home Office, should sufficient public support be forthcoming in the shape of signatures.

The petition which Wilde drafted in his prison cell at Reading, and which lay in the Home Office archives for nearly sixty years, unseen by any outside eye, is without doubt one of the most remarkable documents of its kind ever written. It is also one of the longest, consisting of approximately 2,000 words, which the petitioner had some difficulty in getting into the two-and-a-half foolscap pages allowed for the purpose. Wilde made it a powerful plea *ad misericordiam*, beginning with a confession of guilt, and analysing his homosexual tendencies on the lines that his condition was a pathological one, which should be the subject of medical treatment and not of imprisonment.[1]

[1] H–D, 401.

PETITION

OSCAR WILDE *H.M. Prison,*
Reading.
2nd July 1896.

To the Rt. Hon. H.M. Principal Secretary of State for the Home Department.

THE PETITION OF THE ABOVE-NAMED PRISONER HUMBLY HEWETH—

that he does not desire to attempt to palliate in any way the terrible offences of which he was rightly found guilty, but to point out that such offences are forms of sexual madness and are recognised as such not merely by modern pathological science but by more modern legislation, notably in France, Austria and Italy where the laws affecting these misdemeanours have been repealed, on the ground that they are diseases to be cared for by a physician, rather than crimes to be punished by a judge. In the works of eminent men of science such as Lombroso and Max Nordau, to take merely two instances out of many, this is specially insisted on with reference to the intimate connection between madness and the literary and aesthetic temperament. Professor Nordau in his book on 'Degenerescence' (*sic*)[1] published in 1894 having devoted an entire chapter to the Petitioner as a specially typical example of his fatal law. The Petitioner is now keenly conscious of the fact that while the three years preceding his arrest were from the intellectual point of view the most brilliant years of his life, (four plays from his pen having been produced on the stage with immense success, and plays not merely in England, America and Australia, but in almost every European capital, and many books that excited much interest at home and abroad having been published), still that during the entire time he was suffering from the most horrible form of erotomania, which made him forget his wife and children, his high social position in London and Paris, his European distinction as an artist, the honour of his name and family, his very humanity itself, and left him the helpless prey of the most revolting passions, and of a gang of people who for their own profit ministered to them, and then drove him to his hideous ruin.

It is under the ceaseless apprehension lest this insanity, that displayed itself in monstrous sexual perversion before, may now extend to the entire nature and intellect, that the Petitioner writes this appeal which he earnestly entreats may at once be considered.

[1] This work was originally published in Germany in 1893 as *Entartung*. An English edition entitled *Degeneration* appeared in 1895. Dr Max Simon Nordau (1849–1923) was a German author, physician and sociologist, who in *Entartung* applied the theory of physical degeneration to the intellectual side of civilised man, citing Wilde among others as an example, notably in his aesthetic phase.

Horrible as all actual madness is, the terror of madness is no less appalling and no less ruinous to the soul.

For more than thirteen dreadful months now, the Petitioner has been subject to the fearful system of solitary cellular confinement: without human intercourse of any kind: without writing materials whose use might help to distract the mind: without suitable or sufficient books, so essential to any literary man, so vital for the preservation of mental balance: condemned to absolute silence: cut off from all knowledge of the external world and the movements of life: leading an existence composed of bitter degradation and terrible hardships, hideous in its recurring monotony of dreary task and sickening privation, the despair and misery of this lonely and wretched life having been intensified beyond words by the death of his mother, Lady Wilde, to whom he was deeply attached, as well as by the contemplation of the ruin he has brought on his young wife and two children.

By special permission the Petitioner is allowed two books a week to read: but the prison library is extremely small and poor: it hardly contains a score of books suitable for an educated man: the books kindly added at the prisoner's request he has read and re-read till they have become almost meaningless to him: he is practically left without anything to read: the world of ideas, as the actual world, is closed to him: he is deprived of everything that could soothe, distract, or heal a wounded and shaken mind: and horrible as all the physical privations of modern prison life are, they are nothing compared to the entire privation of literature to one to whom Literature was once the first thing of life, the mode by which perfection could be realised, by which, and by which alone, the intellect could feel itself alive.

It is but natural that living in this silence, this solitude, this isolation from all human and humane influences, this tomb for those who are not yet dead, the Petitioner should, day and night in every waking hour, be tortured by the fear of absolute and entire insanity. He is conscious that his mind, shut out artificially from all rational and intellectual interests, does nothing, and can do nothing, but brood on those forms of sexual perversity, those loathesome modes of erotomania, that have brought him from high place and noble distinction to the convict's cell and the common gaol. It is inevitable that it should do so. The mind is forced to think, and when it is deprived of the conditions necessary for healthy intellectual activity, such as books, writing materials, companionship, contact with the living world, and the like, it becomes in the case of those who are suffering from sensual monomanias, the sure prey of morbid passions, and obscene fancies, and thoughts that defile, desecrate and destroy. Crimes may be forgotten and forgiven, but vices live on: they make their dwellinghouse in him who by horrible mischance and fate has become their victim: they are embedded in his flesh: they spread over him like a leprosy: they feed on him like a strange disease: at the end they become an essential part of the man: no remorse however poignant can drive them out: no tears however bitter can wash them away: and prison life, by its horrible isolation from all that could save a wretched soul, hands the victim over, like one bound hand and foot, to be possessed and polluted by the thoughts he most loathes and so cannot escape from.

For more than a year the Petitioner's mind has borne this. He can bear it no longer. He is quite conscious of the approach of an insanity that will not be confined to one portion of the nature merely, but will extend over all alike, and his desire, his prayer is that his sentence may be remitted now, so that he may be taken abroad by his friends and may put himself under medical care so that the sexual insanity from which he suffers may be cured. He knows only too well that his career as a dramatist and writer is ended, and his name blotted from the scroll of English literature never to be replaced: that his children cannot bear that name again and that an obscure life in some remote country is in store for him: he knows that bankruptcy having come upon him, poverty of a most bitter kind awaits him, and that all the joy and beauty of existence is taken from him for ever: but at least in all his hopelessness he still clings to the hope that he will not have to pass directly from the common gaol to the common Lunatic Asylum. Dreadful as are the results of the prison system—a system so terrible that it hardens their hearts whose hearts it does not break, and brutalises those who have to carry it out no less than those who have to submit to it—yet at least amongst its aims is not the desire to wreck the human reason. Though it may not seek to make men better, yet it does not desire to drive them mad, and so, earnestly does the Petitioner beg that he may be allowed to go forth while he has still some sanity left, while words have still a meaning, and books a message: while there is still some possibility that, by medical science and humane treatment, balance may be restored to a shaken mind and health given back to a nature that once knew purity: while there is still time to rid the temperament of a revolting madness and to make the soul, even for a brief space, clean. Most earnestly indeed does the Petitioner beg the Home Secretary to take, if he so desires it, the opinion of any recognised medical authorities on silence and isolation on one already suffering from sexual monomania of a terrible character.

The Petitioner would also point out that, while his bodily health is better in many respects here than it was at Wandsworth, where he was for two months in the hospital for absolute physical and mental collapse caused by hunger and insomnia, he has since he has been in prison, almost entirely lost the hearing of his right ear, through an abscess that has caused a perforation of the drum. The Medical Officer here has stated that he is unable to offer any assistance, and that the hearing must go entirely. The Petitioner, however, feels sure that under the care of a specialist abroad his hearing might be restored to him. He was assured by Sir William Dalby,[1] the great aurist, that with proper care there was no reason at all why he should lose his hearing. But though the abscess has been running now for the entire time of his imprisonment and the hearing getting worse every week, nothing has been done in the way of an attempted cure. The ear has been syringed on three occasions with plain water for the purposes of examination, that is all. The Petitioner is naturally apprehensive lest, as often happens, the other ear may be attacked in a similar way, and to the misery of a shattered and debilitated mind be added the horrors of complete deafness.

His eyesight, of which like most men of letters he has always been obliged to take great care, has also suffered very much from the enforced living in a whitewashed cell with a flaring gas-jet at night: he is conscious of great weakness and pain in the nerves of the eyes, and objects even at a short distance become blurred. The bright daylight, when taking exercise in the prison-yard, often causes pain and distress to the optic nerve, and during the last four months the consciousness of failing eyesight has been a source of terrible anxiety, and should his imprisonment continue, blindness and deafness may in all human probability be added to the certainty of increasing insanity and the wreck of the reason.

There are other apprehensions of danger that the limitation of space does not allow the Petitioner to enter on: his chief danger is that of madness, his chief terror that of madness, and his prayer that his long imprisonment may be considered with its attendant ruin a sufficient punishment, that that imprisonment may be ended now, and not uselessly or vindictively prolonged till insanity has claimed soul as well as body as its prey, and brought it to the same degradation and the same shame.

OSCAR WILDE

As soon as it was finished, the petition was brought to the Governor's office. When he had read it, Major Isaacson showed it to the prison doctor and asked him for a short medi-

[1] Sir William Dalby (1840–1918), the well-known aural surgeon.

cal report, which he could attach to it. Dr Maurice's report was as follows:

> The health of the Prisoner Wylde (*sic*) has improved considerably since he came to Reading and he has gained flesh.
>
> I have never been able to see any evidence of insanity or approaching insanity, and, while fully recognising the trial it must be to a man of his antecedents to be in the position that he now is, having carefully read the Petition, it is to my mind, from the lucid way in which he quotes authorities and gives his own ideas of insanity, clear evidence of his present sanity, and I confess I see no reason to think there is any evidence of his mind giving way.
>
> It is perfectly true that he has a slight perforation of the drum of the right ear, but there is no evidence of mischief in the left, nor of any defect of vision.
>
> OLIVER MAURICE
> M.O. H.M. Prison, Reading
> 3rd July, 1896.

On the same day Major Isaacson forwarded the petition and the medical report to the Prison Commissioners. It was one of his last official acts at Reading, since the decision had already been taken by the Commissioners to transfer him to another post in the Prison Service.

2

The first step taken by Ruggles-Brise, on receiving Wilde's petition and the accompanying report of the prison doctor, was to refer the matter to the Visiting Committee. The members of this statutory body were required to make regular visits of inspection to every prison in the country, and, although they were primarily concerned with breaches of discipline, for which they had the power to award punishments like flogging, which Governors could not order, they were also expected to report from time to time on the health of the prisoners and on prison conditions generally. Four Prison Visitors duly appeared at Reading and carried out an inquiry, studying the petition and interviewing the prisoner as well as the Governor, Medical Officer and chaplain. On July 10, they reported that in their opinion Wilde had been well treated and was in as good health, mental and physical as could be expected in a prisoner of his education and antecedents, for whom 'prison life must of course be more irksome and severe' than the ordinary prisoner. 'He himself states that his treatment has been good and the dietary sufficient', they stated, 'he has been relieved of oakum picking, has been allowed more books and more exercise than the other prisoners. He has increased eight pounds in weight since he entered the prison.' They did not consider that there was any danger of Wilde becoming insane; but, 'as this prisoner's petition is based upon the fear of insanity, always a difficult subject', the Committee recommended 'an expert medical inquiry' to include hearing and eyesight.[1]

On July 15 Ruggles-Brise sent the petition and two reports, with a minute, to Kenelm Digby, the Permanent Under-Secretary at the Home Office. In the light of the Visiting Committee's report, and 'having regard to the fact that the prisoner is in a very morbid state of mind and living under artificial conditions, calculated to intensify any tendency to unsoundness', Ruggles-Brise endorsed the recommendation for an independent medical inquiry. In due course the papers reached the Secretary of State's desk, with a note from Kenelm Digby advising that the petition should be shown to the medical officer at Broadmoor Criminal Lunatic Asylum who had examined Wilde at Wandsworth. 'I think it would be well to let Dr Nicolson see this remarkable petition, which certainly does not contain internal evidence of failure of brain-power, and then discuss the matter with him.' To this course the Home Secretary agreed, although at the same time he expressed himself in favour of 'a special medical inquiry' as recommended by the Visiting Committee.

MINUTE FROM PERMANENT UNDER-SECRETARY
TO SECRETARY OF STATE

Home Office,
July 24, 1896.

Dr Nicolson has seen these papers and does not advise any inquiries into Wilde's mental condition. He says there is no indication of insanity or approaching insanity in this petition. He thinks the reports show that Wilde is better than when he saw him at Wandsworth last December.[2] As more than half his sentence has

[1] The Visiting Justices' Book, which contains this Report, is preserved at Reading. I am obliged to the late Governor for kindly letting me see it.

[2] This is a mistake. The visit to Wandsworth took place in the previous October; see above, p. 35.

elapsed he thinks the morbidity in his mind will diminish as time goes on and the period of his release approaches. He thinks it would be well to give him increased and exceptional facilities as to books and writing materials.

As to his bodily health I think it hardly necessary to call in further medical assistance at present, unless the M.O. desires it.

To these proposals the Home Secretary again assented, and consequently nothing more was heard of the Visiting Committee's recommendation. The papers were returned to the Prison Commissioners with a direction that appropriate instructions should be sent to the Governor of Reading in the light of Dr Nicolson's opinion. The instructions were drafted on July 27 by Ruggles-Brise personally and sent to the Governor on the same day.

Confidential

INSTRUCTIONS SENT TO GOVERNOR, READING PRISON, IN THE CASE OF OSCAR WILDE

July 27, 1896.

With reference to the Petition of Oscar Wilde, dated 20th instant, the Secretary of State has decided that this prisoner should be provided with foolscap paper, ink and pen, for use in his leisure moments in his cell, as you will be good enough to act accordingly.

I. This privilege is only conceded on these conditions

(1) that no communication is made to outside persons otherwise than consistently with the ordinary rules;

(2) that use is not made of the writing materials to such a degree as to interfere with his ordinary prison occupation.

You will personally superintend this matter and will exercise your discretion as to the time during the day when the privilege may be exercised.

It will also be exercised in such a way as not to needlessly arouse comment among other prisoners.

(3) all writing materials will be withdrawn from the prisoner's cell at locking up and all written matter will be subject to your inspection, and you will be responsible for seeing that no improper use is made of this privilege.

II. The prisoner has complained of the absence of suitable and sufficient books and of his 'privation of all literature' he having read and reread the books that have hitherto been provided for him. You will please report whether this is the fact: and, if so, you will give the prisoner his choice of any suitable books in the prison library. Failing these, you will ask the prisoner to name any work with which he desires to be provided, and will report to the Commissioners, who will give further instructions thereon.

The Prison rules limiting the issue of books to two per week may be relaxed in the case of this prisoner, and you will use your discretion as to allowing to the prisoner sufficient books to occupy his mind, always provided that any indulgence granted in this respect is not extravagant, and does not interfere with the ordinary labour required of the prisoner in fulfilment of his sentence.

III. The prisoner has complained of an affection of the ear, which, he alleges, has received insufficient treatment, and of an affection of the eyesight. Having regard to the certificate of the Medical Officer no special inquiry seems necessary at the present time as to his state of health but the Medical Officer will watch the general health of the prisoner and in particular matters complained of with care, and should he consider that an *outside* opinion would be desirable he is authorised to call for it, this second opinion could in all probability be obtained locally, be it either of a special or a general nature.

By the time these instructions arrived, a change of Governors had taken place, which was to prove of great significance for Wilde. Major Isaacson had been transferred to another prison and his place at Reading had been taken by Major James Osmond Nelson. Frank Harris always claimed that it was his report which got Isaacson relieved and Nelson appointed in his stead. While there may be some doubts as to the extent of this claim, there is happily no doubt about the truth of Harris's description of Isaacson's successor as 'an ideal governor'.[1]

3

Major Nelson was about thirty-six years of age at the time of his appointment to Reading. He immediately made his influence felt in a thoroughly unaccustomed manner. The number of punishments was more than halved and soon the chaplain was able to report that the punishment list 'is always very light here'. Wilde was among the first to experience the effects of the change, since he and Nelson were to become firm friends. 'The present Governor of Reading is a man of gentle and humane character, greatly liked and respected by all the

[1] Harris. II, 606.

prisoners', Wilde wrote a few days after his release. 'Though he cannot alter the rules of the prison system, he has altered the spirit in which they used to be carried out under his predecessor. He is very popular with the prisoners and with the warders. Indeed he has quite altered the whole tone of prison life. Upon the other hand, the system is, of course, beyond his reach as far as altering its rules is concerned. I have no doubt that he sees daily much of what he knows to be unjust, stupid and cruel. But his hands are tied. . . . I merely judge him by the complete change he brought about to Reading Prison. Under his predecessor the system was carried out with the greatest harshness and stupidity.'[1] A little later in conversation with an acquaintance, Wilde stated that, whilst Isaacson was 'not able to enjoy his breakfast unless someone was punished before he ate it', Nelson was 'the most Christ-like man' he had ever met.[2]

Wilde now availed himself of the privilege of seeing the new Governor whenever he could. 'I looked forward to those morning talks,' said Major Nelson afterwards. 'I always allowed Wilde to stay the full quarter of an hour to which a prisoner was entitled for an interview with the Governor—or rather I kept him the full time. For it was a pleasure to me. Wilde certainly was the most amazing and brilliant talker I have ever met'. In gratitude after he left prison Wilde was to send Nelson a copy of *The Ballad of Reading Gaol.* Robert Ross thought at the time that Nelson was a little hurt by the *Ballad*, which he fancied rather reflected on him, though Major Isaacson was the Governor at the time the soldier was executed.[3] On the other hand, when Nelson was asked many years later whether or not Wilde had exaggerated the effect on the prison inmates of an impending execution, Nelson replied that 'it was not only a faithful description of the effect produced by the hanging of the soldier to whom Wilde's verses refer, but that the same dreadful atmosphere of doom affecting warders and prisoners alike, permeated our gaols on the morning of an execution even today'.[4]

It was not long before Wilde experienced an example of the new Governor's kindness. Wilde's next quarterly visit from

[1] Letter to the *Daily Chronicle*, May 27, 1897.
[2] See 'A Reminiscence of 1898' by Wilfred Hugh Chesson in *The Bookman* (New York), Vol. XXXIV (December, 1911) at p. 390.
[3] Harris. II, 606.
[4] *Manchester Guardian*, October 13, 1914. See also, below, p. 178.

two friends, whom he was entitled to see, became due in August. More Adey, whom he had not seen for six months, and Arthur Clifton, another friend, who was a solicitor and whom he had not seen at all, both applied for visiting orders, and Wilde asked that the necessary orders should be sent to them. Just after this had been done, Robert Sherard requested permission to come as well. Although he had told Sherard on the occasion of his previous visit that he would be glad to see him next time, Wilde did not think he would be in England in August, for Sherard habitually lived in Paris. He was naturally disappointed since he felt particularly grateful to Sherard for having succeeded in stopping the publication of his letters to Alfred Douglas. To compensate him Major Nelson allowed Wilde to send Sherard a special letter. 'I often think of you and of our uninterrupted friendship of twelve years standing,' he wrote to Sherard on August 26, 'and, while I bitterly regret the sorrow that I have brought on you and other of my friends, I remember with pride and gratitude your chivalry and courage on my behalf. Should the end of my terrible punishment ever come, you are one of the few people I should like to see, and be with from time to time.'[1]

In acknowledging receipt from the Prison Commissioners of the instructions about the provision of more books and writing materials for the prisoner, Major Nelson recommended a manuscript notebook, strongly but coarsely bound, for Wilde's use, in preference to the foolscap sheets. 'The book could be used and withdrawn every day without arousing any comment amongst other prisoners', the Governor remarked, 'and would afford less facilities for improper use than sheets of foolscap, although I do not for one moment anticipate abuse of this privilege.' At the same time the Governor enclosed a long list of books which Wilde had asked for and which was in the prisoner's handwriting, with his comments on certain titles. They included the works of Tennyson, Marlowe, Keats, Chaucer and Spencer, Bishop Percy's *Reliques of Ancient Poetry*, Carlyle's *Sartor Resartus*, a prose translation of Dante's *Divina Comedia*, Renan's *Vie de Jésus* and *Les Apôtres* ('The Chaplain sees no objection to these if they are in the original French'), Ranke's

[1] H–D, 407. The original of this letter, with the official regulations governing the writing and receiving of letters by prisoners on the reverse side, is in my possession.

OVERLEAF

LETTER FROM OSCAR WILDE
TO ROBERT SHERARD

Written from Reading Gaol, August 26, 1896

'While I bitterly regret the sorrow that I have brought on you and other of my friends, I remember with pride and gratitude your chivalry and courage on my behalf.'

Address
Oscar Wilde

20 August 1896

Wednesday

My dear Robert

The Governor has told me that you have written to ask to see me. It is most kind and affectionate of you, but an order has already been sent to More Adey, and Arthur Clifton (whom I have not seen yet) and, as you know, I am only allowed two visitors. I did not think there would have been any chance of your being in town. I hope you are well, and writing a great deal. I often think of you and of our uninterrupted friendship, of twelve years standing, and while I bitterly regret the sorrow that I have brought on you and other of my friends, I remember with pride and gratitude your chivalry and courage on my behalf: should the end of my terrible punishment ever come you are one of the few people I would like to see, and be with from time to time.

Please remember me very kindly to George Ives. I was greatly touched at hearing of his desire to come and see me. In the terrible solitude and silence in which one lives a message or a memory means a great deal. I hope he is hard at work writing books. I am very glad you know him. He is such a good fellow, and so clever.

Should you have anything special to communicate to me – something separate from the sympathy and affection you have, I know, for me – More Adey who is to write to me in the course of the next fortnight will communicate it in his letter. He has to write to me on business.

I was so disappointed at not seeing you that I have been allowed as a favour to write this letter to you. Pray remember me to any of my friends who may ask after me, and Believe me, dear Robert, Sincerely yours

Oscar

History of the Popes, and Cardinal Newman's *Critical and Historical Essays*. 'The library here contains no example of any of Thackeray's or Dickens's novels', noted Wilde on the list. 'I feel sure that a complete set of their works would be as great a boon to many amongst the other prisoners as it would certainly be to myself.' The Prison Commissioners approved the purchase of a manuscript notebook for Wilde, and they also authorised the Governor to spend £10 for the prison library for the ensuing year on all the books which Wilde had requested, except the works of Thackeray.[1]

Adey's visit was principally concerned with business, since he had been constituted a kind of unofficial trustee in Wilde's bankruptcy; it was through him that the negotiations with the Official Receiver about the life interest in the marriage settlement took place. Then Wilde wished to have another solicitor, since he was dissatisfied with Humphreys, whom he blamed, somewhat unfairly, for allowing him to be made bankrupt. He thought that Clifton might agree to act for him in any further proceedings and also might become the guardian of his two children, since he felt that, although they no longer bore his name, 'for their own sake as well as for mine they should not be brought up to look on me with hatred or contempt', and 'a guardian amongst my wife's relations would be for this reason impossible'. Finally, Adey was busy getting up another petition for Wilde's release. Copies were being printed, he told the prisoner, and he was going to write to the Home Secretary about it. This petition was drafted in similar terms to that previously prepared by Adey, with an important additional plea. It contained a reference to the recent Report of the Departmental Committee on Prisons (the Gladstone Committee), which recommended that the power to earn remission of sentence should be extended to prisoners serving terms of imprisonment.[2] At that time only convicts undergoing penal servitude could earn such remission. Wilde would shortly have completed eighteen months of his sentence, which under the convict rule would entitle him to release subject to good conduct.

On September 23, soon after Adey and Clifton had visited Reading, Wilde wrote to the former of these friends:

[1] Major Nelson to Prison Commissioners, July 29, 1896: Home Office (Prison Commission) Papers.
[2] *Oscar Wilde: Three Times Tried*, 470.

I thank you very much for writing to the Home Secretary. I do hope it will have some effect. But pity seems to beat in vain at the doors of officialism: and power, no less than punishment, kills what else were good and gentle in a man. The man without knowing it loses his natural kindliness, or grows afraid of its exercise. Still, I hope something may be done.

I admit that I look forward with horror to the prospect of another winter in prison. There is something terrible in it. One has to get up long before day-break and in the dark cold cell begin one's work by the flaming gas-jet. Through the small barred window only gloom seems to find an entrance, and days often go over without one's being even once in the open air, days on which one stifles, days that are endless in their dull monotony of apathy or despair.

On November 19th I will have had eighteen months of this black loathsome hell. Perhaps then something may be done. I know you will do your best: I have no words for my sense of your great wonderful kindness to me.[1]

As events turned out, the petition, which Adey had printed, was never presented. On the day after Wilde had written the above lines, a letter was sent to Adey on the instructions of the Home Secretary informing him 'that the case of this prisoner has been the subject of careful inquiry and consideration and that, as a result, he has come to the conclusion that no grounds, medical or other, exist which would justify him in advising any mitigation of the sentence'.[2] The petition was thereupon abandoned.

This news apparently did not reach Wilde for some time, since a little later he himself addressed another petition to the Home Secretary.[3]

PETITION

OSCAR WILDE

H.M. Prison,
Reading.
10th November, 1896.

THE PETITION OF THE ABOVE NAMED PRISONER HUMBLY SHEWETH

that in the month of June last the Petitioner, having been at that time a prisoner for more than a year, addressed to the Secretary of State a petition praying for his release on the grounds chiefly of mental health,

[1] Clark MSS; H–D, 407.
[2] *Oscar Wilde: Three Times Tried*, 468; Sherard, *The Real Oscar Wilde*, 392.
[3] Home Office Papers; H–D, 411.

that the Petitioner has received no answer to this petition, and would earnestly beg that it be taken into consideration, as on the 19th inst. the Petitioner will have completed eighteen months of solitary confinement, a sentence of terrible severity in any case, and, in the case of the Petitioner rendered all the more difficult to bear, as it has been inflicted for offences which are in other countries of Europe, more rightly recognised as tragic forms of madness coming chiefly on those who overtax their brain, in art or science.

Some alleviations have been granted to the Petitioner since the date of his former petition: his ear, that was in danger of total deafness, is now attended to daily and spectacles have been provided for the protection of his eyes: he is allowed a manuscript book to write in, and out of a list of books selected by himself and approved by the Prison Commissioners, a few have been added to the Prison Library: but these alleviations, for which the Petitioner is naturally very grateful, count for but little in relieving the terrible stress and mental anguish that the silence and solitude of prison-life intensify daily—of all modes of insanity—and the Petitioner is fully conscious now, too conscious it may be, that his whole life, for the two years preceding his ruin, was the prey of absolute madness—the insanity of perverted sensual instinct is the one most dominant in its action on the brain. It taints the intellectual as well as the emotional energies. It clings like a malaria to the soul and body alike. And while one may bear up against the monotonous hardships and relentless discipline of an English prison; endure with apathy the increasing shame and the daily degradation: and grow callous even to that hideous grotesqueness of life that robs sorrow of all its dignity, and takes from pain its power of purification; still, the complete isolation of everything that is humane and humanising plunges one deeper and deeper into the very mire of madness, and the horrible silence, to which one is, as it were, eternally condemned, concentrates the mind on all that it longs to loathe, and creates those insane moods from which one desires to be free, creates them and makes them permanent.

Under these circumstances the Petitioner prays for his release on the expiration of his eighteen months confinement, or at any rate before Christmas comes. Some friends have promised to take him abroad at once, and to see that he has the treatment and care that he requires. There is of course before him no public life, nor any life in literature any more: nor joy or happiness of life at all: he has lost wife, children, fame, honour, position, wealth: poverty is all that he can look forward to: obscurity all that he can hope for: yet he feels that, if released now, somewhere, unknown, untormented, at peace, he might be able to recreate the life of a student of letters, and find in literature an anodyne from pain, first, and afterwards a mode by which sanity and balance and wholesomeness might be restored to the soul. But the solitary confinement, that breaks one's heart, shatters one's intellect, too; and prison is but an ill physician: and the modern modes of punishment create what they *should* cure, as, when they have on their side time with its long length of dreary days, they desecrate and destroy whatever good, or desire even of good, there may be in a man.

To be at length, after these eighteen months of lonely sorrow and despair, set free, for whatever brief space of time, health of mind or body may follow, is the earnest prayer of the Petitioner,

OSCAR WILDE

As in the case of the former appeal, this petition was shown to the prison doctor, and then forwarded with his report to the Prison Commissioners. 'I have carefully read the Petition of the prisoner Wilde,' wrote Dr Maurice, 'I have seen him frequently and I am of the same opinion as when I last reported that his mental and bodily health are good. His ear which was more a serious case is better and need cause no anxiety.' It will be remembered that the Prison Commissioners in their instructions to the Governor of Reading on July 27 had authorised the prison doctor to call for a second opinion on Wilde's health. This had been done and Dr Maurice accordingly enclosed this opinion with his report. It was from a local practitioner, Dr J. A. Price, who had examined Wilde's ear, and found a perforation of the left tympanic membrane. He had prescribed 'daily syringing of the ear with diluted carbolic lotion'.

The petition was duly minuted by a senior Home Office official before being laid on the Secretary of State's desk. 'This petition affords no ground for apprehending any injurious effect from further imprisonment', wrote this official. 'The prisoner's fear of mental breakdown or a decay of his literary capability is expressed in too lucid orderly and polished a style to cause apprehension on that point.' His chief agreed with this diagnosis, and the Home Secretary accordingly directed that Wilde should be informed that the petition had been rejected. The news was conveyed to Wilde on the day on which the final six months of his sentence was due to begin.[1]

'The refusal to commute my sentence has been like a blow from a leaden sword', he wrote to Robert Ross a few days later.

[1] Home Office Papers.

'I am dazed with a dull sense of pain. I had fed on hope, and now anguish grown hungry feeds her fill on me as though she had been starved of her proper appetite.' But there was a consolation in the 'kinder elements in this evil prison air' than there were formerly. 'Sympathies have been shown to me and I no longer feel entirely isolated from humane influences which was before a source of terror and trouble to me.' He was reading Dante and making excerpts and notes 'for the pleasure of using pen and ink'. And he was going to take up the study of German. 'Indeed,' he added with a touch of his old humour, 'this seems to be the proper place for such a study.'[1]

4

The last six months of his imprisonment were relatively comfortable for Wilde. Since Major Isaacson's departure he had done no oakum picking; and now, under the beneficent rule of Major Nelson, he appears to have been excused all other forms of manual work. Instead he was appointed 'schoolmaster's orderly', which meant in effect that he was in charge of the prison library, although he also continued to work in the garden. His task was to go round the cells, collecting the books which the prisoners had read, and issue them with new ones. The books, which reached him from time to time from his friends, were subsequently used to augment the meagre library with the approval of the Prison Commissioners. 'They are sentenced to perpetual imprisonment', Wilde told his friend Adey, who had arranged for many of them to be sent to Reading. 'But they may soothe and heal other troubled minds and breaking hearts.' When Arthur Humphreys, the publisher and bookseller, heard that Wilde was now allowed as much to read as he wished subject only to Home Office approval, he arranged for a 'really lavish' consignment to be despatched to him as a free gift. Wilde was deeply touched by this spontaneous act of kindness. 'It is a very dear remembrance on his part of a pleasant literary friendship', he wrote at the time.

In this parcel, which reached him about Christmas time, was a Greek Testament. Every morning, after he had cleaned his cell and polished his tins, he read a little of the Gospels, a dozen or so verses, chosen at random. 'It is a delightful way of

[1] *De Profundis* (1908 ed.), 5–6; H–D, 412.

opening the day', he wrote in *De Profundis*. 'Every one, even in a turbulent, ill-disciplined life, should do the same. Endless repetition, in and out of season, has spoiled for us the freshness, the naiveté, the simple romantic charm of the Gospels. We hear them read far too often and far too badly, and all repetition is anti-spiritual. When one returns to the Greek, it is like going into a garden of lilies out of some narrow and dark house.'

For the first time, on his own admission, he now had enough to eat, and with the beginning of the New Year, 1897, came an additional dietary privilege. He was allowed by the prison doctor to have white bread instead of the coarse black and brown bread of ordinary prison fare. Although unbuttered, he found it a great delicacy. 'It will sound strange that dry bread could possibly be a delicacy to anyone', he wrote at this time. 'To me it is so much so that at the close of each meal I carefully eat whatever crumbs may be left on my tin plate, or have fallen on the rough towel that one uses as a cloth so as not to soil one's table; and I do so not from hunger—I get now quite sufficient food—but simply in order that nothing should be wasted of what is given to me.'[1]

Among the books, which were sent to him at his request during this period, were *The Amazing Marriage* by George Meredith, *The Well Beloved* by Thomas Hardy, the *Letters* of D. G. Rossetti and R. L. Stevenson, and *En Route* by Huysmans. After reading them he sent some characteristic comments to Robert Ross. 'Meredith's novel charmed me. What a sane artist in temper! He is quite right in his assertion of sanity as the essential in romance.' Hardy's novel he found 'pleasant and the style perfect'. But Rossetti's letters were 'dreadful—obviously forgeries by his brother'. Nevertheless he was interested to note that two of the books which had fascinated Rossetti in his youth were *Melmoth the Wanderer* by Wilde's great-uncle, C. L. Maturin, and *Sidonia* by his mother, Lady Wilde. Stevenson's correspondence he also found disappointing. 'I see that romantic surroundings are the worst surroundings possible for a romantic writer. In Gower Street Stevenson could have written a new *Trois Mousquètaires*. In Samoa he wrote letters to *The Times* about the Germans. I see also the traces of a terrible strain to lead a natural life. To chop wood

[1] *De Profundis*, 104, 105.

with any advantage to oneself or profit to others, one should not be able to describe the process. In point of fact the natural life is the unconscious life. Stevenson merely extended the sphere of the artificial by taking to digging. The whole dreary book has given me a lesson. If I spent my future life reading Baudelaire in a café, I should be leading a more natural life than if I took to hedgers' work or planted cacao in mud swamps.' As for Huysmans's book it was 'most overrated', 'sheer journalism', 'it never makes one hear a note of the music it described' and, though the subject was 'delightful', the style was slipshod and flaccid. 'It is worse French than Ohnet's. Ohnet tries to be commonplace and succeeds. Huysmans tries not to be and is.'

Wilde's work as 'schoolmaster's orderly' made him familiar with the defects of the prison library, consisting of about 350 volumes in all, of which 100 ranked as 'school books' and another 100 as 'moral books'. He wrote to Ross on the subject. 'There being hardly any novels in the prison for the poor imprisoned fellows I live with I think of presenting the library with about a dozen good novels.' There was nothing by Thackeray, nothing by Jane Austen, and nothing by Stevenson except *The Black Arrow*. He suggested 'some good Dumas-père-like books, by Stanley Weyman, for instance, and any modern young man'. Ross had mentioned that W. G. Henley had a protégé, whose name Wilde could not remember. What about him? (This was H. G. Wells.) Then there was Anthony Hope. 'After Easter you might make out a list of 14 and apply to let me have them', he told Ross. 'Don't forget I would pay myself for them.'[1]

It had taken Wilde many weeks to get accustomed to using the writing materials with which he was now supplied. His first task had been to try to fill in the missing parts of *A Florentine Tragedy*, the blank-verse play which he had not completed at the time of his arrest. But the effort was too much for him, and he had to give it up. 'Only bits of it remain with me, and I find that I cannot invent', he told Adey. 'The silence, the utter solitude, the isolation from all humane and humanising influences kill one's brain-power: the brain loses its life, becomes fettered to monotony of suffering. But I take notes of books I read, and copy lines and phrases in poets. The mere

[1] *De Profundis* (1908 ed.), 21–5; H–D, 521.

handling of pen and ink help me. The horror of prison is the horror of complete brutalisation: that is the abyss always in front of one, branding itself on one's face daily, and the faces of those one sees. I cling to my note book: it helps me. Before I had it my brain was going in very evil circles.'[1]

He wrote mostly in the evenings, after the other prisoners had been locked in for the night, and he knew he would be undisturbed. For this purpose the gas was turned down in his cell, but it was not turned out. For a table he used his plank bed, which he laid across two wooden trestles. 'It was a very good table too', he told one of the warders. On it, during the month of January, 1897, he began a long letter to Alfred Douglas, parts of which were to be published after his death by Robert Ross under the title *De Profundis*. The letter, which surely must constitute a record in literary history, commenced 'Dear Bosie' and ended 'Your affectionate friend, Oscar Wilde'. It was composed on twenty folio sheets of blue prison paper, stamped at the head of each sheet with the Royal Arms, thus amounting in all to eighty ruled foolscap pages, each page having 33 lines and measuring 13 by 8 inches.[2] Wilde was allowed one sheet of this paper at a time, and, when it was complete, it was supposed to be taken away for Major Nelson to see and replaced by another. It was also supposed to be removed each evening at locking-in time. 'Of the many, many things for which I have to thank the Governor,' he told Robert Ross, 'there is none for which I am more grateful than for his permission to write fully to A[lfred] D[ouglas] and at as great length as I desired.'[3] However, he was also warned by Major Nelson that nothing he wrote in this could leave the gaol without reference to the Prison Commissioners. As will be seen, he never revised the finished version, which he half-humorously suggested might be called *Epistola: in Carcere et Vinculis*; in the circumstances of its composition it runs remarkably smoothly.

On February 18, he wrote to More Adey explaining the reasons which had led him to undertake this work:

[1] Wilde to Adey, September 23, 1896: Clark MSS; H–D, 410. The notebook has not survived. I have in my collection five quarto pages of MS in Wilde's handwriting of part of the unfinished first scene of *A Florentine Tragedy*. Although they have clearly been torn out of a ruled exercise book, there is no evidence to show that they date from the prison period. The text of this interesting fragment has been printed by Mason in his bibliography (pp. 464–5).

[2] Stuart Mason. *Bibliography of Oscar Wilde* (1914), p. 450.

[3] Wilde to Ross, April 1, 1897: Clark MSS; H–D, 514.

I told you I was going to write to Alfred Douglas. I am still at work at the letter. It is the most important letter of my life, as it will deal ultimately with my future mental attitude towards life, with the way in which I desire to meet the world again, with the development of my character: with what I have lost, what I have learned, and what I hope to arrive at. At last I see a real goal towards which my soul can go simply, naturally, and rightly. Before I see you and Robbie I must finish the letter, that you may understand what I have become, or rather desire to become in nature and aim. My whole life depends on it.

I will send the letter to Robbie, who must read it carefully and *copy it out carefully every word* for me. Then you having read it, and seen that it is copied rightly, will send it for me to A.D. I don't know his address. I hope to have it finished by Tuesday.[1]

Much of this now famous letter, in its allusions to Douglas and his conduct, was marked by passages of long and sustained invective. But, towards the end, a softer note is perceptible. Wilde suggested that on his release a meeting between them might be possible 'in some quiet foreign town like Bruges, where grey houses and green canals and cool still ways had a charm for me years ago'. But Douglas would have to change his name. 'The little title of which you were so vain—and indeed it made your name sound like the name of a flower!—you will have to surrender if you wish to see me, just as my name once so musical in the mouth of Fame will have to be abandoned by me in turn.' In conclusion, Wilde felt that he had yet to know his former friend, and perhaps they had yet to know each other. 'How far I am away from the true temper of the soul, this letter in all its changing, uncertain moods, its scorn and bitterness, its aspirations and its failures to realise those aspirations, shows you quite clearly. But do not forget in what a terrible school I am sitting at my task. And incomplete, imperfect, as I am, yet from me you may have still much to gain. You came to me to learn the pleasure of life and the pleasure of art. Perhaps I am chosen to teach you something much more wonderful—the meaning of sorrow and its beauty.'[2]

Wilde intended to enclose the manuscript with his next letter to Ross. In this letter, which was dated April 1, 1897, and was afterwards partly published in the later editions of *De Profundis*, Wilde told Ross that he wished him to be his literary executor

[1] Clark MSS; H–D, 419. [2] *De Profundis*, 145, 148.

in the event of his death, with complete control over his plays, books and papers. At the same time he elaborated the reasons he had already given Adey which had prompted him to write such a remarkable letter to Douglas, and he also repeated in detail the instructions he wished followed for copying it.[1]

> Well, if you are to be my literary executor, you must be in possession of the only document that really gives any explanation of my extraordinary behaviour with regard to Queensberry and Alfred Douglas. When you have read the letter, you will see the psychological explanation of a course of conduct that from the outside seems a combination of absolute idiocy with vulgar bravado. Some day the truth will have to be known—not necessarily in my lifetime or in Douglas's. But I am not prepared to sit in the grotesque pillory they put me into for all time; for the simple reason that I inherited from my father and my mother a name of high distinction in literature and art, and I cannot for eternity allow that name to be the shield and catspaw of the Queensberrys. I don't defend my conduct, I explain it.
>
> Also there are in the letter certain passages which deal with my mental development in prison, and the inevitable evolution of character and intellectual attitude towards life that has taken place: and I want you, and others who still stand by me and have affection for me, to know exactly in what mood and manner I hope to face the world. Of course, from one point of view I know that on the day of my release I shall be merely passing from one prison to another, and there are times when the whole world seems to me no larger than my cell and as full of terror for me. Still I believe that at the beginning God made a world for each separate man, and in that world which is within us one should seek to live.

As to the mode of copying, Wilde felt that 'the only thing to do is to be thoroughly modern and have it typewritten'. He suggested that a girl from the agency, where he had sent his last play to be typed, might be sent to Adey's flat in London to do the work under Ross's supervision. 'Women are the most reliable, as they have no memory for the important.' Wilde went on: 'I assure you that the typewriting machine, when played with expression, is not more annoying than the piano when played by a sister or near relation. Indeed many among those most devoted to domesticity prefer it.' He playfully suggested that the typist 'might be fed through a lattice in the door, like the Cardinals when they elect a Pope, till she

[1] Clark MSS; H–D, 512; partly published in *De Profundis* (1908 ed.), 12–19, and *Dulau Sale Catalogue*, 22–4.

comes out on the balcony and can say to the world "*Habet mundus Epistolam*"; for indeed it is an Encyclical letter, and as the Bulls of the Holy Father are named from their opening words, it may be spoken of as the "*Epistola: in Carcere et Vinculis*".' He asked that copies should be made of certain passages—those that were in fact later published as *De Profundis*—and sent to two particular women friends, Miss Adela Schuster and Mrs Frank Forbes-Robertson. 'I know both these sweet women will be interested to know something of what is happening to my soul, not in the theological sense, but merely in the sense of that spiritual consciousness that is separate from the actual occupations of the body.' Otherwise the letter was to be 'a strict secret from the general world'. Two typed copies only of the whole were to be made, one for Ross and the other to be kept for Wilde himself. When the copies had been checked with the manuscript, the letter was to be dispatched to Douglas by Adey.

> There is no need to tell A.D. that a copy has been taken, unless he should write and complain of injustice in the letter or misrepresentation. Then he should be told that a copy has been taken.
>
> I earnestly hope the letter will do him good. It is the first time that anyone has ever told him the truth about himself. If he is allowed to think that the letter is merely the result of a plank bed on style, and that my views are distorted by the privations of prison life, no good will follow. I hope someone will let him know that the letter is one he thoroughly deserves and that, if it is unjust, he thoroughly deserves injustice. Who indeed deserves it more than he who was always so unjust to others?

As events turned out, there was to be some delay in carrying out these directions. Wilde was not allowed by the Governor to send the manuscript with his letter to Ross. Had the matter rested with Major Nelson alone, he could probably have done so, but the Governor was bound to refer it to the Prison Commissioners. On hearing from them he sent for Wilde and told him that the manuscript would be kept safely and handed to him with his other belongings on the day he left Reading.[1]

[1] On April 2 Major Nelson requested instructions as to whether Wilde 'should be allowed to send out to Lord A. Douglas the enclosed manuscript, which is practically an autobiography of the prisoner's life during his acquaintance with that gentleman'. The MS was returned by the Prison Commissioners to the Governor four days later with a note to the effect that 'this correspondence cannot be allowed to go out—it may be kept and handed over to the Prisoner when he is discharged': Home Office (Prison Commission) Papers.

Whether or not the letter would do good to Douglas's 'narrow nature and hectic brain', Wilde felt that it had done 'great good' to himself. 'I need not remind you that mere expression is to an artist the supreme and only mode of life,' he told Ross. 'It is by utterance that we live. . . . For nearly two years I had within me a growing burden of bitterness, much of which I have now got rid of. On the other side of the prison-wall there are some poor black soot-besmirched trees that are just breaking out into buds of an almost shrill green. I know quite well what they are going through. They are finding expression.'[1]

5

While the prisoner was working on *De Profundis*, another friend made an attempt to secure the remission of the last few months of his sentence. This was Frank Harris, who again visited the office of the Prison Commissioners and sought an interview with the Chairman. 'Oscar Wilde is just about to face life again', he told Ruggles-Brise: 'he is more than half reconciled to his wife; he has begun a book, is shouldering the burden. A little encouragement now and I believe he will do better things than he has ever done.' After more arguments to this effect, Harris concluded by asking Ruggles-Brise to apply his mind to discovering how the Home Secretary might be induced to cancel the remainder of the sentence.

Ruggles-Brise replied that it rested with Harris to put forward some reason for his proposed action, which could be avowed and defended. 'We live under parliamentary rule', he went on. 'Suppose the question were asked in the House—and I think it very likely in the present state of public opinion that the question would be asked—what should we answer? It would not be an avowable reason that we hoped Wilde would write new plays and books, would it? That reason ought to be sufficient, I grant you. But, as you see yourself, it would not be so regarded.'

'You are right, I suppose,' Harris had to admit. 'But if I got you a petition from men of letters, asking you to release Wilde for his health's sake, would that do?'

According to Harris, Ruggles-Brise jumped at the sugges-

[1] Clark MSS; *De Profundis* (1908 ed.), 18–19; H–D, 514.

tion. 'Certainly,' he exclaimed, 'if some men of letters, men of position, wrote asking that Wilde's sentence should be diminished by three or four months on account of his health, I think it would have the best effect.'

Harris said he would see Meredith and others at once and he did not anticipate any difficulty. 'You will find it harder than you think,' Ruggles-Brise remarked. 'But if you get one or two great names, the rest may follow.'[1]

Harris went back to his office in the *Saturday Review* and drafted a brief petition on these lines: 'In view of the fact that the punishment of two years' imprisonment with hard labour has been condemned by a Royal Commission as too severe, and inasmuch as Mr. Wilde has been distinguished by his work in letters and is now, we hear, suffering in health, we, your petitioners, pray etc.' His idea was to get Meredith's signature first and then distribute copies of the petition to other likely signatories.

To Harris's astonishment Meredith refused point-blank. He even refused to see Harris to discuss the matter. Long afterwards, when they did meet, Meredith said he had 'rather a low opinion of Wilde's capacities, instructive, deep-rooted contempt, too, for the showman in him, and an absolute abhorrence of his vice'. He added: 'That vile, sensual self-indulgence puts back the hands of the clock and should not be forgiven.'

With the others whom he approached Harris had a similar experience to that of More Adey and Stuart Merrill with their petitions, and eventually his went the same way as theirs. The excuses varied. One man said his name was not good enough for the purpose. Another said how sorry he was but 'public opinion was against Wilde'. Others were afraid to sign. 'Of course Wilde ought to get out,' said Professor Churton Collins, 'the sentence was a savage one and showed bitter prejudice. But I have children, and my own way to make in the world, and if I did this I should be tarred with the Wilde brush. I cannot afford to do it. . . . I cannot think I am called upon to bell the British cat in his defence: it has many claws and all sharp.' In the end Harris only secured one signature, and that was entirely

[1] Harris. II, 345 *et seq*. I have accepted this account as substantially correct, since it was later corroborated by Lady Ruggles-Brise: see Leslie, *Sir Evelyn Ruggles-Brise*, 135.

voluntary and unsolicited. It came from Professor R. Y. Tyrell, Regius Professor of Greek at Trinity College, Dublin, who remembered Wilde in college and through Harris sent him a friendly message in prison. 'Confusion take all their English Puritanism', he said as he wrote his name underneath the petition.[1]

Some time later, at the beginning of April, Harris paid his second visit to Reading. Wilde, whom he found vastly improved since their meeting nearly a year previously, greeted him with a cheerful jest. 'It's you, Frank,' he cried, pretending to be surprised. 'Always original! You come back to prison of your own free will!' This was more like the old Wilde. He declared that the Governor, Major Nelson, had been as kind as possible to him and that he had not had a punishment for months. 'Oh, Frank, the joy of reading what you like and writing as you please,' he exclaimed, 'the delight of living again!' As the books, which he had received from various friends were to remain prison property, he asked for Harris's help in getting together a small library of about a score of authors, which he could have when he came out of prison. Harris readily promised to get whatever books he wanted. He also told Wilde of a driving tour which he had made through France a couple of years previously, which was 'full of delightful episodes', and he proposed that as soon as Wilde was released, they should make a similar tour together. According to Harris, 'he jumped at the idea, said nothing would please him better, he would feel safe with me and so forth'. Harris said he would engage an American mail phaeton, 'so that a pair of horses would find the load, even with luggage, ridiculously light'.

According to Wilde, Harris, who had come of his own accord, had made two applications to see him, giving 'financial business' as the reason for this visit. 'When I saw him', Wilde wrote a few days later, 'he was most cordial and friendly, and told me that he had made a very large sum of money—some £23,000 in South Africa—and that he had come to place his cheque book at my disposal. I was greatly touched, I admit, at his spon-

[1] Robert Yelverton Tyrell (1844–1914) successively occupied the chairs of Latin, Greek and Ancient History at Dublin University. He also founded and edited the college magazine, *Kottabos*, to which Wilde contributed poems between 1876 and 1879. Tyrell later included several of these in the anthology, *Echoes of Kottabos*, which was published in 1906.

taneous and unsolicited kindness, and told him that, if I were set free from money anxieties, I thought I could produce some good art. He said he had come for the purpose of doing so, and would send me a cheque for £500 before my release. I admit that in my unnerved state, I was very deeply moved at his generous present, and made no attempt to conceal my feelings which were indeed beyond my control.'

Some days afterwards Wilde heard through More Adey that Harris had sent him a message that he was 'very sorry' but he found he could not let Wilde have the promised cheque after all. Wilde was naturally upset, especially as he learned at the same time that several similar promises, on which he had been relying, had fallen through. 'Of course nothing would induce me to go on this driving tour with him after that,' he told Adey in evident pique. 'I hardly suppose he expects it. Would you kindly write to him that you gave me his message and that I was a good deal distressed, as I had unfortunately received similar messages from everyone else who had been kind enough to promise me money, and that I found myself in such a painful and parlous state as regards my finances that I could not think of any pleasant pleasure excursion such as he had promised till I had in some way settled my affairs and seen a possible future? This will end the driving tour, and there is nothing in the message that could hurt his feelings, so pray give it in my own words. In fact Frank Harris has no feelings. It is the secret of his success. Just as the fact that he thinks that other people have none either is the secret of the failure that lies in wait for him somewhere on the way of Life.'[1]

The history of the monies promised and supplied to Wilde at this time is complex but not without interest. Alfred Douglas's elder brother, Lord Douglas of Hawick, who had gone surety for Wilde along with the Rev Stewart Headlam when he was released on bail before the last trial, had like

[1] Wilde to Adey, May 12, 1897: Clark MSS; H–D, 538. This was a brilliant summing up of Harris's character. The incident caused a temporary coolness between them, and Harris refused to accompany More Adey to meet Wilde on the day of his release. But he soon relented and sent Wilde clothes and a cheque immediately after his arrival in Dieppe. 'You have been a real good friend to me, and I shall never forget your kindness,' Wilde wrote from Dieppe. 'To remember such a debt as mine to you, a debt of kind fellowship, is a pleasure. About our tour—later on let us think about it.' The tour never took place, but Wilde later stayed with Harris in the south of France and dedicated *An Ideal Husband* to him as 'a slight tribute to his power and distinction as an artist, his chivalry and nobility as a friend', when the play was published in book form in 1899.

Harris promised a substantial sum. Since, along with his brother Alfred, he had assured Wilde at the time of the original prosecution of his father, Lord Queensberry, by Wilde, for criminal libel, that the family would be responsible for the costs, he promised to set aside for Wilde's use £700, which was approximately the amount of the costs and incidentally the sum for which, on Queensberry's petition, Wilde had been made bankrupt. But, when he was applied to by Adey to redeem his promise, the utmost Lord Douglas could do was to offer to pay £75, being half of the solicitors' costs in the bankruptcy proceedings.[1] Furthermore, when Wilde had been out on bail, another friend, Miss Adela Schuster ('the Lady of Wimbledon') had given him £1,000 for his personal use. As he was staying in Ernest Leverson's house at the time, he handed this sum to Leverson, who agreed to hold the money as trustee[2]. But Leverson had already advanced £500 towards the cost of Wilde's defence in the two trials in which Wilde was prosecuted. Leverson now reimbursed himself to the amount of £250 and proposed to do likewise with the balance. Later on, when he saw Wilde at Reading with Ross, he told him that 'money was tight in the city' and for the moment he could not let him have what was owing to him. 'As if I cared whether money was tight in the city, or knew what it meant', commented Wilde. 'I suppose it means that he was speculating with trust money. That is a dangerous amusement. . . .[3] As for Leverson's action in reimbursing himself of his original loan, he has already had 50 per cent, the only one of my creditors who has had anything. For him to swoop down illegally and collar the balance is not to be thought of.' Besides all this, an anonymous stranger had sent Adey £150 for Wilde's use, most of which, much to Wilde's annoyance, had been used by More Adey in the legal costs incurred in the unfortunate negotiations over Wilde's contingent interest in his wife's marriage settlement. Wilde found that, in addition to the costs of Mr Arthur D. Hansell, of the firm of Stokes and Hansell, solicitors, whom it was found necessary to instruct on his behalf, he also had to pay those of

[1] In 1906, when Wilde's bankruptcy was annulled, the Queensberry family received the whole of the amount with 4 per cent interest.

[2] According to a letter in my possession from Reginald Turner, who originally acted as co-trustee, the money was sent anonymously through the post, and at first Wilde thought it came from Ellen Terry, the actress.

[3] Here Wilde is unjust to Leverson, who had in fact discharged his trusteeship most honourably. For details, see Leverson's letter, cited in H–D, 551–2.

Adey's solicitor, Holman. 'I need not say', he wrote to Adey, 'that had you told me, as you should have, that you had £150 for me and for my use, I should have absolutely prohibited you from squandering it away into a useless, annoying, and meaningless litigation.' In fact, all that Adey had left to hand over when he came out of Reading was £37, though he had told Wilde he need be in no apprehension at all of being in want of money. 'It is grotesque', wrote Wilde to Ross. 'He might just as well remind me that I am entitled to a gratuity of 10/- from the Prison.'[1]

It will be remembered that, although Wilde had asked his friends not to oppose his wife's desire to purchase the whole of his life interest in the marriage settlement, they had offered the Official Receiver £50 for a half-share, being anxious that he should not give up his legal rights over his children, which withdrawal of this offer and acceptance of his wife's offer of an amount of £200 during her lifetime, to be increased by one-third of her interest after her death, would have involved. After a lengthy delay, due to the necessity of consulting Wilde's creditors, the Official Receiver announced that he was going to accept the £50 offer. Whereupon Mr Hargrove, Mrs Wilde's solicitor, wrote to Wilde to say that, if this was not withdrawn, her offer, which by this time had been reduced to £150 without any further increase, would likewise be withdrawn. At this point Wilde, to whom his wife's proposal appeared 'a cruel and heartless one, and as inconsiderate of the children's interest as well as of my existence', told Adey that he felt he had better trust himself entirely to his judgment, and that he was now of opinion that the course he had followed was a wise one. 'What Hargrove's next move will be I do not know', he went on. 'If my wife leaves me absolutely without a penny, I can only trust that for a year at any rate I will be looked after and I may be able to write again.'

It is unnecessary to follow the details of the subsequent negotiations between the various solicitors and the Official Receiver. Mr Hargrove's first move was to advise his client that an originating summons under the Protection of Infants Act should be served on her husband with a view to obtaining the legal custody and guardianship of the two children. In the second place, Hargrove advised Constance Wilde to file a peti-

[1] Wilde to Adey, May 15, to Ross, May 17, 1897: Clark MSS; H–D, 549, 559.

tion for divorce so as to ensure provision for the children after her death. Thirdly, he advised his client not to make any move to purchase the other half of the life interest, but to withdraw altogether from the contest, thus leaving the field open to Wilde's friends to purchase the whole of the contingent interest. The object of this last manœuvre soon became apparent, when the Official Receiver had accepted a bid from More Adey of £75 for the whole life interest. Afterwards Wilde reminded Adey of what had happened: 'I asked you how it was that Mr. Hargrove had not bid for the life interest, but allowed it to go for such a purely nominal sum as £75. You said that Mr. Holman had "bluffed" Mr. Hargrove by saying that there was unlimited money at my disposal. You said it yourself. I remarked that I did not think it probable that Mr. Hargrove was "bluffed" by Mr. Holman or anyone else, and that I thought his conduct very curious. I suppose you know why Mr. Hargrove did not bid against me? I presume you know that? It was because he had in his pocket the opinion of Inderwick, the Q.C., to the effect that on my being divorced my settlement, and consequently my prospective interest in it, was not worth seventy-five brass pennies. The value of my life interest depended on my wife's good will.'[1] In these circumstances all that Wilde's friends could do, in the hopes that the divorce proceedings would be dropped, was to offer no opposition to the summons for custody of the children and to re-open negotiations with Hargrove with a view to a new settlement on the lines that the amount to be settled on the children should be proportionate the allowance Constance might be persuaded to make her husband during his life.

The originating summons was duly issued and the relevant application was heard before Mr Justice Kekewich in the Chancery Division of the High Court, sitting in chambers, on February 12, 1897. In the result an order was made appointing Mrs Constance Wilde, now known as Mrs Constance Holland, and her cousin Mr Adrian Hope, guardians of the children, and directing that the children should remain in her custody. It was made clear at the same time that their father would be restrained from attempting to remove the children from their mother's custody or 'interfering with the same in any manner'. However the father was given liberty to apply to the Court, if

[1] Wilde to Adey, May 15, 1897: Clark MSS; H–D, 549.

he learned that they were not being properly maintained or educated.

To Wilde it was an appalling blow. 'My two children are taken from me by legal procedure', he wrote shortly afterwards in *De Profundis*. 'That is, and always will remain to me a source of infinite distress, of infinite pain, of grief without end or limit. That the law should decide and take upon itself to decide that I am one unfit to be with my own children is something quite horrible to me. The disgrace of prison is as nothing compared with it. I envy the other men who tread the yard along with me. I am sure that their children wait for them, look for their coming, will be sweet to them.'[1] About the same time he wrote to More Adey:

> As regards my children. I sincerely hope that I may be recognised by the Court as having some little, I won't say right, but claim to be allowed to see Cyril from time to time: it would be to me a sorrow beyond words if I were not. I do hope the Court will see in me something more than a man with a tragic vice in his life. There is so much more in me, and I always was a good father to both my children. I loved them dearly and was dearly loved by them and Cyril was my friend. And it would be better for them not to be forced to think of me as an outcast, but to know me as a man who has suffered. Pray let everything be done on my behalf that is possible. A little recognition by the Court would help me so much. And it is a terrible responsibility for the Law to say to a father that he is unfit to see his own children—the consciousness of it often makes me unhappy all day long.[2]

Wilde's only consolation was that Adrian Hope, whom his wife had chosen to help her as the children's guardian, was 'a man of high birth and culture and character'. With him, Wilde felt, Cyril and Vyvyan would have 'a good chance of a beautiful future'.[3] A few days after his release from prison his wife was to send him photographs of them, 'such lovely little fellows in Eton collars'. But she made no promise to allow him to see them. 'She says *she* will see me, twice a year,' he told Robert Ross, 'but I want my boys.'[4] In fact no variation of the Court order was made, and he never saw the boys again.[5]

[1] *De Profundis*, 75.
[2] Wilde to Ross, May 17, 1897: Clark MSS.
[3] *De Profundis*, 128.
[4] *After Berneval*, 14.
[5] Their childhood and upbringing have been most feelingly and vividly described by the younger son, Vyvyan Holland, in his autobiography, *Son of Oscar Wilde* (1954).

CHAPTER V

Last Months in Reading

1

As the date for Wilde's release drew nearer, the subject began to attract attention in the Press, much to the apprehension of the prisoner and his friends, when they heard about it. Among the latter were Max Beerbohm[1] and Reginald Turner.[2] 'Is there any way of getting Oscar out of the country without benefit of journalism?' wrote Beerbohm to Robert Ross. 'There are sure to be a dozen reporters at the prison gate and they will follow him to the English shore, as of course you know, and they will ask him if he has anything to say to them and so on and so on. I suggested to Reggie a decoy-brougham which should be driven out of the prison-yard with blinds drawn down on each side. This the journalists would follow—or else they would go away. Then Oscar could be brought out in another brougham and driven to some obscure way-side station *en route* for the shore. This sounds rather absurd, I suppose—and would have commended itself to the Boy Stevenson,[3]—but surely it is rather important to let Oscar be spared a gang of gaping and offensive pressmen. Isn't there some way of arranging the matter? Personally I think the brougham rather a feasible idea.'[4]

Although Wilde had begun to serve his sentence on May 25, 1895, he was due to be released on May 19, 1897, since the rule is that a sentence runs from the date on which the Sessions or Assizes commence. It seemed to Ross and Wilde's other friends

[1] Sir Max Beerbohm (1872–1956), critic and caricaturist.

[2] Reginald Turner (1869–1938) was the illegitimate son of a well-known newspaper proprietor and wrote several novels. He was with Wilde at the time of his arrest in the Cadogan Hotel in London on April 5, 1895, and he helped Ross to nurse Wilde during his final illness in Paris in November, 1900. He spent his latter years in Florence, where he became friendly with the bookseller G. Orioli, whom he eventually made his heir. Wilde's letters to him, of which I have made use, are now in the collection of Mr and Mrs Donald Hyde of Somerville, New Jersey.

[3] R. L. Stevenson.

[4] Margery Ross. *Robert Ross: Friend of Friends*, 48.

that in these circumstances there was a good case for the Home Secretary remitting the last few weeks of the sentence, particularly since Wilde had spent nearly a month in Holloway Prison after his arrest and this period was not reckoned as part of his sentence. Ross accordingly wrote to Sir Edward Clarke, who had acted as Wilde's leading counsel in the three trials, and as a former Conservative Solicitor-General was well acquainted with Sir Mathew Ridley. Ross begged him to use his influence with the Home Secretary. The answer was disappointing. Clarke spoke to Ridley and was informed that the Home Secretary had no power to interfere with any sentence of the Court, although he could of course advise the Queen to remit a part of the sentence. Clarke told Ross he did not think there would be any use in applying, except on medical grounds, for such a remission in this case. 'I am glad Mr Wilde should still have faithful friends like yourself to stand by him,' Clarke went on, 'but it is impossible for me to forget that before I undertook the most painful case which I have ever been engaged in, he gave me his word of honour as a gentleman that there was no foundation whatever for the charges which were afterwards so completely proved.'[1]

About the same time More Adey wrote in similar terms to Mr Ernest Flower, a Conservative M.P., well known for his philanthropic work.[2] As an additional reason for urging the Home Secretary to release Wilde before May 19, Adey gave 'the persecution of certain disorderly persons', since it was quite possible that Lord Queensberry and his prize-fighting companions would pursue the unfortunate Wilde as they had done when he was released on bail during the trials. Adey undertook that he and other responsible friends, such as Ernest Leverson, Arthur Humphreys and the Rev Stewart Headlam, would see that Wilde left the country 'in strict privacy' on the day of his release. On March 25, Adey's letter was forwarded by Flower to the Home Secretary, who sent it into the Prison Commission for comment. Ruggles-Brise replied on April 2: 'The Commissioners do not anticipate any difficulty in carrying out the discharge of this prisoner without publicity at Reading, but if the Secretary of State so desires he can be transferred

[1] Ross, *op. cit.*, 46; cf. also Hyde, *Trials of Oscar Wilde*, 38.

[2] Ernest Flower (1865–1926) was M.P. for Bradford West from 1895 to 1906. He was knighted in 1903.

to London the day before he becomes due for release. He can be handed over either at Reading or in London to the care of any friends who may arrange to receive him.' While determined that there could be no remission, the Home Secretary instructed the Prison Commissioners to see Adey 'and make such arrangements as may be mutually agreed upon as best in the circumstances of the case'.

A few days later Adey called at the offices of the Prison Commission by request to discuss the details of how and when the prisoner could best be met by his friends on the morning of his release. He was told that it was possible that Wilde would be transferred to a London prison on the previous day. This news Adey duly passed on to Wilde in his next letter. As might be expected, it had a very disturbing effect on the prisoner, who remembered with feelings of horror the terrible circumstances of his journey from Wandsworth to Reading. He asked the Governor for a petition form, and, when it was given to him, he drafted a final plea for the remission of his sentence, praying that he should be discharged from Reading four days before the legal expiry date.[1]

PETITION

OSCAR WILDE

H.M. Prison,
Reading.
22nd April, 1897.

THE PETITION OF THE ABOVE NAMED PRISONER HUMBLY SHEWETH

that the petitioner was sentenced to two years imprisonment on the 20th May 1895.[2] and that his term of imprisonment will expire on the 19th of next May, four weeks from the date of this petition;

that the Petitioner is extremely anxious to avoid the notoriety and annoyance of newspaper interviews and descriptions on the occasion of his release, the date of which is of course well known. Many English, French and American papers have already announced their intention of attending the ceremony of his release for the purpose of seeking and publishing interviews with him on the question of his treatment in prison, the real circumstances that led to his original trial and the like. The Petitioner is anxious to avoid any intrusion of the kind threatened, as he considers that such interviews at such a moment would be from every point of view unseemly. He desires to go abroad quietly without attracting public attention, and his petition is that he may be released on the Saturday preceding

[1] Home Office Papers; H–D, 528.
[2] In fact, Wilde was sentenced on May 25, 1895: see above, p. 1.

the 19th May—Saturday the 15th in fact—so that he may go abroad unobserved and incognito.

The Petitioner would beg to be allowed to mention that he was for three weeks confined in Holloway Prison before his first trial: that he was then released on bail and surrendered to his bail to stand his trial a second time, the second trial resulting in his conviction. The Petitioner will accordingly have had more than two years detention should he be released on the 15th May as his prayer is.

The Petitioner, however, is most anxious that he should not under any circumstances be transferred to another prison from the one in which he is at present confined. The ordeal he underwent in being brought in convict dress and handcuffed, by a midday train from Clapham Junction to Reading was so utterly distressing, from the mental no less than the emotional point of view, that he feels quite unable to undergo any similar exhibition to public gaze, and he feels it his duty to say that he was assured by the former Governor of Reading prison that he would not under any circumstances be again submitted to so terrible an experience.

Should the Petitioner's request to be released on the 15th May be granted, Mr Frank Harris, the Editor of the *Saturday Review*, who has kindly invited the petitioner to go on a driving tour in the Pyrenees with him would at once proceed abroad with him crossing the Channel either in a yacht, or by night, so as to avoid observation and annoyance.

And your Petitioner will ever pray etc.

OSCAR WILDE

At the same time, the Governor in a letter to Ruggles-Brise confirmed that representatives of both the British and foreign Press were likely to attend outside the prison gates on the day of Wilde's discharge in the hope of securing the first interview. In fact, a reporter from one daily newspaper had already been on the scene. Major Nelson recommended that, as some of the prisoner's friends were going to meet him with a cab, all possible annoyance might be avoided if the discharge took place an hour earlier than the usual time, and he suggested to Adey that, if he drove off with Wilde in a closed carriage, he should avoid Reading railway station, where Wilde would be sure to be recognised, and go instead to the small nearby station of Twyford.

Meanwhile Wilde was chafing at the delay in answering his petition, which added to the worries he already had about his finances and the projected divorce proceedings. On May 1, he wrote to Adey:

> The thing I want is to know everything quite clearly as it really is. That is what one wants to know in prison. What kills one is uncertainty, with its accompanying anxiety and distress.
>
> At the present moment, for instance, I am in great trouble because I cannot get an answer from the Home Secretary with regard to the date of my release. I sent a petition to him last Thursday week to ask to be released on Saturday the 15th on the ground of the anxiety of the newspapers to revive public interest in my ruin and its cause by interviewing me and the like, and also for other reasons. The *Morning* newspaper has already been here making inquiries and preparations, and of course others will be in readiness. No notice has been taken of the petition, and I suppose I shall be kept in this horrible suspense till the evening of the 18th when I shall no doubt be informed that the petition has been refused. Or perhaps the news will be broken to me on the morning of the 19th before my release. It is a hideous method of dealing with people who are in distress or misery, but I believe it is entirely in accordance with the ordinary rules of the Office.
>
> To me I confess the prospect of being pursued by interviewers is horrible, especially considering the terrible change in my appearance. I know, of course, that I have become brutalised and horrible in appearance: punishment produces the effect. Nor have I, I need hardly say, any vanity left of any kind. But the consciousness of being degraded of aspect and grotesque is dreadful, and I am anxious to avoid the coarse pen and pencil of the English journalist always so keen to inflict pain or excite ridicule by means of offensive personalities.
>
> I have not much hope that the Home Secretary will accede to my request for privacy in my leaving prison, as regards the day and moment. They brought me down here handcuffed and in convict dress, by a midday train, mobbed and hooted at every station, and I don't expect them to care very much about my feelings on release or to sympathise with my desire for privacy. Still I wish they would convey to me even the usual verbal 'No' that is the stereotyped formula of answer to all requests. I can make no plans till I know one way or the other.[1]

On receiving this letter More Adey prepared to make a final appeal to the Home Secretary. First of all, he wrote to Major Nelson, acquainting him with his intention, mentioning the inquisitive *Morning* reporter and asking if he might quote his views on the possibility of Wilde being subjected to embarrassing activities on the part of the Press. His letter somewhat alarmed the Governor, who had evidently told Wilde about the reporter and seemed to have felt that he had exceeded his authority in doing so.

At all events he wrote to Adey privately by return, asking him to treat this information as confidential. 'It would be quite wrong and open to censure for me', he continued, 'to give an opinion on the probabilities of journalistic annoyance upon the day of release with the object of strengthening your petition for an earlier discharge. I feel sure you will accept this refusal in the spirit that is meant, as you must by this time have a good knowledge of the red tape-ism (*sic*) which is if possible even more rampant in the prison service than any other public department. That being the case I must ask you on no account to mention my views on this subject either to the Home Secretary or the Commissioners.'[1]

While the Governor was writing this letter, the official decision on the subject of Wilde's petition was actually in the post to Reading. The prisoner was immediately informed of it, so that he was able to add a postscript to a letter to Adey which he had just finished: 'The answer has just come from the Home Secretary. It is the customary refusal.' By this time Adey had heard definitely that Queensberry had threatened to be present and create a disturbance, as happened when Wilde was released on bail, and he again appealed to Ernest Flower, M.P. 'Wilde must stop somewhere on his way abroad from prison in order to shave,' he told Flower, 'as razors are not permitted inside the prison. This I have particularly inquired of the Governor. Wilde cannot grow a beard properly so called. He might almost as well wear a broad arrow on his overcoat as travel with the sort of beard he wears now . . . If the Home Secretary will order his release on either of the two previous days, there is no difficulty at all about effecting it privately. Otherwise I do not see how it is to be done without a strong chance of a cruel and disgraceful exhibition.' Adey repeated his request in writing to the Home Secretary 'for the sake of humanity and public order', on May 12. 'The Secretary of the Prison Commission sent for me according to your directions and discussed the arrangements attending it,' he wrote, 'and I am endeavouring to secure strict privacy. But this task be-

[1] Major Nelson to Adey, May 5, 1897: Clark MSS.

comes more and more difficult as the time approaches. The Press shows no diminution of interest in Oscar Wilde, and I continue to receive every few days from a Press-cutting agency paragraphs from journals of all kinds referring to his release.' After mentioning Lord Queensberry's admitted intentions, Adey stated that he would have a carriage ready and that Wilde would leave for the Continent on the same day. Mr Ernest Flower, M.P., had guaranteed that these plans would be carried out. 'I have very little hope that this can be accomplished without public scandal on May 19th,' Adey concluded, 'and I am reluctant, without previously laying the case before you, to expose myself and anyone else who is kind enough to assist me to the curiosity of the Press and the demonstrations of the Marquess of Queensberry.'

For the satisfactory outcome of these representations Wilde had to thank Ruggles-Brise and the other Prison Commissioners, to whom Adey's letter and Flower's supporting note were referred for their observations. While the Commissioners saw no reason for discharging the prisoner before the day he became due for release, they proposed to transfer him to Pentonville on the evening of May 18 in plain clothes and without handcuffs. 'He can then be discharged to the care of his friends from Pentonville at any hour which may suit them', wrote Ruggles-Brise to the Home Secretary. Wilde breathed a sigh of relief when the Governor gave him this piece of news. Although he was to be sent to London, 'the one place I wished to avoid', so he told Adey, at the same time he had to admit that 'the transference is to be conducted with humanity'.[1]

2

About two months before Wilde was due to be released, a new warder was appointed to the prison. He was a young man of thirty named Tom Martin, a native of Belfast, who had spent some years in the army before transferring to the prison service. On his arrival at Reading he was put in charge of Gallery C, in which Wilde was confined, so that Wilde saw him constantly. They immediately became friends, for Martin was unlike many other warders in the service. 'I was struck by the singular kindness and humanity of the way in which he

[1] Wilde to Adey, May 17, 1897: Clark MSS; H–D, 557.

spoke to me and to the other prisoners', Wilde wrote of him after his release. 'Kind words are much in prison, and a pleasant "Good-morning" or "Good-evening" will make one as happy as one can be in prison. He was always gentle and considerate.' More than that, Martin consistently broke the prison rules to gave Wilde and the other prisoners in Gallery C some unexpected relaxations. Every day, for instance, he used to smuggle a copy of the *Daily Chronicle* into the prison for Wilde, an action which was of course a most serious breach of the regulations. He would also bring him and the others little delicacies of food. It was his conduct, as will be seen, which ultimately landed him in trouble and led to his dismissal.

Wilde was in the habit of writing him notes on the backs of envelopes and other odd scraps of paper, and pushing them under the cell door. Several of these have survived.[1] This is the first.

> My dear Friend,
>
> What have I to write about except that if you had been an officer in Reading Prison a year ago my life would have been much happier? Everyone tells me I am looking better and happier.
>
> That is because I have a good friend who gives me the *Chronicle* and *promises* me ginger biscuits!
>
> O.W.

At the foot of this note Warder Martin wrote in pencil: '*Your ungrateful I done more than promise.*'

In another note, Wilde asked for the address of a fellow-prisoner, who was due for release and to whom he wished to send a small sum of money to help him to get started again in life. 'Of course I would not for worlds get such a friend as you are into *any danger*. I quite understand your feelings.' Yet the kindly Warder Martin ran great risks to procure for Wilde the reading matter he wanted. On one occasion, when Wilde was reading the *Daily Chronicle* in his cell, he suddenly heard footsteps in the gallery outside and the key turned in the lock. He had no time to do more than fold up the paper and put it with his books on the trestle table where he worked. Then the Governor walked in. Wilde immediately stood to attention in front of the table and remained in this position throughout the interview, which happened to be unusually long that day. Fortunately Major Nelson did not see the incriminating newspaper,

[1] Mason, 50–1. The originals are in the Clark Library, University of California, Los Angeles. See below, Appendix E, p. 209.

or, if he did, he pretended not to notice it. But Wilde was not content with the *Daily Chronicle*; he persuaded the warder to get him the *Saturday Review* and other weekly periodicals, which presented much greater difficulties than the newspaper. 'To give him the *Chronicle* to read was easy enough, as I had it delivered to me at the prison,' Warder Martin afterwards told Sherard, 'but what gave me a lot of trouble was getting him the weeklies that he wanted, because I could not have those sent to the prison, as that would have attracted attention. Prison warders don't read *Spectator*s and *Saturday Review*s. I had to go out into the town to fetch them, and was often anxious lest my absence might be noticed, and then there was always the risk of my being questioned as to what I had been to fetch and what it was for.'[1]

Another kindhearted act of Martin, which is worthwhile describing in detail, had somewhat painful consequences for the warder, although all was well in the end. It happened on a certain bleak, raw morning in March, when Martin entered Cell C.3.3. and, to his surprise found its occupant still in bed. 'I have had a bad night,' Wilde explained. 'Pains in my inside, which I think must be cramp, and my head seems splitting.' The warder asked whether he ought not to report sick. 'No, not for anything,' said Wilde. 'I shall be better, perhaps, as the day advances. Come back in a few minutes, when I will be up.' Martin returned to the cell a little later, and found the prisoner was up, but looking so ill that he again advised him to see the doctor. Wilde refused, saying he would be all right when he had had something warm to drink.

The warder knew that in the ordinary course of events Wilde would have nothing for at least another hour, so he resolved to find something to give him in the meanwhile himself. He hurried off, and warmed up some beef tea, poured it into a bottle, placed the bottle inside his jacket, and returned towards Wilde's cell. While he was ascending the staircase to Galley C, the bottle slipped down between his shirt and skin. It was very hot. Martin knew that there was an unoccupied cell in the next gallery, and he decided to go there and withdraw the bottle from its painful position. But at that moment a voice called out to him from the central hall below. Martin looked down and saw the Chief Warder. He beckoned him towards him.

[1] Sherard. *The Real Oscar Wilde*, 258–60.

There was a discrepancy in the previous night's muster report, and the Chief Warder wished to speak to him about it. Martin went back and tried to elucidate the mystery of two prisoners being in the prison, who apparently had no claim on its hospitality. Meanwhile the hot bottle burned into his skin like molten lead. 'I could have cried out in my agony, but dared not', wrote Martin afterwards in his account of the incident. 'The cold, damp, beads of perspiration gathered on my brow; I writhed and twisted in all manner of ways to ease myself of the dreadful thing, but in vain. I could not shift that infernal bottle—try as I might. . . . And the strange thing about it was the longer it lay the hotter it became. The Chief eyed me curiously. I believe he thought I had been drinking. I know I was incoherent enough for anything. At last he walked off, and left me, for which I was truly thankful.'

Martin thereupon bounded up the iron stairs to Wilde's cell, where he pulled out the bottle and, 'amid gasps and imprecations' related his awful experience. Wilde smiled when he heard the story and then, to Martin's surprised indignation burst out laughing. The warder, who thought it was a poor reward for all he had undergone to be laughed at, left the cell angrily, slamming the door after him with a bang.

A little later when Martin brought Wilde his breakfast he looked a picture of contrition. He said he would not touch it unless the warder promised to forgive him. 'Not even the cocoa,' the prisoner replied, looking at it longingly. 'Well, rather than starve you, I'll forgive you.' 'And supposing I laugh again,' said Wilde, with a smile. 'Then I shan't forgive you again.' Next day Martin received a charming written apology, full of subtle humour and characteristic epigrams. 'Yesterday morning I laughed, which showed my perversity, for I felt really sorry for you,' Wilde told Martin, after he had read the apology. 'I didn't mean to laugh: I had vowed never to laugh again. Then I thought it fitting when I had broken one vow to break the other also. I had made two, and I broke both, but now I have made them again. I never intend to laugh, nor do I intend ever again to write anything calculated to produce laughter in others. I am no longer the Sirius of Comedy. I have sworn solemnly to dedicate my life to Tragedy. If I write any more books, it will be to form a library of lamentations. They will be written in a style begotten of sorrow, and in sentences composed in solitude, and punctuated by tears. They will be written exclusively for those who have suffered or are suffering. I understand them, and they will understand me. I shall be an enigma to the world of Pleasure, but a mouthpiece for the world of Pain.'[1]

After he came out of prison, Wilde described a characteristic act of kindness by Warder Martin to one of the other prisoners. This man had recently been convicted, and was suffering from violent diarrhoea in consequence of the food, as was usually the case. Since no prisoner was allowed under any circumstances to leave his cell after 5.30 p.m., he had to use his cell as a latrine. About two hours after locking up time, Martin was going the rounds with one of the senior warders for the purpose of collecting the oakum and tools of the prisoners. When they came to this man's cell the prisoner asked the senior warder if he might empty his slops on account of the horrible odour of the cell and the possibility of illness again during the night. 'The senior warder refused absolutely; it was against the rules. The man had to pass the night in this dreadful condition. Martin, however, rather than see this wretched man in such a loathsome predicament, said he would empty the man's slops himself, and did so. A warder emptying a prisoner's slops is, of course, against the rules, but Martin did this act of kindness to the man out of the simple humanity of his nature, and the man was naturally most grateful.'[2]

For his part Martin developed a tremendous admiration for Wilde, whom he used to call 'the Poet', and later on when Sherard was writing his biography, he was to contribute an interesting chapter of reminiscences, which is a remarkable composition for a prison warder. Amongst others he described the effect of the order issued by the Prison Commissioners, during the latter part of Wilde's time at Reading, that first offenders were to be kept apart from other prisoners. They were distinguished by two red stars, one of which was worn on the jacket and the other on the cap, the consequence of which they were known as 'star-class men'. The order was not retrospective and therefore did not apply to Wilde, who was obliged to stand with his face to the wall, when any of the

[1] Sherard. *Life*, 394–7. This account is taken from 'The Poet in Prison', the chapter which Martin contributed to Sherard's *Life of Oscar Wilde* (1906).

[2] Letter to the *Daily Chronicle*, May 28, 1897.

'star-class' were passing nearby. 'The framers of the order were, no doubt, actuated by the best of motives,' wrote Warder Martin in the chapter alluded to, 'but its too literal interpretation caused it to look rather ludicrous. I have seen the Poet having to stand with his face to the wall while a villainous-looking ruffian, who had been convicted of half killing his poor wife passed him. In fact nearly every day he was forced to assume this undignified position, which might have been obviated but for the crass stupidity of officialdom.'[1]

3

Wilde's scribbled messages to Warder Martin are among the most convincing proofs of his essential kindness of heart and humanity. The following example was written during the last week of his imprisonment.

> Please find out for me the name of A.2.11. Also the names of the children who are in for the rabbits, and the amount of the fine.
>
> Can I pay this and get them out? If so, I will get them out tomorrow. Please dear friend do this for me, I must get them out.
>
> Think what a thing for me it would be to be able to help these three little children. I would be delighted beyond words: if I can do this by paying the fine tell the children they are to be released tomorrow by a friend, and ask them to be happy and not to tell anyone.[2]

Wilde had noticed A.2.11 for the first time among the other prisoners at exercise about three months previously. He was a young man who seemed to him to be silly or half-witted. 'Every prison, of course, has its half-witted clients, who return again and again, and may be said to live in the prison', Wilde wrote after his release. 'But this young man struck me as being more than usually half-witted on account of his silly grin and idiotic laughter to himself and the peculiar restlessness of his eternally twitching hands. He was noticed by all the other prisoners on account of the strangeness of his conduct.' From time to time A.2.11 did not appear at exercise, which showed that he was being punished by being confined to his cell. Finally, Wilde discovered that he was under observation, and was being

[1] Sherard. *Life*, 390. For further reminiscences by Warder Martin, see below, Appendix E.
[2] Reproduced in facsimile in Harris, II, 576.

watched day and night by warders. 'When he did appear at exercise, he always seemed hysterical, and used to walk round crying or laughing. At chapel he had to sit right under the observation of two warders, who carefully watched him all the time. Sometimes he would bury his head in his hands, an offence against the chapel regulations, and his head would be immediately struck up by a warder so that he should keep his eyes permanently in the direction of the Communion table. Sometimes he would cry—not making any disturbance—but with tears streaming down his face and an hysterical sobbing in his throat. Sometimes he would grin idiot-like to himself and make faces. He was on more than one occasion sent out of chapel to his cell, and of course he was continually punished.' As the bench on which Wilde used to sit in chapel was directly behind the bench at the end of which this unfortunate young man was placed, he had full opportunity of observing him. 'I also saw him, of course, at exercise continually,' wrote Wilde, 'and I saw that he was becoming insane, and was being treated as if he was shamming.'

On the Saturday before his release Wilde was in his cell about one o'clock occupied in cleaning and polishing the tins he had been using for dinner. Suddenly he was startled by the most horrible and revolting shrieks, or rather howls, which broke the prison silence and made him think at first that some animal like a bull or a cow was being unskilfully slaughtered outside the prison walls. He soon realised, however, that the howls proceeded from the basement of the prison, and he knew that some wretched man was being flogged. 'I need not say how hideous or terrible it was for me,' Wilde observed, 'and I began to wonder who it was who was being punished in this revolting manner. Suddenly it dawned on me that they might be flogging this unfortunate lunatic.' They were. Wilde subsequently found out from another prisoner at exercise that the wretched creature had received twenty-four lashes in the cook-house, by order of the Visiting Justices on the report of the doctor.

On the next day, Wilde saw the poor fellow at exercise, his weak, ugly, wretched face bloated by tears and hysteria almost beyond recognition. 'It was my last Sunday in prison, a perfectly lovely day, the finest day we had had the whole year,' Wilde recalled later, 'and there in the beautiful sunlight, walked this poor creature—made once in the image of God—grinning like an ape, and making with his hands the most fantastic gestures, as though he was playing in the air on some invisible stringed instrument, or arranging and dealing counters in some curious game. All the while these hysterical tears, without which none of us ever saw him, were making soiled runnels on his white swollen face. The hideous and deliberate grace of his gestures made him like an antic. He was a living grotesque. The other prisoners all watched him, and not one of them smiled. Everybody knew what had happened to him, and that he was being driven insane—was insane already.'

From Warder Martin, in response to his note, Wilde learned that the man's name was Prince, that he was a soldier and that he had been sentenced to six months for some military offence by a court martial. 'This man is undoubtedly becoming insane', Wilde wrote in a letter of protest which he sent to the *Daily Chronicle* a few days after leaving Reading. 'The case is a special instance of the cruelty inseparable from a stupid system.' As for the medical officer, who passed the man as fit for punishment in these circumstances, Wilde was justly severe in his criticism. 'Prison doctors have no knowledge of mental disease of any kind', he wrote. 'They are as a class ignorant men. The pathology of the mind is unknown to them. When a man grows insane, they treat him as shamming. They have him punished again and again. Naturally the man becomes worse. When ordinary punishments are exhausted, the doctor reports the case to the justices. The result is flogging. Of course, the flogging is not done with a cat-of-nine tails. It is what is called birching . . . the result on the wretched half-witted man may be imagined. . . . This man A.2.11 will, I have no doubt, be able to tell his name, the nature of his offence, the day of the month, the date of the beginning and expiration of his sentence, and answer any ordinary simple question; but that his mind is diseased admits of no doubt. At present it is a horrible duel between himself and the doctor. The doctor is fighting for a theory. The man is fighting for his life. I am anxious that the man should win. But let the whole case be examined into by experts who understand brain-disease, and by people of humane feelings who have still some common sense and some pity. There is no reason that the sentimentalist should be asked to interfere. He always does harm.'[1]

On the subject of the half-witted Prince, it only remains to add that Wilde's protest does not seem to have had any effect on the authorities. The last that Wilde heard of him, some weeks after his own release, was that he had again been flogged.

As for the three children, about whom Wilde also wrote to Warder Martin, he was able to do more for them. They had been committed to prison for snaring rabbits. The bench of magistrates, which had convicted them, had given them the option of paying fines. They, of course, had no money of their own, and their parents were either unwilling or, more probably, unable to pay the fines for them. Wilde did so, and so secured their release. To the youngest of them Warder Martin also performed an act of humanity—the child was crying with hunger and the warder gave him some biscuits—and for this kindness he was dismissed.

Wilde saw them for the first time just after they had been convicted. They were standing in a row in the central hall in their prison dress, carrying their sheets under their arms before being sent to the cells allotted to them. Wilde happened to be passing along one of the galleries on his way to the reception room, where he was to have an interview with his solicitor. The description of these children and of their treatment, in the form of a letter, which he subsequently sent to the *Daily Chronicle*, is a vivid and moving example of his writing.

> They were quite small children, the youngest—the one to whom the warder gave the biscuits—being a tiny little chap, for whom they had evidently been unable to find clothes small enough to fit. I had, of course, seen many children in prison during the two years during which I was myself confined. Wandsworth Prison especially contained always a large number of children. But the little child I saw on the afternoon of Monday the 17th, at Reading, was tinier than any of them. I need not say how utterly distressed I was to see these children at Reading, for I knew the treatment in store for them. The cruelty that is practised by day and night on children in English prisons is incredible, except to those that have witnessed it and are aware of the brutality of the system.
>
> . . . . . .
>
> The present treatment of children is terrible, primarily from

[1] Letter to the *Daily Chronicle*, May 28, 1897.

people not understanding the peculiar psychology of a child's nature. A child can understand a punishment inflicted by an individual, such as a parent or guardian, and bear it with a certain amount of acquiescence. What it cannot understand is a punishment inflicted by society. It cannot realise what society is. With grown people it is, of course, the reverse. Those of us who are either in prison or have been sent there, can understand, and do understand, what that collective force called society means, and whatever we may think of its methods or claims, we can force ourselves to accept it. Punishment inflicted on us by an individual, on the other hand, is a thing that no grown person endures, or is expected to endure.

The child consequently, being taken away from its parents by people whom it has never seen and of whom it knows nothing, and finding itself in a lonely and unfamiliar cell, waited on by strange faces and ordered about and punished by the representatives of a system that it cannot understand, becomes an immediate prey to the first and most prominent emotion produced by modern prison life—the emotion of terror. The terror of a child in prison is quite limitless. I remember once in Reading, as I was going out to exercise, seeing in the dimly lit cell right opposite my own a small boy. Two warders—not unkindly men—were talking to him with some sternness apparently, or perhaps giving him some useful advice about his conduct. One was in the cell with him, the other was standing outside. The child's face was like a white wedge of sheer terror. There was in his eyes the terror of a hunted animal. The next morning I heard him at breakfast-time crying, and calling to be let out. His cry was for his parents. From time to time I could hear the deep voice of the warder on duty telling him to keep quiet. Yet he was not even convicted of whatever little offence he had been charged with. He was simply on remand. That I knew by his wearing his own clothes, which seemed neat enough. He was, however, wearing prison socks and shoes. This showed that he was a very poor boy whose own shoes, if he had any, were in a bad state. Justices and magistrates, an entirely ignorant class as a rule, often remand children for a week and then perhaps remit whatever sentence they are entitled to pass. They call this 'not sending a child to prison'. It is, of course, a stupid view on their part. To a little child, whether he is in prison on remand or after a conviction is not a subtlety of social position he can comprehend. To him the horrible thing is to be there at all. In the eyes of humanity it should be a horrible thing for him to be there at all.

This terror that seizes and dominates the child, as it seizes the grown man also, is of course intensified beyond power of expression by the solitary cellular system of our prisons. Every child is confined to its cell for twenty-three hours out of the twenty-four. This is the appalling thing. To shut up a child in a dimly lit cell, for twenty-three hours out of the twenty-four, is an example of the cruelty of stupidity. If an individual, parent or guardian, did this to a child, he would be severely punished. The Society for The Prevention of Cruelty to Children would take the matter up at once. There would be on all hands the utmost detestation of whomsoever had been guilty of such cruelty. A heavy sentence would undoubtedly follow conviction. But our own actual society does worse itself, and to the child to be so treated by a strange abstract force, of whose claims it has no cognisance is much worse than it would be to receive the same treatment from its father or mother, or some one it knew. The inhuman treatment of a child is always inhuman, by whomsoever it is inflicted. But inhuman treatment by society is to the child the more terrible because there is no appeal. A parent or guardian can be moved, and let out a child from the dark lonely room in which it is confined. But a warder cannot. Most warders are very fond of children. But the system prohibits them from rendering the child any assistance. Should they do so, as Warder Martin did, they are dismissed.

The second thing from which a child suffers in prison is hunger. The food that is given to it consists of a piece of usually badly-baked prison bread and a tin of water for breakfast at half-past seven. At twelve o'clock it gets dinner, composed of a tin of coarse Indian meal stirabout; and at half-past five it gets a piece of dry bread and a tin of water for its supper. This diet in the case of a strong grown man is always productive of illness of some kind, chiefly, of course, diarrhoea with its attendant weakness. In fact, in a big prison astringent medicines are served up regularly by the warders as a matter of course. In the case of a child, the child is, as a rule, incapable of eating the food at all. Anyone who knows anything about children knows how easily a child's digestion is upset by a fit of crying, or trouble and mental distress of any kind. A child who has been crying all day long, and perhaps half the night, in a lonely dimly lit cell, and is preyed upon by terror, simply cannot eat food of this coarse, horrible kind. In the case of the little child to whom Warder Martin gave the biscuits, the child was crying with hunger on Tuesday morning, and utterly unable to eat the bread and water served to it for its breakfast. Martin went out after the breakfasts had been served, and bought the few sweet biscuits for the child rather than see it starving. It was a beautiful action on his part, and was so recognised by the child, who, utterly unconscious of the regulation of the Prison Board told one of the senior warders how kind this junior warder had been to him. The result was, of course, a report and a dismissal.

. . . . .

As regards the children, a great deal has been talked and written lately about the contaminating influence of prison on young children. What is said is quite true. A child is utterly contaminated by prison life. But the contaminating influence is not that of the prisoners. It is that of the whole prison system—of the governor, the chaplain, the warders, the lonely cell, the isolation, the revolting food, the rules of the Prison Commissioners, the mode of discipline, as it is termed, of the life. Every care is taken to isolate a child from the sight even of all prisoners over sixteen years of age. Children sit behind a curtain in chapel, and are sent to take exercise in small sunless yards—sometimes a stone-yard, sometimes a yard at the back of the mills—rather than that they should see the elder prisoners at exercise.

. . . . .

I am not proposing that the children should not sit behind a curtain in chapel, or that they should take exercise in a corner of the common yard. I am merely pointing out that the bad influence on children is not, and could never be, that of the prisoners, but is, and will always remain, that of the prison system itself. There is not a single man in Reading Gaol that would not gladly have done the three children's punishment for them. When I saw them last it was on the Tuesday following their conviction. I was taking exercise at half-past eleven with about twelve other men, as the three children passed near us, in charge of a warder, from the damp, dreary stone-yard in which they had been at their exercise. I saw the greatest pity and sympathy in the eyes of my companions as they looked at them. Prisoners are, as a class, extremely kind and sympathetic to each other. Suffering and the community of suffering makes people kind, and day after day as I tramped the yard I used to feel with pleasure and comfort what Carlyle calls somewhere 'the silent rhythmic charm of human companionship'. In this, as in all other things, philanthropists and people of that kind are astray. It is not the prisoners who need reformation. It is the prisons.

Of course no child under fourteen years of age should be sent to prison at all. It is an absurdity, and, like many absurdities, of absolutely tragic results. If, however, they are to be sent to prison, during the daytime they should be in a workshop or schoolroom with a warder. At night they should sleep in a dormitory, with a night-warder to look after them. They should be allowed exercise for at least three hours a day. The dark, badly ventilated, ill-smelling prison cells are dreadful for a child, dreadful indeed for any one. One is always breathing bad air in prison. The food given to children should consist of tea and bread-and-butter and soup.

> Prison soup is very good and wholesome. A resolution of the House of Commons could settle the treatment of children in half an hour. . . . The way that children are treated at present is really an outrage on humanity and common sense. It comes from stupidity.[1]

4

It will be remembered that the reason why Wilde's wife had offered no opposition to the purchase of the whole of his interest in the marriage settlement from the Official Receiver was the advice of her solicitors that a divorce would break the settlement and that she should file her petition forthwith so as to make sure that their children should be provided for in the event of her death. She had originally been advised to take this course by Sir George Lewis immediately after her husband's conviction, but had refrained from doing so as a result of her two meetings with Wilde in prison. As Wilde himself had anticipated, she now reluctantly agreed to begin divorce proceedings, since she felt she had been deceived in the matter of the marriage settlement. 'My wife was very sweet to me,' Wilde told Robert Ross, 'and now she very naturally goes right against me. Of her character also a wrong estimate was made. She warned me that if I let my friends bid against her, she would proceed to a certain course and she will do so.'[2] In due time he learned the name of the witness on whose evidence his wife's solicitors were relying. He was horrified and wrote to Lord Alfred Douglas:

> At the present moment my wife, estranged from me over the important question whether I should have £3 or £3.10.0 a week to live on, is preparing a divorce suit, for which, of course, entirely new evidence and an entirely new trial, to be followed perhaps by more serious questions, will be necessary. I, naturally, know nothing of the details. I merely know the name of the witness on whose evidence my wife's solicitors rely. It is your own Oxford servant, whom at your special request I took into my service for our summer at Goring.[3]

At first Wilde thought that he could successfully resist the divorce suit by pleading his wife's condonation. But he soon

[1] The imprisonment of children was abolished by the Children Act, 1908, which also instituted juvenile courts.

[2] Wilde to Ross, April 1, 1897: Clark MSS; H–D, 515.

[3] *De Profundis*, 45.

discovered to his dismay that this plea would only cover that one offence and that particulars of other offences would be alleged to justify the petition. More Adey wrote to tell him that details of each separate offence would have to be given, apparently suggesting that, as Wilde had never committed sodomy, he would have no difficulty in preparing his defence. Wilde quickly brushed aside this consolatory argument.

> . . . though the particular offence required by the law did not find part amongst my perversities of passion, still perversities there were, or else why am I here? It may be a terrible shock to my friends to think that I had abnormal passions and perverse desires; still, if they read history they will find I am not the first artist so doomed any more than I shall be the last. To talk of my defending the case against Sir George Lewis is childish. How can I expect to be believed on a mere detail? What limit is there to the amount of witnesses he may produce? None. He and Queensberry can sweep Piccadilly for them. It makes me sick with rage when I am told of the opportunities I shall have of defending the case. What commonsense have my friends got to write such twaddle to me?[1]

In another letter to Ross, written about the same time, Wilde put his point of view even more clearly.

> . . . really my friends must face the fact that setting aside such details in my indictment as belonged to my bosom-friend,[2] three in number, I am not in prison as an innocent man. On the contrary, my record of perversities of passion and distorted romances would fill many scarlet volumes. I think it right to mention this—however surprising, and no doubt shocking it will sound to many—because More Adey in his letter tells me that the opposite side will be obliged to furnish strict details of the dates and places and exact circumstances of the terrible charges to be brought against me. Does he seriously imagine that, if I submitted to more cross-examination I would be believed? Does he propose I should do so, and repeat the Queensberry fiasco? It is the case that the charges are not true. But that is a mere detail. If a man gets drunk, whether he does so in white wine or red is of no importance. If a man has perverse passions, their particular mode of manifestation is of no importance either.
>
> I said from the first that I relied on my wife's condonation. I now learn that no condonation is of any value where more than one

[1] Wilde to Ross, April 6, 1897: Clark MSS; H–D, 519.

[2] Lord Alfred Douglas: see *Trials of Oscar Wilde* (ed. Montgomery Hyde) at p. 80.

offence may be charged. My wife has simply to say that she condoned X, but knew nothing of Y, and would not hear of condoning Z. There is a little shilling book—ninepence for cash—called *Every Man His Own Lawyer*. If my friends had only sent it to me, or even read it themselves, all this trouble, expense and worry would have been saved. . . .

My friendship with A[lfred] D[ouglas] brought me first to the dock of the Criminal Court, then to the dock of the Bankruptcy Court, and now to the dock of the Divorce Court. As far as I can make out (not having the shilling primer on the subject), there are no more docks into which he can bring me. If so, I can draw a breath of relief.[1]

Having carefully considered the matter, Wilde came to the conclusion that his best course would be to agree to the divorce, and he asked his friends to let the lawyers know he would not attempt to defend it. 'A grave mistake has been made', he told Ross. 'Submission has to follow.' He proposed that his life interest should be restored to his wife as a parting gift from him. 'It will render my exit from marriage less ignominious than to wait for its being done by legal coercion. Whether I am married or not is a matter that does not concern me. For years I have disregarded the tie. But I really think it is hard on my wife to be tied to me. I always thought so. And, though it may surprise some of my friends, I am really very fond of my wife and very sorry for her. I sincerely hope she may have a happy marriage, if she marries again. She could not understand me, and I was bored to death with married life. But she had some sweet points in her character and was wonderfully loyal to me.' As for his admissions, or at least failure to deny the allegations, in the anticipated divorce suit, on second thoughts he was inclined to doubt the likelihood of their leading to another criminal trial. 'I don't think the Government could possibly prosecute me again', he wrote to Ross. 'Even for a British Government it would be too brutal a procedure. . . . I don't think that even a British Government with Labouchère, Stead and the Social Purity League to back them would rearrest me and send me to prison again. It would be a ridiculous thing to do. I must live in England if I am to be a dramatist again, so I must face it if they do, but it would be a bestial infamy to again send me to prison for offences that in all civilised countries

[1] Wilde to Ross, April 1, 1897: Clark MSS; H–D, 515–16.

are questions of pathology and medical treatment if their cure is desired.'[1]

In fact the situation was not so serious as Wilde envisaged. His wife was still anxious to avoid a divorce and her solicitors had reopened negotiations with Adey's solicitors. They had suggested that, if Adey and Ross were prepared to surrender Wilde's interest in the marriage settlement, which they had bought from the Official Receiver, to Wilde's wife, she would undertake to allow him £150 a year during her lifetime; but this annuity was to be forfeited, should Wilde misconduct himself in the future. She also pledged herself not to institute divorce proceedings based on any misconduct by Wilde previous to the trials, which she was thus willing formally to condone.[2] After some correspondence and discussion had passed between the various lawyers these terms were accepted by Wilde's friends, it being mutually agreed at the same time that the decision as to whether any future action of Wilde's constituted misconduct should lie with his own solicitor, Mr Hansell, who agreed to act as arbitrator for this purpose. These arrangements were embodied in a draft Deed of Arrangement, and the draft was sent by Hansell to Wilde in Reading.

'It is couched in legal language and of course quite unintelligible to me', commented Wilde when he read it. 'The only thing I can make out is the close, where it is laid down that I am to be deprived of my £150 if I know any "disreputable" people. As good people, as they are grotesquely termed, *will* not know me, and I am not to be *allowed* to know *wicked* people, my future life, as far as I can see at present, will be passed in comparative solitude. I have written to Hansell that artists and the criminal classes are the only people who will know me, and that the conditions would place him in an absurd position. But what I want now is a legal condonation from my wife of the past, so as not to have it raked up again and again. For the rest, to have been divorced would have been horrible of course, but now that the children are publicly taken from me by a Judge's order, and it is decided that I am unfit to be with Cyril, I am very disheartened. All I want is peace. All I ever wanted was peace. I loathe legal worries.'[3]

[1] Wilde to Ross, April 6, 1897: Clark MSS; H–D, 519.
[2] Adey MSS.
[3] Wilde to Adey, May 6, 1897: Clark MSS; H–D, 534.

5

We have seen how incensed Wilde was that the sum of £150, which had been given to More Adey for his use by an anonymous well-wisher, had been mostly expended in the litigation with his wife over the marriage settlement. For this purpose Adey had instructed his solicitor, Mr Martin Holman of the firm of Parker, Garrett & Holman. 'In the whole of this law business my life has been gambled for and staked on the board with the utter recklessness', wrote Wilde to Adey. 'In the centre of it all has been a man whom I don't know, but who I now understand has secretly been my solicitor for more than a year, of the name of Holman.' Wilde reminded his friend of the two retired solicitor's clerks called Bouvard and Pecuchet in Flaubert's novel *La Bêtise Humaine*. 'The opinions of this man Holman, my secret solicitor, if collected as Holmaniana, would prove a serious rival to Flaubert's grotesques. For sheer crass stupidity they, if correctly reported, are perfectly astounding. The reckless gambling with my life has had, if a Tragedy to me, at least the comic choragus in Holman, the leader of the Dances.'[1]

In a series of letters, written from his prison cell to Ross and Adey, Wilde castigated his friends for the way in which they had mismanaged his affairs, through the instrumentality of the unfortunate Holman. 'The rushing in to try to get more money for me was wrong', he told Adey. 'It has resulted in less money, and in a separation and in the deprivation of my children, the last quite appalling.'

In the first place, wrote Wilde, there was a complete misapprehension of his wife's solicitor, Mr Hargrove. The latter had been the family solicitor for three generations and owed much of his own wealth, which was quite considerable, to Constance's grandfather, Horatio Lloyd, who had made a fortune in the railway boom of the 1840s. 'He was regarded as a solicitor of the Humphreys class—one who would threaten to gain an end, bluster, extort and the like. Quite the contrary. He is a man of very high character and extremely good social position. The idea of putting me, a wretched prisoner and pauper, up to fight Mr. Hargrove and Sir George Lewis was grotesque. The idea of bidding against them was absurd.

[1] Wilde to Ross, May 13, 1897: Clark MSS; H–D, 543.

Mr. Hargrove, the family solicitor of the Lloyds for thirty years, would advance my wife £10,000 if she wanted it and not feel it.'[1] Secondly, Adey, Ross and Holman all begged him not to surrender his legal rights over his wife and children. He wrote to Ross:

What absurd nonsense! I have no rights over my wife's children. That is not a right which a formal application by a solicitor's clerk can deprive one of in twenty minutes. You should read Carlyle. A right is an articulated might. Mr. Holman, I was told, was specially strong on the subject of my not surrendering 'my legal rights over my wife and children'. Mr. Hargrove warns me, warns More Adey, warns Holman. I am told that Holman considers that Mr. Hargrove is merely trying to frighten you by threats. That he has no intention of carrying them out. Poor Holman! His psychological estimate of Mr. Hargrove was sadly to seek.

My friends, reckless, as it was with my life and my money they were gambling, procure from the Official Receiver my Life Interest at the cost of £75. To achieve this, they think of two *clever* lies, as they fancy them to be. Holman tells Mr. Hargrove that a large sum of money is at my disposal and that I am in no want of money at all. It is supposed—*O sancta simplicitas*!—that this will overawe Mr. Hargrove and prevent his bidding against you! The sole result is that Mr. Hargrove tells me that he has it on the authority of Holman that I am going to be in no want of money, so that there is not the smallest necessity for increasing the £150. So my wife writes to me at Christmas and advises me to invest the money in an annuity so as to increase my income! She naturally supposed that it was about £3,000, something that one could buy an annuity with. So did I. I find that the entire sum was £150, of which everything except about thirty-five shillings has to go in law expenses.

The other clever lie is to pretend to Mr. Hargrove that you are not my agents but quite independent people, while assuring the Registrar of Bankruptcy that you are really my agents. As for me, you tell me that you are acting independently, but I find it is with my money. More Adey really expected Mr. Hargrove to believe in the ridiculous comedy. So did Holman. I need not say that Mr. Hargrove was not taken in for a single moment. He directed all his attacks on me. That is why More Adey and Holman and you were so brave. Nothing could exceed the heroism with which you exposed me to danger. . . .

Mr. Hargrove, there being no necessity to take the smallest

[1] Wilde to Ross, April 1, 1897: Clark MSS; H–D, 515.

notice of any one who had bought my life interest, suddenly deprives me of my children. This and the death of my mother are the two terrible things of my prison life. Holman didn't care, they were not his children. More was not interested. Even you, who were fond of them, of whom they were fond, who knew my idolatrous love of Cyril, even you took no notice. You never wrote me a line to say you were sorry at such a tragedy coming on me. You were absolutely indifferent. To me it was a blow appalling. I shall never get over it. That a Court of Law should decide that I am unfit to be with my own children is so terrible that to expunge it from the scroll of History and of Life I would gladly remain in this lonely cell for two more years—or for ten years if needs be. I don't care to live if I am so degraded that I am unfit to be with my own child.

What does Holman say? Well, I received a message from More Adey to say 'Holman declares himself very well satisfied so far'. Can one conceive such nonsense! But he gives Holman's sapient reasons.

(1) 'No costs were given against me.' As regards this, the costs would not have been more than £3.10.0 and no one gives costs against a bankrupt. I have no estate.

(2) 'An account is to be furnished of the progress of the education of my children twice a year to me.' As to this, it is quite untrue. The Court naturally requires an account to be handed in by the Guardians for the Court's information. I get no account. I can employ a Queen's Counsel and make an application to know if Cyril is learning to cipher, or if Vyvyan's spelling is improved. That is all.

(3) 'I have liberty to make an application if I like.' Certainly, but only on points of common ordinary law: viz. if I heard that the children are badly fed, or insufficiently clothed. What a privilege! Do you think they are likely to be?

(4) 'Mr. Holman is of opinion that this action shows that Mr. Hargrove will *not* apply for a divorce.' This is a typical specimen of Holmaniana. If he knew anything about law or equity, this ignorant and absurd solicitor would know that it was absolutely necessary for my wife to apply for and gain a divorce once she has charge of the children. Why? Because she had to make an affidavit that she could adequately provide for the suitable education of my children before the Court would even listen to an application to remove them from me. She was pledged to secure the life interest. By buying it you had forced her to do so. Step by step More Adey has forced my wife to bring the divorce suit. She had no option. She struggled for two years not to do it. It was reserved

for my friends to force it on her. Try and realise that, my dear Robbie, and you will understand my feelings.

But you and More Adey say now, 'you are *not* deprived of access to your children' . . . It is true that thro' a technical error it is not specified that I am to have no access, but perhaps you would like to hear a letter from Hansell on the subject dated April 10th. He writes as follows: 'The Court does not expressly forbid access. But it is understood that should you try to make any attempt to communicate with them an order would be issued expressly restraining you.' Note the words: '*any attempt to communicate with them*'. Are you satisfied now?

But you said with triumphant emphasis on Tuesday, 'Holman says that the order of the Court does not restrain you abroad!' This is an excellent bit of Holmaniana. Of course it does not. The byelaws of the Reading Vestry are not binding on the green water-streets of Venice. The laws passed by the English Parliament do not bind the inhabitants of France. But who ever said they did?

If I try to see the children two things happen. (1) I lose my entire income as, the children being in charge of my wife, it comes under the head of 'molestation or annoyance'. (2) She at once is forced to deprive the boys of the advantage of a foreign education, to remove them to England to the jurisdiction of the Court. In England if I try to write to them even I can be put in prison for contempt of Court. Do you understand all this? Is it dawning on you what More Adey and you and my friends have done?

The most shameful conduct on More Adey's part and the part of my friends was when my wife proceeded to the divorce. You were utterly regardless of me and my safety and my position. You simply were gambling with my life. My father used to have a story about an English landlord who wrote from the Carlton to his Irish agent and said, 'Don't let the tenants imagine that by shooting you they will at all intimidate me'. More Adey and you took up exactly the same position with regard to me. You did not care what happened. Do you think I am writing mere rhetoric? Let me quote to you your friend More Adey's letter conveying to me the news that George Lewis was going to divorce me on appalling charges of a new and more infamous character. 'We', he said—'your friends', that is—'we will have nothing whatever to do with your relations to your wife and we will not be *influenced by threats of a divorce, a matter in which we have no concern.*' There are your friend's words: that is the attitude of you, More Adey, and your brother Aleck, apparently.

You were all keen to repeat the Queensberry scandal and affair. First a civil trial, with me cross-examined by Carson. Then a report by the Judge to the Treasury. I am divorced and re-tried and sent to prison! That is what you are working for. 'Oh! but', says More Adey, 'when we advised you to resist and meet the "tainted" evidence, we didn't mean it. We meant that you might have time to get abroad.' So the great scheme was that I should be divorced on hideous grounds, and should live in exile. As my divorce would annul my settlement, I would of course have had no income at all. And, when I was skulking abroad, More Adey would have written to me and said, 'We have succeeded in all we aimed at: You have now no longer (1) any wife, (2) any children, (3) any income, (4) any possibility of ever coming to London to produce a play. Mr. Holman says he is very well satisfied on the whole.'

. . . In point of fact, dear Robbie, you had better realise that of all the incompetent people on the face of God's earth in any matter requiring wisdom, common sense, straightforwardness, ordinary intelligence, More Adey is undoubtedly the chief. I have written to him a letter about himself which I beg you will at once go and study.[1]

The relevant portion of Wilde's letter to Adey was as follows:

My dear More, the time is come when you should recognise one thing that is that in all business matters, even of the simplest kind, your judgment is utterly incompetent, your opinion either foolish or perverted, and your capacity to understand the most ordinary circumstances of actual life absolutely *nil*. You are a man of singular culture, of grave and castigated taste in style, you can discern the intellectual architecture of work that seems to others flamboyant or fantastic by an immediate sympathy of recognition: to discern the classical element in contemporary work is your function, one that you should more fully recognise than you do. You have not in literature ever tried to do yourself justice. In your nature you are most sympathetic. You would love to help others. You are patient in excess. Your forbearance is beautiful. But you have not got enough commonsense to manage the affairs of a tom-tit in a hedge.

Everything you do is wrong and done in the wrong manner. Robbie is better as a guide; for, if he is quite irrational, he has the advantage of being always illogical, so he occasionally comes to a right conclusion. But you not merely are equally irrational, but are absolutely logical: you start always from the wrong premises, and arrive logically at the wrong conclusion. As soon as I see in

[1] Wilde to Ross, May 12, 1897: Clark MSS; H–D, 544. (Partly quoted in the *Dulau Catalogue*, at p. 26, where his letter is misdated April 13.)

your letters (1), (2), (3), I know you have been doing something utterly foolish and are giving utterly foolish reasons.

The crowning example of Adey's folly, in Wilde's view, was his acceptance of a post-dated cheque from Leverson, who had now agreed to hand over the balance of the sum which he had been holding in trust for Wilde. 'Of your accepting a post-dated cheque from Leverson it is useless to speak', he wrote to Adey. 'A boy of ten years of age would know that a post-dated cheque is not a legal tender. It is the one thing you should not have done.' Wilde went on to tell his friend that he had so mismanaged his affairs that he had to do a few things for him, 'not as a reparation, for that is out of your power, but simply as an attempt to show your regret'. The first was to go immediately to Leverson. 'Get from him £200 either in notes or in an open cheque payable to bearer (if he *writes* the word "bearer" across the word "order" in the cheque see that he initials the word.) Lodge £100 in your bank for me: the other £100 convert into five £10 notes, nine £5: gold. Buy a pocket book for me in Bond Street, a good one with silver clasps—suitable for carrying money—*not too thick*: one that I could carry in a breast pocket: put the notes into it. . . . Remember, go to Leverson at once: see him at breakfast in presence of his wife: do not go away without the £200 . . . kindly do not mismanage anything.'[1]

[1] Wilde to Adey, May 16, 1897: Clark MSS; H–D, 550.

CHAPTER VI

Release

1

THERE were various other questions which remained to be settled before the date of Wilde's release. Chief among them was his destination on the Continent, for he had no desire to stay in England, at least for the time being, nor did his friends wish him to do so. Various places were considered. At one time Wilde fancied having a flat in Brussels, but this idea was dismissed apparently on the grounds of expense. Boulogne was also thought of until it was discovered that Alfred Douglas was a frequent visitor there. By this time he had forgiven Frank Harris, who had brought him some clothes, and for a while he reverted to the plan of a driving tour in the Pyrenees. Eventually Wilde's friends fixed on Dieppe, to which he agreed with some reluctance. 'I am so well known there that I dislike it and the air is relaxing,' he told Adey, 'but I suppose one can move on.' He asked Ross, who had undertaken to cross over to Dieppe ahead of him and arrange accommodation, to see if he could find some 'little quiet place' about ten miles away by rail to which they could go together. 'I am well known at all the Dieppe hotels, and of course my arrival will be telegraphed to London.'[1]

Several friends had contributed to provide him with such articles as a dressing-case, books, clothes and toilet necessities on his release. The dressing-case came from Reggie Turner, who had the initials 'S.M.' specially stamped on it and its contents since Wilde had decided to adopt the name 'Sebastian Melmoth'.[2] Besides Frank Harris, Ross gave him a suit of

[1] Wilde to Ross, May 17, 1897: Clark MSS; H–D, 559.

[2] From the title of a novel by his great-uncle, Charles Maturin, about whom Ross and Adey had collaborated in writing a book. In a letter to Mr Louis Wilkinson in 1900, the original of which is in my possession, Wilde wrote: 'You asked me about "Melmoth". Of course I have not changed my name: in Paris I am as well known as in London: it would be childish. But to prevent postmen having fits, I

clothes and an overcoat and More Adey the sum of £25, which he expended on hats, gloves, collars, socks, handkerchiefs, mother-of-pearl studs ('by the way I want to make "nacred" an English word'), French soap, tooth powder, toilet water, and a lotion for his hair, which had become very grey. ('I am under the impression that it is quite white, but I believe that is an exaggeration. There is a wonderful thing called Koko Marikopas, to be got at 233 Regent Street, which is a wonderful hair tonic. The name alone seems worth the money, so please get me a large bottle.') He also asked for two travelling Scotch rugs and some long nightshirts with turndown collars, and a breast pocket for a handkerchief. 'I want, for psychological reasons, to feel entirely physically cleansed of the stain and soil of prison life,' he told Adey, 'so these things are all, trivial as they may sound, really of great importance.'[1]

These matters were discussed with Ross and Adey on the occasion of their last visit to Reading, which took place about ten days before Wilde's release. On this occasion the two friends were accompanied by Charles Ricketts, the artist, who had drawn the cover design for Wilde's poem *The Sphinx*.[2] As they had so much business to discuss with the prisoner, neither Ross nor Adey was very anxious to have Ricketts with them, but he had asked for a visiting order several times in the past without success and, as Wilde put it to Adey, 'I thought, as he had applied so often, it was not for me to refuse a kindly offer from an artist of whom I am very fond'. Unfortunately this visit proved to be both painful and unsatisfactory for everyone, except possibly for Ricketts. For one thing Wilde was smarting under a sense of grievance at what he considered the mismanagement of his affairs by Adey and Ross, and the atmosphere was consequently strained. Then he was upset by the behaviour of the additional visitor. 'I was wrong to have Ricketts present', he told Ross afterwards. 'He meant to be cheerful, but I thought

sometimes have my letters inscribed with the name of a curious novel by my grand-uncle Maturin, a novel that was part of the romantic revival of the early century, and though imperfect, a pioneer—it is still read in France and Germany.' See Louis Marlow, *Seven Friends* (1953), at p. 13.

[1] Wilde to Adey, May 6, 1897: Clark MSS; H–D, 535.

[2] Charles Ricketts (1866–1931) was a painter, printer, stage-designer and writer, and is perhaps best remembered for his fine publications from the Vale Press, which he directed jointly with his friend, C. H. Shannon. His posthumously published *Self Portrait: Letters and Journals*, compiled by T. Sturge Moore (1939), contains some interesting references to Wilde, as well as his *Recollections of Oscar Wilde* (1932).

him trivial. Everything he said, including his remark that he supposed time went very fast in prison (a singularly unimaginative opinion and one showing an entirely inartistic lack of sympathetic instinct), annoyed me extremely.'[1]

Ricketts has left an account of this meeting, in which he has recorded some of the conversation, although he does not mention the tactless remark which Wilde attributed to him.[2] According to the artist, the behaviour of the three visitors resembled that of men about to attend a funeral, Ross even developing a touch of hysteria on reaching the prison gate. The arrangement was that the other two should see Wilde first for their business talk, and after half an hour Ricketts should join them. Ricketts was accordingly put to wait 'in a small putty coloured writing room, decorated with a chocolate dado and an ebonized clock'. After a few minutes alone he was joined by a friendly warder.

'You know Wilde?'

'Yes, very well.'

'Know his books and all that?'

'Yes, they are very good.'

'So I should think . . . a queer chap . . . but very nice.'

As Ricketts again agreed, the warder continued his interrogation.

'Seen his plays?'

'Yes, often. Have you?'

'No.' The warder spoke in an obvious tone of regret at having missed something good. 'But one of my mates went to see *Lady Windermere's Fan*. He says it was splendid. Miss Marion Terry did it. I wish I had been there. Wish I had half his brains.'

Presently Ricketts was summoned and conducted through ochre-coloured corridors and past iron staircases until he reached the visiting-room. Here Wilde was seated at a green-baize covered table with his back to the window. To Ricketts he seemed 'radiant with health and humour' and looked 'stouter than formerly in his loose-fitting prison clothes'. The sight of these made Ricketts wince. Two warders and several other prison officials were standing at some distance by the wall and seemed interested in the appearance of Ricketts. But the faces

[1] Wilde to Ross, May 13, 1897: Clark MSS; H–D, 541.
[2] Charles Ricketts. *Recollections of Oscar Wilde* (1932), pp. 44–9.

of his two fellow-visitors showed constraint, since the business discussion had not gone at all well, particularly on the question of his future destination. Of this nothing was visible on Wilde's countenance. The words with which he cordially greeted Ricketts and his inquiries about him might have been spoken in Bond Street, in a new frock coat with a large buttonhole, instead of in the special visitors' room of Reading Gaol in the drab prison uniform with its broad arrows.

'Both my dear friends would wish me to retire to a monastery,' he exclaimed laughingly, as he threw a glance in the direction of Ross and Adey. 'Why not La Trappe? Or worse still to some dim country place in England. I believe it was Twyford.'

He paused for a moment before continuing. 'They speak of Venice later with its silence and dead waterways. No. I have had enough silence.'

'But, Oscar,' murmured Ricketts. 'Is not Venice with its beauty and stillness, the very place for work and privacy? There you could see your friends if——'

'No!' Wilde interrupted. 'Privacy! Work! My dear Ricketts, I wish to look at life, not to become a monument for tourists!'

He seemed to favour somewhere in France, although he was not enamoured of Dieppe. 'The French have produced *Salomé* during my stay here and it was reviewed in the English Press. France understands the value of an artist for what he is, not for what he may have done. Privacy! I have had two years of it . . . save for that other self—the man I once was.'

They all seized on the mention of *Salomé* as an excuse for turning the conversation to this play. Wilde asked Ross for details of the Paris production, which had appeared in the *Daily Telegraph* but which he had not been allowed to see in prison.

Ricketts asked whether he had thought of a new play, since he had had ideas for several on hand at the time of his arrest.

'A play, the theatre! My dear boy, what folly was mine! I held the future of the English stage in the hollow of my hand, to make or mar. Today, in London, who would produce a work of mine?'

Ricketts then mentioned *Lady Windermere's Fan*, which had recently been given at Richmond, and he spoke of the friendly warder. He also quoted some praise of him from the lips of Ellen Terry and the sympathy expressed for him by Henry Irving.[1]

Wilde inquired about Ricketts's publishing activities. 'I want to return to literature and you must print *A Portrait of Mr. W. H.'* he added. 'I know it needs retouching, but it is one of my early masterpieces.'

In this essay, which had originally appeared in *Blackwood's Magazine*, Wilde set out to prove that the 'W.H.', to whom the sonnets of Shakespeare are dedicated, was a boy actor named Willie Hughes. At Wilde's suggestion Ricketts had painted an imaginative portrait of the actor, which he intended to use as a frontispiece for a revised and enlarged version of the essay. In fact, his publisher, John Lane, actually announced this work for publication. But fear of losing other authors had obliged Lane to drop Wilde from his list, which of course involved the abandonment of the contemplated publication.[2] At the same time Rickett's picture had been acquired by a dealer when the contents of Wilde's house in Chelsea were sold up during the trials, and its whereabouts could not be traced.[3]

'Your picture, Robbie tells me, has vanished,' remarked Wilde to the artist. 'But you will design me another wonderful frontispiece.'

'My dear Oscar, of course I will publish a book of yours,' said Ricketts. 'But for the moment, let it be some other work, your *Sainte Courtesane*, for instance.'

'Alas,' exclaimed Wilde. 'She no longer says marvellous

[1] Irving's grandson has written: 'A veiled lady, generally believed to be Ellen Terry, had left a bouquet of violets with a message of sympathy at Wilde's house where, in dazed resignation, he was spending the interval between the two trials; the violets suggest that Irving and Ellen Terry were partners in this kindly gesture. . . . Wilde had an almost childish love of the theatre that Irving had created —though his own work ushered in the new school of sophisticated comedy. No doubt Irving was grateful to Wilde for not having involved in any way the all too vulnerable world of the theatre in his own calamity.' Laurence Irving. *Henry Irving* (1951), at p. 579.

[2] The MS of the enlarged version of *The Portrait of Mr. W. H.*, which was thought to have been stolen at the time of the sale of the contents of Wilde's house in Tite Street in 1895, turned up many years later in the offices of Lane's publishing firm, being discovered in a drawer used by a member of the staff named George Chapman, who had died and who had no doubt been engaged in preparing the book for the press at the time of Wilde's arrest. It was sold on behalf of Chapman's widow by the publisher, Mitchell Kennerley, to the well-known American dealer, Dr W. S. Rosenbach, and is now in the possession of the Rosenbach Foundation in New York. The complete text was published by Kennerley in New York in a limited edition in 1921, and was republished in England with an Introduction by Mr Vyvyan Holland in 1958. Further details will be found in my letter to *The Times Literary Supplement*, December 5, 1958.

[3] Mason, 7.

things, the robbers have buried her white body and carried away her jewels.'

There was a pause, as Wilde reflected for a moment or two. 'Yes, perhaps you are right,' he went on. '*Mr. W. H.* might be imprudent. The English public would have to read Shakespeare's sonnets.'

They all joined in the nervous laughter which followed. Then Ross asked 'Why not the play about Pharaoh?'

'Yes,' replied Wilde. 'Of course, the King is tremendous when he cries to Moses "Praise be to thy God, O prophet, for he has slain my only enemy, my son".' He laughed repeatedly. 'But I must have books about Egypt, full of the names of beautiful things, rare and curious meat for the feast, not the mere flesh-pots the Jews regretted.'

His face began to cloud over. 'At night in the cold . . . when I felt hungry . . . I have often thought of fantastic feasts . . . yes, I have sometimes been cold and hungry . . . not here . . . my gaolers are kind, excellent fellows . . . it has not always been thus with some others.'

He then spoke of the kindly warders in the dock at the Old Bailey, of the chaplain at Pentonville who had questioned him about morning prayers, and of Major Isaacson's harsh rule at Reading. 'Yes,' he repeated. 'I have been cold and hungry. Cold is worse than hunger . . . in time one gets used to this . . . but many of my warders have been my friends.'

He leaned across in his chair and spoke in a confidential tone about the warders. 'Don't mention this, it might lead to trouble . . . knowing that I had not enough food, they have brought me curious things to eat, Scotch scones, meat pies and sausage rolls, believing that a hungry man can eat anything, just as the British throw Bibles to the bears.'

He laughed, and on this note of forced gaiety the visit ended.

During the business discussion with Ross and Adey, Wilde had mentioned the draft Deed of Arrangement, which legally embodied the terms on which his wife undertook to make him an allowance of £150 a year. It so happened that on the same day a meeting took place in the offices of Constance Wilde's solicitors in London, at which the terms of the deed were finally settled. Besides the three lawyers, Hargrove, Holman and Hansell, whose clients were interested, Adrian Hope was present as guardian of Wilde's two children.

Holman, who represented Adey and Ross as assignors of Wilde's life interest in the marriage settlement under the deed, considered it 'a very satisfactory interview'. He now wrote to inform Adey that after Constance Wilde's death the £150 would be paid to Wilde unconditionally. During her life she undertook to pay the same amount subject to Wilde doing nothing 'which would entitle his wife to a divorce or a decree for judicial separation, or be guilty of any *moral* misconduct, or *notoriously* consort with evil or disreputable companions'. Wilde's solicitor, Hansell, had agreed to act as arbitrator in the case of any alleged misconduct on the part of his client, he and Holman having obtained the insertion of the words in italics above, 'which we think meets the case'. In addition, Holman and Hansell persuaded Hargrove to add another paragraph to the effect that any decision from Hansell as arbitrator was to be for the purpose of the deed only and was not to be used in Court in any other proceedings against his client.

At this interview Adrian Hope stated that he was now practically the sole adviser of Constance Wilde, both in her own interests and in those of her children, and that it was immaterial to him what kind of life Wilde led after he came out of prison, 'provided he did not molest his wife and provided he kept out of the newspapers'. He also said that in the event of there being 'any public scandal', in which Wilde was mixed up, he would at once put the matter before Hansell and ask for his authority to stop the allowance. 'These terms are, I think all that we can ask,' Holman told Adey, 'and the deed will therefore be engrossed in triplicate on these lines. Mr. Wilde has approved it, and he has been made a party to it (though this is not necessary) in order that he may never in the future be able to accuse you or his other friends, or Mr. Hansell, or myself, of entering into any arrangement with which he was not fully conversant.'

Adey's solicitor concluded this letter to his client with what he considered a piece of advice of paramount importance for Wilde. 'I do hope', he wrote, 'you will impress upon him, as Mr. Hansell has already done, how absolutely fatal to him any further intercourse with Lord Alfred Douglas will be. Apart from the fact that Lord Alfred is a "notoriously disreputable companion", Lord Queensberry has made arrangements for being informed if his son joins Mr. Wilde and has expressed his intention of shooting one or both. A threat of this kind from most people could be more or less disregarded, but there is no doubt that Lord Queensberry, as he has shown before, will carry out any threat he makes to the best of his ability.'[1]

2

After the Deed of Arrangement had been engrossed in Hargrove's office, one of the copies was sent out for signature to Mrs Wilde, who had now apparently decided to come to England for the purpose of executing it. Holman asked Hargrove for its return in time to enable Hansell to take it with him to Reading on the Saturday (May 15) preceding the date on which Wilde was due to be released. Wilde was expecting his solicitor on that day, when he received a message to the effect that Hansell was unable to come down until after the weekend, that is on the following Monday.

'I was greatly disappointed at not seeing Hansell today', wrote Wilde to Adey on the Saturday night. 'Monday is so late that I fear he will be of little service to me beyond getting my signature to the deed arranging the terms of separation from my wife. . . . The question of the children has been settled by the Court ultimately and finally. They are taken from me, and on my wife's death should that terrible event occur, they will belong to Adrian Hope. As regards our own personal relations, all that is settled on the strictest terms by this deed. If I attempt to write to her without her permission or reside near her against her wishes, I at once lose my sole income of £3 a week. I am to keep away. If we make friends and live together again, I am to lose the income just as much as if I annoyed her. The matter is out of my wife's control.'[2]

The reason for the postponement of Hansell's visit may have been that Constance Wilde wished to come to Reading as well and had not arrived or had only just arrived in England on the Saturday. At any rate, it has been asserted by the warder who was on duty, 'in sight but out of hearing', for the purpose of this visit, that Mrs Wilde accompanied the solicitor but did not wish her husband to see her. According to the warder the interview took place in what was known as the 'solicitors' room', and Wilde sat at a table with his head in his hands oppo-

[1] H. Martin Holman to More Adey, May 10, 1897: Adey MSS.
[2] Wilde to Adey, May 16, 1897: Clark MSS; H–D, 548.

site the lawyer. Outside in the passage, with the warder, waited a figure dressed in black. It was Constance Wilde—in tears. While the consultation was proceeding, Mrs Wilde turned to the warder and begged a favour. 'Let me have one glimpse of my husband,' she said. The kindly warder, who was himself deeply touched by the occasion, could not refuse her. He stepped back silently, so as to enable her to look through the glass peep-hole in the door. In the warder's words, 'Mrs Wilde cast one long lingering glance inside, and saw the convict-poet, who, in deep mental distress himself, was totally unconscious that any eyes save those of the stern lawyer and myself witnessed his degradation'. At that precise moment Wilde was in the act of putting his signature to the deed. She drew back, 'apparently labouring under deep emotion', and a few minutes later left the prison with the solicitor, still unperceived by her husband. To the warder it remained 'the saddest story' he knew of the prisoner.[1]

Until this visit Wilde had been in doubt as to where he was to go on the morning of his release from Pentonville, in order to shave, bath, change and breakfast, before continuing his journey to the Continent. Hansell now told him his friends had arranged for him to be met with a closed carriage at the prison early in the morning of May 19 by More Adey and the Rev Stewart Headlam, the kindly clergyman who had gone bail for him during the trials, and that they would take him to Headlam's house in Bloomsbury, where he could wait until it was time to leave to catch the boat-train for Newhaven. This plan did not appeal to Wilde. 'I do not like the idea of going to Stewart Headlam's at all', he wrote to Reginald Turner immediately the solicitor had left. 'I don't know him very well, and I am afraid of strangers. Please will you consider the possibility of an Hotel? Some quiet place—Euston Road or anywhere like that, I would much prefer it. Thank Stewart Headlam for me, but tell him I am very nervous and ill and upset. If you really wish it, I will go to his house: but I would sooner not. Any quiet Hotel would be better for me.'

[1] *Evening News*, March 2, 1905. This account received some corroboration from Major Nelson, the Governor of Reading, who later stated that he 'well remembered Mrs Wilde' and described her as 'a beautiful and loyal woman': *Manchester Guardian*, October 13, 1914. Presumably this was the sole occasion on which he could have seen her, since her only other visit to Reading took place in the time of Major Isaacson.

These words were put in a postscript at the end of a letter to Turner, which Wilde had finished before he saw the solicitor and in which he asked his friend to meet him at Pentonville and take him to a hotel. 'At the Hotel I want to find all my clothes, your dressing bag to which I look forward with joy and gratitude, a room to dress in and a sitting room. In fact, dear Reggie, you had better go yourself to an Hotel tomorrow evening, and sleep there. I can dress in your room and breakfast in the sitting room adjoining . . . I would like coffee for breakfast, as I have been living on cocoa, and don't think I could taste tea . . . Try to find an Hotel with a good bathroom close to bedroom—this is most essential.' He also asked Turner to travel with him to the Continent and spend a week with him. 'If you consent to come away with me, you will be doing a service beyond words to a very heart-broken man.'[1]

Wilde reinforced this plea in a second letter to Turner, written later the same day and apparently smuggled out of the prison. Because of being uncensored, it is perhaps the frankest of all Wilde's prison letters.

This is a contraband letter, my first and last. I have found a mode of getting it out of prison unread and unseen. I send it to you because your kind and sweet and generous affection for me, as evinced in your lovely present, of which I have received the tidings, has so touched and so charmed me that I must write specially and freely to you . . . I can't tell you how touched I am: I shall never forget it.

. . . I am ill, and unnerved. Already the American interviewer and the English journalist have arrived in Reading: the Governor of the Prison has just shown me a letter from the American interviewer stating that he will be here with a carriage on Wednesday morning for me, and offering any sum I like if I will breakfast with him! Is it not appalling? I who am maimed, ill, altered in appearance so that no one can hardly recognise me, brokenhearted, ruined, disgraced—a leper and a pariah to men—I am to be gibbetted for the public of two worlds! The Home Secretary, an ignorant man, has refused to let me go out one half hour before the time! So I want to escape somewhere where I can find you, my good dear simple-hearted friend—and I beg you to keep yourself in readiness. . . .

I won't tell you all I have suffered, my dear Reggie—the eternal silence, the hunger, the sleeplessness, the cruelty, the hard and

[1] Wilde to Turner, May 17, 1897: Turner MSS; H–D, *556*.

revolting punishments, the utter despair, the ignoble dress and loathsome mode of life—it would only distress you. . . .

There are many good nice fellows here. I have seven or eight friends—they are capital chaps. Of course we can't speak to each other, except a word now and then at exercise, but we are great friends, they take their punishment so well, so cheerfully.

I go out with an adder in my heart and an asp in my tongue, and every night I sow thorns in the garden of my soul. But you will do me good. If I don't see you on Wednesday, I shall be so disappointed—no one must give me the dressing bag but yourself.[1]

It is doubtful whether Turner received this letter in time to act on it, since he left next day with Ross for Dieppe so as to make advance arrangements for Wilde's accommodation there. Ross had been present with Turner at the moment of Wilde's arrest in the Cadogan Hotel in Sloane Street, and for that among several reasons Wilde had begged Ross not to come to Pentonville on the morning of his release. 'I think that for many reasons, social emotional and others', he had written to Adey on May 12, 'it is much better he should not meet me.' No doubt Turner thought it preferable for him to keep in the background too, and anyhow he did not wish to interfere with the arrangements which had been made by Adey. Wilde had written to Adey on the same day as he had written to Turner, telling Adey that he had asked Turner to come abroad with him, adding that, if Adey came too, 'it would only distress us both'. He was evidently in a highly neurotic state, as he wrote this, while waiting for Hansell's visit. Later in the same letter, which he completed after the solicitor had departed, he wrote more calmly. 'Of course I really will be glad to see you the morning of my release, and I know you have taken a great deal of trouble about it. So come either to the prison with Reggie or to his rooms if that is more convenient. But we must not talk about business.' He had previously made a particular request. 'As I no doubt shall be very much upset and hysterical would you ask your doctor for any *nerve sedative*? Nerves are not treated in prison.' Incidentally Wilde's condition had not escaped the attention of Major Nelson, who wrote to the Prison Commissioners on May 15: 'The prisoner each day becomes more hysterical and fearful of any annoyance that may be caused by the importunity of the Press.'

Tuesday, May 18, 1897, was Wilde's last day in Reading. 'I hope', he had written to Adey, 'through my good and kind friend, as I must call him, the Governor, to be allowed to escape on Tuesday about 6 o/c. Of course, there will be people waiting then, to see me transferred to Wormwood Scrubs, as the newspapers announced I would be: still there won't be so many.' It was, in fact, nearer eight o'clock when Warder Martin came into cell C.3.3 with the clothes in which Wilde had been sentenced, frock coat, silk hat and patent leather boots. After Wilde had dressed, he shook hands with the warder and asked Martin to think of him sometimes. (Years later the kindly warder wrote: 'I have thought of you always, scarcely one single day has passed since then that I have not thought of you—you who were at once my prisoner and my friend.') He was then conducted to the main hall, where the Governor, Chief Warder and other prison officials were waiting to see him off. So as to spare him the possibility of being recognised at Reading railway station, Major Nelson had arranged that he should catch the London train from the small neighbouring station at Twyford. The Chief Warder and another warder were to act as the prisoner's escort, and it had also been arranged that instead of going to Paddington, which as a terminus was open to the same objections as Reading, the party should alight at Westbourne Park and from there complete the journey to Pentonville by cab.

Wilde shook hands with the Governor and thanked him. Major Nelson wished the prisoner luck. Before saying goodbye Major Nelson handed the departing prisoner a bulky package. This contained the manuscript of *De Profundis.* Then Wilde and the two warders got into the cab, which was waiting in the courtyard and drove off through the prison gates. Only two reporters were waiting outside the gates, one from a London daily paper, *Morning*, and the other from an American journal. The two newspapermen followed Wilde's cab to Twyford station, where the prison party immediately retired to the waiting-room to wait for the train which was due at 8.52 p.m. 'I had an opportunity of observing Mr Wilde while he was in the waiting room at Twyford', wrote the correspondent of the *Morning* for the information of its readers next day.' He looked very well. His build and general appearance were—as of old—distinguished and attractive. In short Oscar

Wilde of today is the Oscar Wilde, so far as appearance goes.'[1]

A second-class compartment had been reserved for the party on the London train; on its arrival they boarded the train and were locked in the carriage by the station master. An hour and ten minutes later they reached Westbourne Park. The remainder of the journey was completed without incident. At Pentonville, where they arrived shortly after 10.30, the Governor was waiting, since he had been instructed by the Prison Commissioners to receive Wilde himself and not to let any of his officers know the prisoner's name.[2] He told Wilde that his friends were sending a carriage for him at 6.15 next morning and that it would be allowed to drive into the prison yard.

3

Fortunately everything went off for the prisoner's release according to plan. 'A private conveyance containing two gentlemen arrived at 6.10 this morning', wrote the Governor of Pentonville to the Prison Commissioners later the same day. 'It was admitted into the courtyard and turned round, the prisoner then got into it and was driven off totally unobserved by anyone. Inquiries were made by strangers soon after 6.30, who continued to watch the prison until after the normal discharges left the prison.'[3] The two occupants of the brougham were More Adey and the Rev Stewart Headlam. 'I was very anxious to avoid reporters', Headlam recalled afterwards, 'and to my surprise we succeeded in doing so, though we saw on a newspaper placard as we drove down the Euston Road the anticipatory announcement RELEASE OF OSCAR WILDE.' Together they drove to Headlam's house—31 Upper Bedford Place—where Wilde was able to change and have breakfast. 'He was given the first cup of coffee after two years', noted his host: 'how grateful he was!' He told Headlam something of his life in prison, mentioning some of the books he had read. He seemed particularly eager to talk about Dante, and he insisted on writing

[1] *Morning*, May 19, 1897.
[2] Prison Commissioners to Governor of Pentonville, May 17, 1897: Home Office (Prison Commission) Papers.
[3] Governor of Pentonville to Prison Commissioners, May 19, 1897: Home Office (Prison Commission) Papers.

down for Headlam's benefit the best way to study the Italian poet and the best books about him.[1]

While he was still at breakfast there was a ring at the front door. It was Ernest Leverson and his wife, Ada, whom Wilde used affectionately to call 'The Sphinx', and at whose house Wilde had stayed when he was out on bail between his two trials.[2] They were shown into the drawing-room, which Mrs Leverson was to remember as 'full of Burne-Jones and Rossetti pictures, Morris wallpaper and curtains, in fact an example of the decoration of the early eighties, very beautiful in its way, and very like the aesthetic rooms Oscar had once loved'. Both Mrs Leverson and her husband felt intensely nervous and embarrassed. ('We had the English fear of showing our feelings.') Presently Wilde entered the room, 'with the dignity of a King returning from exile', and immediately put them both at their ease. According to Mrs Leverson, 'he came in talking, laughing, smoking a cigarette, with waved hair and a flower in his button-hole, and he looked markedly better, slighter, and younger than he had two years previously'. He greeted his friends characteristically. 'Sphinx,' he cried, 'how marvellous of you to know exactly the right hat to wear at seven o'clock in the morning to meet a friend who has been away! You can't have got up, you must have sat up.'

There was some discussion as to where Wilde was to go after Dieppe, and the projected driving tour with Frank Harris was mentioned. According to Headlam, Wilde said 'it would be like a perpetual football match to be with him'. The conversation then got on to the subject of religion. Wilde remarked that he looked on all the different religions 'as colleges in a great university' and that he regarded Roman Catholicism as 'the greatest and most romantic of them'. At length he said he would like to go into a retreat for six months, and he asked Headlam to send a message to this effect to one of the priests at the Jesuit church in Farm Street. His host obligingly wrote a

[1] F. G. Bettany, *Stewart Headlam* (1926), pp. 131–2.

[2] Ada Leverson, who first met Wilde through an anonymous parody of *The Picture of Dorian Gray*, which she had written, was reckoned with her husband among his closest friends. She later became herself a witty novelist. In 1930 she published a selection of Wilde's letters to her, with her own recollections, and an introduction by Robert Ross: *Letters to the Sphinx from Oscar Wilde and Reminiscences of the Author*, re-published in *The New Savoy* in 1946. Sir Osbert Sitwell has written an interesting account of her in the last volume of his autobiography, *Noble Essences* (1950), pp. 127–62. She died in 1933.

letter and despatched it by cab. Whilst waiting for the reply Wilde walked up and down the drawing-room. He continued to talk gaily in response to his friends' inquiries about his life at Reading. 'The dear Governor,' he exclaimed, 'such a delightful man, and his wife is charming. I spent happy hours in their garden, and they asked me to spend the summer with them. They thought I was the gardener.' He began to laugh. 'Unusual, I think? But I don't feel I can. I feel I want a change of scene.'

He chatted on. 'Do you know one of the punishments that happen to people who have been "away"? They are not allowed to read the *Daily Chronicle.*' He explained that on his journey in the train on the previous night, he had asked permission to read it. Apparently one of the warders had a copy. This was refused. Wilde then suggested that he might be allowed to read it upside down. 'This they consented to allow,' he added with a chuckle, 'I read the *Daily Chronicle* upside down all the way, and never enjoyed it so much. It's really the only way to read newspapers.'

The laughter caused by these jests suddenly died away with the return of the messenger from Farm Street. He handed Wilde a letter and the others looked aside while he read it. His face suddenly assumed a serious expression. Then he broke down and sobbed bitterly. The reply was in effect a polite refusal. It was intimated that he could not be accepted in the retreat on the impulse of the moment, but must first consider the matter for at least a year.[1]

The arrangement had been that Wilde and Adey should cross together by the day-boat from Newhaven to Dieppe. But Wilde talked for so long and seemed to be enjoying himself so much that no one seemingly liked to tell him when the time had come for him to leave. He had other visitors too, besides the Leversons, a young couple whom he had befriended in happier days, presenting the husband with a cheque to enable him to get married. Anyhow he and Adey missed the train. In the circumstances the only thing to do was to go for the night-boat, which they accordingly did. So it was the afternoon when they said good-bye to their generous host, 'of whose care, charity and kindness', wrote Robert Ross, 'it would be impossible to

[1] Ada Leverson. *Letters to the Sphinx from Oscar Wilde* (1930), pp. 45–6.

speak too highly'.[1] On Headlam Wilde's visit made a vivid impression. 'I like to think of him as I knew him for those six hours on that spring morning,' this kindhearted clergyman later recalled, 'and to hope that somewhere and somehow the beauty of his character may be garnered and the follies and weaknesses burnt up.'[2]

Taking care to avoid Victoria Station, after being recognized in Hatchard's bookshop in Piccadilly, where they had called for a few minutes, Wilde and Adey went by cab to West Croydon, where they caught the Newhaven train. On reaching Newhaven, Wilde sent the following telegram to Ross at the Hotel Sandwich, Dieppe.[3]

> Arriving by night boat. Am so delighted at prospect of seeing you and Reggie. You must not mind one foolish unkind letter. More has been such a good friend to me and I am so grateful to you all I cannot find words to express my feelings. You must not dream of waiting up for us. In the morning we will meet. Please engage rooms for us at your hotel. When I see you I shall be quite happy. Indeed I am happy now to think I have such wonderful friendship shown to me.
>
> SEBASTIAN MELMOTH

Ross and Turner were on the landing stage at Dieppe when the boat steamed into the harbour at half-past four on the morning. In the first rays of the dawn Wilde's tall figure was easily discernible on deck, dominating the other passengers. As Ross and Turner began to run along the jetty, Wilde recognised them and waved smilingly. At this moment he made an unforgettable impression in appearance. 'His face had lost all its coarseness,' noted Ross afterwards, 'and he looked as he must have looked at Oxford in the early days before I knew him and as he only looked again after death. A good many people, even friends, thought his appearance almost repulsive, but the upper part of his face was extraordinarily fine and intellectual.'

There was the usual irritating delay, and then Wilde, with an odd elephantine gait, which Ross had never seen in anyone else, stalked off the boat. He was holding in his hand a large

[1] Robert Ross, MS Preface to *After Reading*: Clark MSS (*Dulau Catalogue*, item 35). This draft preface, which Ross intended to be used for an edition of Wilde's post-prison letters to him, contains interesting facts about Wilde at this period, and I have used it here. It was never completed. Mason and Adey, who later brought out a selection of the letters under the titles of *After Reading* and *After Berneval*, do not appear to have seen this MS, which has now been partly published by Hart-Davis, *op. cit.*, 564–5.

[2] Bettany, *loc. cit.*

sealed envelope. Inside it was the manuscript of *De Profundis*. 'This, my dear Robbie, is the great MS about which you know,' he exclaimed coming down the gangway. He handed the MS to Ross to deal with according to his instructions. He then broke into what Ross called 'a great Rabelaisian sort of laughter', as he went on to speak in a bantering tone about Adey: 'More has behaved very badly about my luggage and was anxious to deprive me of the blessed bag which Reggie gave me.' Their greetings over, Wilde handed Turner the keys of his luggage and his friend went off to open the suitcases for Customs examination. On his return he found Wilde in the buffet surrounded by other passengers, as he put it, 'sitting at the head of the buffet table drinking his coffee and dominating the whole seasick company'.[1] The four friends then made their way to the hotel, where 'a feast of sandwiches' had been prepared for the travellers. Here Wilde broke down, but this did not prevent him from continuing to talk until nine o'clock, when Ross insisted on going to his room for some rest.

While the others were resting, Wilde went to his own room and wrote a note to Mrs Leverson. The style was quite like the old Wilde, especially the characteristic postscript.[2]

Hotel Sandwich,
Dieppe.

Dear Sphinx,

I was so charmed with seeing you yesterday morning that I must write a line to tell you how sweet and good it was of you to be the very first to greet me. When I think that Sphinxes are minions of the morn and that you got up early before dawn, I am filled with wonder and joy.

I often thought of you in the long black days and nights of my sad life, and to find you just as wonderful and dear as ever was so surprise; the beautiful are always beautiful.

It is my first day of real liberty, so I try to send you a line.

Ever affectionately yours,

OSCAR WILDE

I am stopping here as Sebastian Melmoth—not Esquire, but Monsieur Sebastian Melmoth.

Reggie Turner is staying here under the name 'Robert Ross'. Robbie under the name 'Reginald Turner'. It is better they should not use their own names.

[1] Reginald Turner to Christopher Millard, October 29, 1920: Clark MSS. (*Dulau Catalogue*, Item 53).

[2] Leverson, *op. cit.*, 62; H–D, 566.

The four men met again at midday for *déjeuner*, all of them exhausted except Wilde, according to Ross. In the afternoon they drove over to Arques-la-Bataille, and sat for a while on the ramparts of the old castle. Wilde enjoyed the trees and the grass and the country scents and sounds in a way Ross had never known him do before, just as a city-bred child might enjoy his first day in the country. Ross remembered afterwards that he had a characteristic adjective for everything, such as 'monstrous', 'purple', 'grotesque', 'gorgeous', 'curious' and 'wonderful'.[1] During that day and for many days afterwards he talked principally of Reading Prison and his experiences there. According to Ross, it had already become for him a sort of enchanted castle of which Major Nelson was the presiding fairy; the prison's machicolated turrets were turned into minarets, the very warders were benevolent mamelukes, and his three companions were Paladins reclaiming him after his captivity. He mentioned the various warders by name and of each one of them he had a good story to tell.

On this particular afternoon Ross remembered asking him if he had met any Freemasons in prison, since he knew that Wilde belonged to the brotherhood. Ross, who was a particularly devout Catholic convert, had a great prejudice against the craft, particularly English Freemasonry, but he was bound to admit that Wilde rose to the occasion. 'Yes, it was very terrible,' he replied. 'As I was walking round the yard one day, I noticed that one of the men awaiting trial was signalling to me by masonic signs. I paid no attention until he made me the sign of the widow's son, which no Mason can ignore. I found he was in on a charge of fraud of some kind and was anxious that I should get all my friends to petition for his release. He was quite mad, poor fellow. As he *would* carry on signalling, and I was afraid the warders would get to notice it, I persuaded Major Nelson to let me wear black goggles until he was convicted and sent to Portland.'[2]

[1] *A propos* of this excursion Robert Ross wrote in the unfinished draft Preface to the edition of Wilde's letters, which he had planned: 'It was natural to Wilde to be artificial, as I have often said, and that is why he was suspected of insincerity. I mean when he wrote of serious things, of art, ethics or religion, of pain or of pleasure. Wilde in love of the beautiful was perfectly perhaps too sincere, and not the least of his errors was a suspicion of simple terms. Simplicity is one of the objections he urged against prisons.'

[2] Ross, *op. cit.* See also Sherard, *The Real Oscar Wilde* (at pp. 140–2) for a fuller account of this incident. Wilde became a Freemason in 1876, when he was an undergraduate at Oxford.

At Wilde's request Adey wrote to Major Nelson to let him know of their safe arrival in France and from the Governor he received by return of post this kindly reply.[1]

The Governor's House,
H.M. Prison,
Reading.

22.5.97.

Dear Sir,

It was very kind and thoughtful of Mr. Wilde to let me know through you that all was well and that he had gone abroad without any difficulties or bothers. I only hope he will soon be himself again and feel sure that the new scenes and the new feeling of peace and quietude will work wonders. Please thank him for me and tell him that I shall be only too glad to hear from him when he feels equal to writing a letter.

Again thanking you for your kindness in letting me know that all has gone off so well, and trusting that Mr. Wilde will be restored to health both physically and mentally by leaps and bounds.

Believe me,
Yours truly,
J. O. NELSON

Wilde and his friends made several other excursions through the surrounding countryside and along the coast, partly with the object of finding a quiet little hotel where Wilde could settle. Wilde and Turner usually drove while Adey and Ross, who had hired bicycles, rode behind. Ross did his best to persuade Wilde to take to a bicycle, but the experiment was not a success. As Wilde had occasion later to remind Ross, 'even my leg remembers it'. Eventually they discovered the Hotel de la Plage at Berneval-sur-mer, a few miles from Dieppe, and Wilde arranged to move in there.

Lugné-Poë, who had produced *Salomé* in Paris while Wilde was in prison, came through Dieppe on his way to London for a visit, and he breakfasted with Wilde, Ross and Turner. Wilde was 'quite charmed with him'; he had had no idea he was so young or so handsome, having expected 'a *maladif* edition of the great poet whom America put to death on a clearly proved charge of having written poems entirely composed of those three wonderful things, Romance, Music and Sorrow'.[2] However, one aspect of this meeting troubled Wilde. The young

[1] Clark MSS. [2] Walt Whitman.

French actor-manager had been asked by a newspaper to record his impression of the newly released prisoner. 'I earnestly impressed on him the importance of writing no interview, and giving no details of my strange name, my place of sojourn, my altered appearance, and the like', wrote Wilde after Lugné-Poë had departed: 'but I know how tempted people are to write for their own pleasure about others, thoughtlessly and without care. . . . What I want him to say is how grateful I was and am to France for their recognition of me as an artist in the day of my humiliation, and how my better treatment in an English prison was due to the French men of letters.'[1]

After about a week Adey and Turner went back to London, while Ross remained a few days longer to see Wilde settled in at Berneval. On May 27, Wilde wrote to Turner from the Hotel de la Plage: 'This is my first day here. Robbie and I arrived last night: the dinner was excellent, and we tried to eat enough for eight as we occupy so many rooms. However, we soon got tired. Only the imagination of man is limitless. The appetite seems curiously bounded. This is one of the many lessons I have learnt.'[2]

For the time being Wilde was tolerably contented, although he quickly realised what he called his 'terrible position of isolation' as soon as Ross had left him. Any momentary feelings of annoyance he had felt with Adey and Ross had now disappeared, nor did he nourish any other hard feelings by reason of his imprisonment. 'You will be pleased to know that I have not come out of prison an embittered or disappointed man', he told the artist, William Rothenstein, at this time. 'On the contrary. In many ways I have gained much. I am not really ashamed of having been in prison: I often was in more shameful places: but I *am* really ashamed of having led a life unworthy of an artist. I don't say that Messalina is a better companion than Sporus, or that the one is all right and the other all wrong: I know simply that a life of studied materialism, and a philosophy of appetite and cynicism, and a cult of sensual and senseless ease, are bad things for an artist: they narrow the imagination, and full the more delicate susceptibilities. I was all wrong, my dear boy, in my life. I was not getting the best out of me. *Now*, I think that with good health and the friendship of a few

[1] Wilde to Adey, May 25, 1897: Clark MSS; H–D, 567.
[2] Turner MSS; H–D, 575.

good, simple nice fellows like yourself, and a quiet mode of living, with isolation for thought, and freedom from the endless hunger for pleasures that wreck the body and imprison the soul—well, I think I may do things yet that you may all like.'[1]

4

'I hope to write about prison life and to try and change it for others, but it is too terrible and ugly to make a work of art of. I have suffered too much in it to write plays about it.' Wilde put these words in one of the surreptitious notes which he sent Warder Martin. Little did he think when he scribbled them that his first opportunity of writing about prison life would be provided by the treatment accorded to the friendly warder by the prison authorities. Before leaving Dieppe for Berneval Wilde learned, to his great regret, through the columns of the *Daily Chronicle*, that Martin had been dismissed from the prison service, as we have already seen, 'for having given some sweet biscuits to a little hungry child'. The matter had also reached the ears of Michael Davitt, the Irish Nationalist M.P., who had himself suffered harsh prison experiences; he immediately tabled two questions to the Home Secretary in the House of Commons, asking him to confirm the circumstances of Martin's dismissal, 'whether, in case the giving of the food in the manner mentioned was the only breach of discipline committed by the warder, he will reconsider the penalty inflicted on the erring officer'. However, Sir Mathew Ridley refused to enter into any details beyond stating that 'the dismissal of this warder was a proper one'.[2]

As soon as he read the news of Martin's dismissal, Wilde decided to write a strongly worded letter of protest to the *Daily Chronicle*, which he felt to be the most likely newspaper to publish it. Ross and his other friends seem to have had some doubts as to the wisdom of this course, since they may have thought it better, in the circumstances, for Wilde to keep out of the news. However, Wilde laughed their objections aside and wrote the letter during the first few days he spent in Dieppe with his friends. Besides describing the plight of children in prison in the light of Martin's action, Wilde also drew atten-

[1] John Rothenstein. *Sixteen Letters from Oscar Wilde* (1930), p. 24; H–D, 604.
[2] Hansard, *Parliamentary Debates*, 4th series, Vol. XLIX, cols. 1266–7, 1419.

tion to the repeated punishment of the mentally backward soldier, Prince, whom the Visiting Justices had again ordered to be flogged. The letter, which has been reproduced in substance in the preceding pages, came out in the *Daily Chronicle* on May 28, occupying three columns under the heading THE CASE OF WARDER MARTIN, SOME CRUELTIES OF PRISON LIFE. It caused quite a sensation, since it appeared over Wilde's signature. When he saw it Robert Ross sent Wilde a congratulatory telegram. This pleased him considerably. 'Don't you see how right I was to write to the *Chronicle*?' Wilde replied. 'All good impulses are right. Had I listened to some of my friends I should never have written.'[1]

Wilde purposely delayed writing to the Governor of Reading until he had got his *Daily Chronicle* letter out of the way, as he considered that to do otherwise might embarrass Major Nelson. Fortunately the text of this fine letter to the Governor has been preserved.[2]

Hotel de la Plage,
Berneval-sur-Mer,
près de Dieppe.

Dear Major Nelson,

I had of course intended to write to you as soon as I had safely reached French soil, to express, however inadequately, my real feelings of what you must let me term, not merely sincere, but *affectionate* gratitude to you for your kindness and gentleness to me in prison, and for the real care that you took of me at the end, when I was mentally upset and in a state of very terrible nervous excitement. You must not mind my using the word 'gratitude'. I used to think gratitude a burden to carry. Now I know that it is something that makes the heart lighter. The ungrateful man is one who walks slowly with feet and heart of lead. But when one knows the strange joy of gratitude to God and man the earth becomes lovelier to one, and it is a pleasure to count up, not one's wealth but one's debts, not the little that one possesses, but the much that one owes.

I abstained from writing, however, because I was haunted by the memory of the little children, and the wretched half witted lad who was flogged by the doctor's orders. I could not have kept them out of my letter, and to have mentioned them to you might have put *you* in a difficult position. In your reply you *might* have expressed

[1] *After Reading*, 14.
[2] H–D, 580. The original is in the Berg Collection in the New York City Public Library.

sympathy with my views—I think you would have—and then on the appearance of my public letter you might have felt as if I had, in some almost ungenerous or thoughtless ways procured your private opinion on official things, for use as corroboration.

I longed to speak to you about these things on the evening of my departure, but I felt that in my position as a prisoner it would have been wrong of me to do so, and that it would, or might have put you in a difficult position afterwards, as well as at the time. I only heard of my letter being published by a telegraph from Mr. Ross, but I hope they have printed it in full, as I tried to express in it my appreciation and admiration of your own humane spirit and affectionate interest in *all* the prisoners under your charge. I did not wish people to think that an exception had been specially made for me. Such exceptional treatment as I received was by order of the Commissioners. You gave me the same kindness as you gave to everyone. Of course, I made more demands, but then I think I had really more needs than others—and I lacked often their cheerfulness acquiescence.

Of course I side with the prisoners—I was one, and I belong to their class now—I am not a scrap ashamed of having been in prison. I am honestly ashamed of the materialism of the life that brought me there. It was quite unworthy of an artist.

Of Martin, and the subjects of my letter I of course say nothing at all, except that the man who could change the system—if any one man can do so—is yourself. At present I wrote to ask you to allow me to sign myself, once at any rate in life, your sincere and grateful friend

OSCAR WILDE

My name here is *Mons. Sebastian Melmoth*

Shortly afterwards Martin wrote to Wilde asking if he could help him to get work. In his reply, in which he enclosed £5 10*s*., Wilde had the pleasure of rebuking one by whom, though a friend, he had been rebuked at Reading. 'I must begin by scolding you thoroughly for a piece of carelessness on your part', wrote Wilde. 'I told you I had changed my name, and wrote out most carefully for you my new name and address—in spite of this you write to me on the envelope as "Oscar Wilde, Esqre., care of Sebastian Melmoth". Now this was silly of you. I changed my name so as not to be bothered, and then you must go and write to me as Oscar Wilde. You must be careful and thoughtful about things. Just as much trouble is caused by carelessness as by crime, my friend.' Naturally

Wilde promised to do his best for him to secure a post. 'I have spoken highly of your character and intellect', he added. 'Let me beg of you to deserve all I have said of you. You have, I think, a good chance of a good place, so you must be as sound and straightforward and as good a fellow as possible.'[1]

Wilde also remembered his particular friends among his fellow-prisoners and other warders at Reading, as the dates of their release approached. He wrote to ten of them, sending the letters to Ross with a request to enclose, from his own money, small sums varying from £1 to £1 10*s*. 'They are my debts of honour, and I must pay them', he wrote. 'Of course it is a great deal, but I thought I would have lots . . . How it mounts up!'[2] (The total sum was £22 10*s*.) By a happy chance the text of one of these letters has been preserved.[3] It is a charming letter and an excellent illustration of Wilde's friendly, kind-hearted and generous nature.

c/o Stoker and Hansell,
14 *Grays Inn Square,*
W.C.

My dear Friend,

I send you a line to show you that I haven't forgotten you. We were old friends in gallery C.3., were we not? I hope you are getting on well and in employment.

Don't like a good little chap, get into trouble again. You would get a terrible sentence. I send you £2 just for luck. I am quite poor myself now, but I know you will accept it just as a remembrance. There is also 10s. which I wish you would give to a little

[1] Sherard, *Life*, 405. Martin remained without work for some time. In February, 1898, Wilde's *Daily Chronicle* letter was republished by Murdoch & Co., 26 Paternoster Square, London, under the title *Children in Prison and other Cruelties of Prison Life*. In a prefatory note the publishers stated: 'This pamphlet is tendered to earnest persons as evidence that the prison system is opposed to all that is kind and helpful. Herein is shown a process that is dehumanizing, not only to the prisoners, but to everyone connected with it. Martin was dismissed. It happened in May last year. He is still out of employment and in poor circumstances. Can anyone help him?' Martin eventually rejoined the army and fought in the South African War. For a while after the war he lived by journalism. He subsequently entered the Poor Law service and was employed as a porter at Fulham Workhouse and later as a male nurse in Norwich. A newspaper interview, which he gave while recovering from a serious illness in the Norwich Workhouse Infirmary, shortly before the last war, was published in the *Sunday Dispatch*, February 12, 1939. He died eleven months later in Norwich, aged seventy-three. He was unmarried. See further below, Appendix E.

[2] *After Reading*, 12; H–D, 578.

[3] *Reading Standard*, July 2, 1897. The publication of this letter was due to the fact that its recipient, in an endeavour to trace the other ex-prisoner mentioned in it, handed it to the local agent of the Discharged Prisoners Aid Society, who showed it to a reporter and allowed him to take a copy.

dark eyed chap who had a month in, I think—C.4.14. He was in from February 6th to March 6th—a little chap from Wantage, I think, and a jolly little fellow. We were great friends. If you know him, give it to him from C.3.3.

I am in France, by the sea, and I suppose I am getting happy again. I hope so. It was a bad time for me, but there were many good fellows in Reading. Send me a line c/o my solicitors to my own name.

Your friend,

C. 3. 3.

One of the released prisoners, to whom Wilde also sent £2, was a soldier named Arthur Cruttenden. His letter of thanks so touched Wilde that he invited him to spend a week as his guest at Berneval. 'Now I have asked him to come and stay a week here with me, so that he may have a holiday after eighteen months hard labour', Wilde wrote to Turner. 'His offence . . . He was a soldier, dined too well, or perhaps badly, and "made hay" in the harness room of the regimental stables: the sort of thing one was "gated" for at Oxford, or fined £5 by the Proctor. He has never taken anything by fraud or violence. He is a good chap, and he has a nice sweet nature. I had better say candidly that he is not a "beautiful boy". He is 29 years of age, but looks a little older, as he inherits hair that catches silver lights early, he has also a slight, but still *real* mustache. I am thankful and happy to say that I have no feeling for him, nor could have other than affection and friendship. He is simply a manly simple fellow, with the nicest smile and the pleasantest eyes, and I have no doubt a confirmed "mulierast" to use Robbie's immortal phrase. . . . He is not English, he is American, but has no accent at all. He always wrapped up well at night in his native land.'[1]

The purpose of this testimonial was to persuade Turner to advance £6 10*s*. to enable the young ex-soldier to buy some clothes and also his ticket to Dieppe. 'Next week you shall have the £6.10s', Wilde reassured his friend. 'I simply dare not tell Robbie to give it, because he scolds me, and I hate giving him pain. I know he is right . . . he is very severe on me for having sent some money to four chaps released last week —he says I can't afford it. But, dear Reggie, I must look after my prison friends, if my good friends like you look after me

[1] Wilde to Turner, June, 1897: Turner MSS; H–D, 600.

. . . if you will manage to do all this for me and A[rthur] C[ruttenden], you will, in some other way than the repayment of £6.10s next week, reap a harvest of deep gold in the heart of the great world. I know it. I have been taught it in Cell C.3.3.'

Needless to state, Turner could not remain unmoved by this appeal. He saw the soldier and advanced the money, but at the same time, like Ross, he lectured Wilde on indulging in expenditure which he could ill afford. But Wilde was undeterred. 'Of course, all you said to me, dear Reggie, is quite true', he wrote back: 'but you must understand that I have the deepest desire to try and be of a little help to the other fellows who were in trouble with me. . . . Now I feel that, if I can really help others, it will be a little attempt, however small, at expiation. To be of real assistance to even one of them would give me a joy beyond what I could express to you.'

The ex-soldier duly arrived at Berneval, and his visit proved a success. To Wilde's surprise he turned out to be quite a good musician, being a practised singer and songwriter. Wilde found him 'gentle and unassuming and grateful' and sent him back to England with a letter to Turner. 'I am going to try to help him, through a friend of mine, to re-enter his business', wrote Wilde: 'he was brought up as a saddler, and did very well while his father was alive. He will tell you his prospects. Of course I don't know if I shall be able to get him any start, but I can only try.'[1]

The friend, through whose good offices Wilde hoped to help Cruttenden, may have been Frank Harris, with whom he had now made things up. He had already written to Harris about another ex-soldier, who had been released at the beginning of June. 'If you can give him a trial, do so', wrote Wilde. 'If you see your way to this kind action and write to him to come and see you, kindly state in your letter that it is about a situation. He may think otherwise that it is about the flogging of A.2.11, a thing that does not interest *you*, and about which *he* is a little afraid to talk . . . All soldiers are neat, and smart, and make capital servants. He would be a good *groom*, he is, I believe, a 3rd Hussars man—he was a quiet well-conducted chap in Reading always.'[2]

After the success of his letter to the *Daily Chronicle*, Wilde

[1] Wilde to Turner, July 16, 1897: Turner MSS; H–D, 611. [2] Harris. II, 582.

considered writing an article or a series of articles on his prison experiences. In this apparently he intended to incorporate some parts of the portion of his long letter to Alfred Douglas, which was subsequently published by Robert Ross as *De Profundis*. He thought of sending them to the *Daily Chronicle*, and he wrote to the editor. 'It is interested in prison reform,' he told Ross, 'and the thing would not look like an advertisement . . . Of course much will be psychological and introspective, and one will be on Christ as the Precursor of the Romantic Movement in Life, that lovely subject which was revealed to me when I found myself in the company of the same sort of people that *Christ* liked, outcasts and beggars.' On June 3, Wilde wrote to Ross: 'I think the *Chronicle* people are nervous. They have not yet answered on anything. Of course with them I am all right, if they take my work.'[1] Although nothing seems to have come of these suggestions, later on the newspaper in question did publish a powerful letter from Wilde on the subject of prison reform, which had been inspired by the introduction of the Prison Bill in the House of Commons.

This measure embodied most of the recommendations of the Departmental Committee on Prisons, which had reported in 1895, such as the abolition of the treadmill and crank and the power to earn remissions of sentence. Wilde's letter appeared in the *Daily Chronicle* on March 24, 1898, under the heading DON'T READ THIS IF YOU WANT TO BE HAPPY TODAY and it was signed '*The Author of The Ballad of Reading Gaol*'. Wilde began by stating that he had learned that the chief reform proposed was an increase in the number of prison inspectors and official visitors. He continued:

> Such a reform as this is entirely useless. The reason is extremely simple. The inspectors and justices of the peace that visit prisons come here for the purpose of seeing that the prison regulations are duly carried out. They come for no other purpose, nor have they any power, even if they had the desire, to alter a single clause in the regulations. No prisoner has ever had the smallest relief, or attention, or care from any of the official visitors. The visitors arrive not to help the prisoners, but to see that the rules are carried out. Their object in coming is to ensure the enforcement of a foolish and inhuman code. And, as they must have some occupation, they take very good care to do it. A prisoner who has been

[1] *After Reading*, 11, 14, 28.

allowed the smallest privilege dreads the arrival of the inspectors. And on the day of any prison inspection the prison officials are more than usually brutal to the prisoners. Their object is, of course, to show the splendid discipline they maintain.

Wilde went on to describe the defects of the present system, as he had experienced them, the poor and inadequate food, the dreadful sanitary arrangements, the absence of proper ventilation in the cells, the iniquitous plank bed and its resultant insomnia, the bad mental effects of solitary confinement, the lack of good books in the prison library, the humiliating conditions in which prisoners could see visitors, and the hardship of being able to work and receive letters only four times a year, which in any event were liable to censorship by the Governor. He also discussed the shortcomings of the average prison chaplain and prison doctor, and showed how he thought improvements could be made generally. These remarks have already been quoted extensively in this book.

'I have tried to indicate in my letter a few of the reforms necessary to our English prison system', Wilde concluded. 'They are simple, practical, and humane. They are, of course, only a beginning. But it is time that a beginning should be made, and it can only be started by a strong pressure of public opinion formularised in your powerful paper, and fostered by it. But to make even these reforms effectual, much has to be done. And the first, and perhaps the most difficult task is to humanise the governors of prisons, to civilise the warders and Christianise the chaplains.'[1]

[1] This letter was republished, together with the letter on the dismissal of Warder Martin from Reading, in the 1908 edition of *De Profundis* and has been included in most subsequent editions of this work.

CHAPTER VII

'The Ballad of Reading Gaol'

1

THE idea of *The Ballad of Reading Gaol* came to Wilde when he was in prison. As we have seen, it was suggested by the execution of a guardsman which took place at Reading in July, 1896. 'The prison style is absolutely and entirely wrong', he wrote in *De Profundis*. 'I would give anything to be able to alter it when I go out. I intend to try.' He began the poem immediately after his friends had left him in Berneval to return to England. He had been reading *A Shropshire Lad* by A. E. Housman, and to some extent the metre he adopted, as well as the subject, was inspired by Housman's poem. On June 1, he wrote to Ross: 'I have begun something that I think will be very good.'[1] A few days later, in order to secure quiet for his work he made up his mind to move into a nearby house, the Chalet Bourgeat, which happened to be vacant, and which had a large writing-room, though he continued to take his meals at the Hotel de la Plage. 'Don't be nervous', he reassured Ross, who was worried about the expense. 'I have many irons and a huge fire. But to work I must be isolated. . . . Overhead here is a lady with two children—perfect darlings—and their racket is appalling. There is no peace except in one's own home.' Accordingly he took the chalet and set to work. Here the first draft of the ballad was completed in about six weeks. 'The poem is nearly finished', he wrote to Ross on July 20. 'Some of the verses are awfully good.'[2] But at other moments he had doubts. He read some of the verses to the young American poet, Vincent O'Sullivan, who happened to be on a visit to Dieppe.[3] His hearer noted that he did so with great modesty

[1] *After Reading*, 24. [2] *After Reading*, 32, 37, 48.

[3] Vincent O'Sullivan was a Catholic writer of Irish descent, who was born in New York in 1872, and spent most of his life in France. As a young man just down from Oxford, he contributed to *The Yellow Book* and *The Savoy*. His most successful work was a novel, *The Good Girl*, which appeared in 1912. He saw a good

and hesitation, which seemed to O'Sullivan quite extraordinary for a person of his intellectual position in relation to a young man who had yet to make his way as a writer. 'I feel quite sure you won't like it,' said Wilde at the time. 'I am not sure that I like it myself. But catastrophes in life bring about catastrophes in art.'[1]

The question now arose, how to find a publisher for the poem? John Lane, who had published more of Wilde's writings than any other publisher, had struck his name out of the firm's list after his downfall. No other reputable publisher could be expected to touch anything of Wilde's after what had happened; the risk of injury to his business, if he did so, would be too great. According to Vincent O'Sullivan, it was Robert Ross, who now thought of Leonard Smithers.[2] During the course of the summer this amazing Yorkshireman paid several visits to Dieppe in the company of Aubrey Beardsley and Vincent O'Sullivan, with whom Smithers had become friendly as publisher of the shortlived but brilliant periodical, *The Savoy*, which was illustrated by Beardsley and to which O'Sullivan contributed. On July 26, Wilde wrote to Ross: 'I saw Aubrey at Dieppe. . . . Smithers, the publisher, was with him: very intoxicated but amusing.'[3]

Leonard Smithers, at this date in his middle thirties, was one of the most extraordinary men who has ever ventured into the world of publishing. He originally came from Sheffield, where he had been admitted a solicitor. He already knew Wilde, since as a young practitioner of twenty-six in Sheffield he had written to the author congratulating him on the publication of *The Happy Prince*, which had first appeared in 1888. An amiable reply from Wilde had led to their becoming acquainted, when Smithers migrated to London a few years later.[4]

In London Smithers had gradually dropped the law for printing, publishing and bookselling. His methods were daring and unorthodox. 'I'll publish anything that the others are afraid of,' he said to Vincent O'Sullivan on the occasion of their first meeting. For this reason he refused to advertise and hardly

deal of Wilde during the latter's last years on the Continent and wrote a sympathetic and revealing study of him in this final phase of his life: *Aspects of Wilde* (1936). He died during the German occupation of France in the last war.

[1] O'Sullivan. *Aspects of Wilde*, 97. [2] Ibid., 125. [3] *After Reading*, 53.

[4] H–D, 221. A facsimile of Wilde's reply has been published by Sherard in *The Real Oscar Wilde*, at p. 344. Wilde afterwards gave Smithers the MS of *The Happy Prince*.

ever sent out review copies to the Press. Nevertheless some finely produced books had issued from his offices in the Royal Arcade, off Bond Street, including works of poets like Ernest Dowson and Vincent O'Sullivan and artists like Beardsley, Conder and Max Beerbohm. He also ran a more or less surreptitious business in retailing pornography. There is a story that the widow of a famous High Court judge, finding after his death a large library of erotic books, sent for Smithers to 'take them away', which the obliging bookseller quickly did, having already sold most of them to his late Lordship at a handsome profit. Women were said to be irresistible to Smithers, although those who succumbed to his charms must have been mostly of the *demi-mondaine* class. He was also noticeably fond of the absinthe bottle. 'Since I last wrote to you I have neglected absinthe, and have drunk whiskey and water,' he wrote to Wilde in one of his letters, 'but I have distinctly seen the error of my ways and have gone back to absinthe.'[1] Indeed a combination of drink and drugs eventually killed him. But in the days of his success, he seems to have been a genial and generous friend, who on the whole treated his authors and artists well.[2]

'I do not know if you know Smithers', wrote Wilde to Reggie Turner at this time. 'He is usually in a large straw hat, has a blue tie delicately fastened with a diamond brooch of the impurest water, or perhaps wine, as he never touches water—it goes to his head at once. His face, clean shaven as befits a priest who serves at the altar whose God is literature, is wasted and pale, not with poetry, but with poets, who, he says, have wrecked his life by insisting on publishing with him. He loves first editions, especially of women—little girls are his passion—he is the most learned erotomaniac in Europe. He is also a delightful companion, and a dear fellow, very kind to me.'[3]

Smithers had just sent Wilde a parcel of books, for which Wilde was most grateful. 'How nice it is of you to give them to me', wrote Wilde to the publisher on August 4. 'I hope very much that some day I shall have something that you will

[1] Mason, 416.

[2] Further details about Leonard Charles Smithers (1862–1907) will be found in Vincent O'Sullivan, *Aspects of Wilde* (1936), *Letters from Aubrey Beardsley to Leonard Smithers*, edited by R. A. Walker (1937), and the autobiography of his son, *The Early Life and Vicissitudes of Jack Smithers* (1939).

[3] Wilde to Turner, August 10, 1897: Turner MSS. On the following day Wilde wrote to Turner: 'By my elaborate description of Smithers you are certain not to recognise him.' H–D, 630, 631.

like well enough to publish.' Smithers's chance came about a fortnight later when he was in Dieppe. Wilde mentioned his poem, and in an expansive moment Smithers offered to publish it and to give Wilde the whole profits. 'This offer, I may say, was made before, not after dinner, at the Café Tribunaux', wrote Wilde, recalling the incident afterwards. 'I said I would not agree to it, as I did not think it fair . . . but that I would take half the profits. This was agreed to.'[1]

On August 24 Wilde wrote to Ross from Berneval:

> My poem is still unfinished, but I have made up my mind to finish it this afternoon, and send it to be type-written. Once I see it —even type-written—I shall be able to correct it: *now* I am tired of the MS.
>
> Do you think this verse good? I fear it is out of harmony, but wish you were here to talk about it . . .
>
> The Governor was strong upon
> The Regulation Act,
> The Doctor said that Death was but
> A scientific fact;
> And twice a day the Chaplain called
> And left a little tract.
>
> It is, of course, about the condemned man's life before his execution.[2] I have got in "latrine"—it looks beautiful.[3]

On the same day Wilde sent Smithers the first draft in manuscript with a request to have it typewritten for him. 'I want it done on good brown paper—*not* tissue paper—and bound in a brown paper cover', wrote Wilde in his covering letter. 'It is not yet finished, but I want to see it typewritten. I am sick of my MS.' The manuscript was returned to the author, with the typed copy, ten days later.[4] 'I yesterday sent you back your

[1] *Sale Catalogue of Library of Richard Butler Glaenzer* (New York, 1911), pp. 33–4; Mason, *Bibliography of Oscar Wilde*, 411.

[2] In a note to Smithers, he similarly defended this and the other five opening stanzas in Part III: 'I think this is necessary on the grounds of narrative. And the standard by which the poem is to be judged is not that of lyrical beauty, but of realistic presentation and actuality at least by a sane critic, if there is one outside Bedlam': *Catalogue of the Library of Jerome Kern* (New York, 1929), II, 460.

[3] *After Reading*, 55. The allusion is to Part V, Stanza 7, see above, p. 7.

[4] The whereabouts of the MS. are unknown. It was probably stolen from the villa at Posilippo, where Wilde stayed with Alfred Douglas later the same year (see below, p. 162), and has never been traced. Some additional stanzas in Wilde's handwriting, however, have passed through the sale room from time to time. For instance, a portion of Part III was put up for auction in the Haber Sale in New York in 1909 and realised $100. This increased to $600 at the Stetson Sale. The first six stanzas from Part III and the thirteenth stanza from Part I, together with

poem', Smithers wrote to Wilde on September 2. 'I showed it to Aubrey [Beardsley] and he seemed to be much struck by it. He promised at once to do a frontispiece for it—in a manner which immediately convinced me he will never do it. He has got tired already of *Mlle de Maupin* and talks of *Casanova* instead. It seemes hopeless to try and get any connected work out of him of any kind.'[1]

During the ten days that the MS of the first draft of *The Ballad* was being typed, Wilde came to a fateful and unfortunate decision for himself. He had begun to feel very lonely at Berneval, he was tired of his Dieppe admirers, and was out of patience with his wife who for one reason or another had put off seeing him. Meanwhile he had been in touch with Alfred Douglas. They had narrowly missed meeting at Berneval in June when Douglas was on the point of coming to stay at the Chalet Bourgeat and was put off at the last moment by Wilde, who had just received a letter from his solicitor, repeating his previous warnings of the danger of such a visit. At that time, too, apparently Queensberry had dispatched a private detective to Berneval to report on Wilde's movements and visitors. Wilde now planned to meet his friend clandestinely at some spot between Dieppe and Paris, where Douglas was staying. By a coincidence—for there is no evidence that Constance knew anything of his intention—she wrote to him too late, saying that she would see him, as she had then got their children 'out of the way'. Wilde was so irritated at what he considered his wife's 'extraordinary want of tact', that contrary to the advice

a note about the former from Wilde to Smithers, fetched $1600 at the Kern Sale in 1929: see *Kern Sale Catalogue, loc. cit.* The MS. of the last stanza of Part IV, the first two stanzas of Part V, and an unused stanza are reproduced by Stuart Mason in his *Bibliography of Oscar Wilde* (1914), at p. 416.

[1] Mason, 410. At this time Beardsley was in an advanced state of tuberculosis and had only a few months to live. He died on March 16, 1898, aged twenty-six. Although he had provided the illustrations for Wilde's *Salomé*, he had never cared very much for the author and indeed latterly turned against him, avoiding him in Dieppe and only consenting to edit a new magazine called *The Peacock*, which Smithers contemplated bringing out, 'if it is quite agreed that Oscar Wilde contributes nothing to the magazine, anonymously, pseudonymously or otherwise': see *Letters from Aubrey Beardsley to Leonard Smithers*, 174. Wilde, as was his wont, bore no ill-will. 'It was *lâche* of Aubrey' was his only comment on the Dieppe incident: O'Sullivan, *op. cit.*, 87. On Beardsley's death Wilde wrote to Smithers (March 18, 1898): 'I was greatly shocked to hear of poor Aubrey's death. Superbly premature as the flowering of his genius was, still he had immense development and had not sounded his last stop. There were great possibilities always in the cavern of his soul and there is something macabre and tragic in the fact that one who added another tenor to life should have died at the age of a flower': Clark MSS; H–D, 719.

given him by Ross and other friends he refused to go to her, writing to the effect that he was 'utterly lonely, treated like a pariah and worn out with her perpetual procrastination, and was therefore going to live with the only person ready to give him his companionship', namely, Alfred Douglas.[1]

Wilde set out to meet his friend at Rouen on September 4. Half an hour before he left he scribbled a note to Ross. 'I have not yet finished my poem!' he wrote. 'I have got in about the kiss of Caiaphas: it is very good.'[2] The reunion in Rouen was conclusive. Wilde cried at the station when Douglas met him, and they 'walked about all day, arm in arm, or hand in hand, and were perfectly happy'.[3] Wilde returned to Berneval next day to pack his bags and prepared to join Douglas *en route* from Paris to Naples. Before he left he was writing to Douglas in the old adoring strain. 'I feel that my only hope of again doing beautiful work in Art is being with you. It was not so in the old days, but now it is different, and you can really re-create in me that energy and sense of joyous power on which Art depends. Everyone is furious with me for going back to you, but they don't understand us. I feel that it is only with you that I can do anything at all. Do remake my ruined life for me, and then our friendship and love will have a different meaning to the world. I wish that when we met at Rouen we had not parted at all.'[4]

At Naples they were to spend most of the next two months together. 'I love him and have always loved him', Wilde wrote to Turner shortly after his arrival. 'He ruined my life, and for that reason I seemed forced to love him more: and I think that now I shall do some lovely work. Bosie is himself a poet, far the best of all the young poets of England, an exquisite artist in lyric and ballad. It is to a poet that I am going back. So

[1] More Adey to Miss A. Schuster, March 12, 1898. (Communicated by Mr G. F. Sims.)

[2] *After Reading*, 56. The reference is to the part played by the prison chaplain at the execution:

He does not stare upon the air
  Through a little roof of glass:
He does not pray with lips of clay
  For his agony to pass;
Nor feel upon his shuddering cheek
  The kiss of Caiaphas.

[3] Douglas, *Autobiography* (2nd edition), 152.

[4] A. C. Dennison and H. Post. *Some Letters from Oscar Wilde to Lord Alfred Douglas* (1924), xxxiv; H–D, 637.

when people say how dreadful of me to return to Bosie, do say *No*. Say that I love him, that he is a poet, and that, after all, whatever my life may have been ethically, it has always been *romantic*—and Bosie is my romance. My romance is a tragedy of course, but it is none the less a romance—and he loves me very dearly, more than he loves or can love anyone else, and without him my life was dreary.'[1]

After about a fortnight in the Hotel Royal et des Etrangers at Naples, where they ran up a bill of £68, the two friends moved into a furnished villa at Posilippo. It was called the Villa Giudice and was charmingly situated, overlooking the Bay of Naples, with a terrace and marble steps leading down to the sea. ('The French papers describe me as living broken down in health, in the lovely villa of the son of Lord Douglas!'[2]) There was, however, one initial disadvantage. The villa was infested with rats. These were eventually removed through the combined operation of an orthodox rat-catcher and a bearded old woman, who had the reputation of being the local witch: she came and 'burned odours' and muttered incantations which she assured the two friends that no rats could resist. Anyhow the rats disappeared, and the two friends were able to settle down to work.[3] Here Wilde completed *The Ballad*, while Douglas wrote several sonnets.

Wilde's letters to Ross, Turner and Smithers at this time, most of which have survived, enable us to follow the progress of *The Ballad* in its concluding stages. 'I think bits of the poem very good now', Wilde wrote from the villa on September 24, 'but I will never again out-Kipling Henley.'[4] However, money was fast running out at the villa, and at the beginning of October Wilde appealed to Smithers for an advance of £20 on account of future royalties.

> *Villa Giudice, Posilippo, Naples. Sunday* [*October* 3, 1897]. . . . I am not asking you for an ordinary loan of money at all. I am asking for a small advance on my poem which you are about to publish. . . .
>
> In case you have not grasped the idea that an advance of £20 on my poem is really a thing that I have a perfect right to expect on business grounds, pray do so at once. Application to you for a per-

[1] Wilde to Turner, September 23, 1897: Turner MSS; H–D, 648.
[2] Wilde to Turner, October 19: Turner MSS; H–D, 663.
[3] Douglas. *Autobiography*, 18.
[4] *After Berneval*, 12.

sonal loan may, and, I have no doubt will, follow later on, but up to the present time our relations have been merely the usual ones of poet and publisher, with the usual complete victory for the latter. . . .

I also—such is the generosity of my nature—send enclosed four more verses of great power and romantic-realistic suggestion, twenty-four lines in all, each worth a guinea in any of the market places for poetry. Will you kindly . . . insert them in Part II of the poem, after the sixth stanza, the one ending 'had such a sin to pay'? They come in there splendidly and improve Part II, as it was a little too short compared to the others.[1]

On the same day he wrote to Ross:

. . . I have just sent Smithers four more stanzas for insertion—one of them very good, in the romantic vein that you don't quite approve of, but on the whole it will, I think, make a balance to the poem. Here it is:—

It is sweet to dance to violins
When Life and Love are fair:
To dance to flutes, to dance to lutes,
Is delicate and rare:
But it is not sweet with nimble feet
To dance upon the air.

On the whole I like the poem now, except the second and third stanzas of Part III. I can't get that part right.[2]

At Wilde's request, Smithers had sent Ross a typed copy of the first draft of the poem, which Ross now proceeded to criticise in a letter to Wilde. Although Wilde appreciated his friend's suggestions, in fact he declined to act on most of them. 'I don't think I can do much more with the poem', he wrote to Ross about this time. 'All your suggestions were very interesting, but of course, I have not taken them all. "Black dock's dreadful pen", for instance, is my own impression of the place in which I stood: it is burned into my memory.'[3]

[1] Mason. *Bibliography*, 411; H–D, 651. The additional stanzas begin with the line 'For oak and elm have pleasant leaves' and end with 'His sightless soul may stray'.

[2] *After Berneval*, 14.

[3] *After Berneval*, 26. Ross was even more critical of the verses, which were added at Posilippo. 'I do not know what you will think,' he later told Frank Harris, 'but to me they prove the mental decline due to the atmosphere and life that Wilde was leading at the time. Let us be just and say that perhaps Douglas assisted more than he was conscious of in their composition. To me they are terribly poor stuff, but then, unlike yourself, I am a heretic about *The Ballad*': Harris, II, 607. Vincent O'Sullivan shared this view: see O'Sullivan, *Aspects of Wilde*, 97. On the other hand, Douglas claimed that it was his influence, which persuaded Wilde to controvert many of Ross's criticisms. 'It is exceedingly lucky

Posilippo. Friday [*October* 8, 1897]. . . . With much of your criticism I agree. The poem suffers under the difficulty of a divided aim in style. Some is realistic, some is romantic: some poetry, some propaganda. I feel it keenly but, as a whole, I think the production is interesting: that it is interesting from more than one point of view is artistically to be regretted.

With regard to the adjectives, I admit there are far too many 'dreadfuls' and 'fearfuls': the difficulty is that the objects in prison have no shape or form. To take an example: the shed in which people are hanged is a little shed with a glass roof, like a photographer's studio on the sands at Margate: for eighteen months I thought it *was* the studio for photographing prisoners. There is no adjective to describe it. I call it 'hideous' because it became so to me after I knew its use.

A cell may be described psychologically with reference to its effect on the soul: in itself it can only be described as 'white-washed' or 'dimly lit'. It has no shape, no contents, it does not exist from the point of view of form or colour.

In point of fact, describing a prison is as difficult artistically as describing a water-closet would be. If one had to describe the latter in literature, prose or verse, one could say merely that it was well or badly papered, or clean or the reverse. The horror of prison is that everything is so simple and commonplace in itself, and so degrading and hideous and revolting in its effect.

October 19. . . You are quite right in saying the poem should end at 'Outcasts always mourn'—but the propaganda, which I desire to make begins there. I think I shall call the whole thing '*Poésie et Propagande*' or '*Dichtung und Wahrheit*'.[1]

On October 14 Wilde triumphantly announced to Reggie Turner: 'I have finished the great poem—600 lines now—I hope it will make a good effect. I like much of it myself—much is, I feel, for a harsher treatment than the languorous flute I love.' A few days later he told this same friend that Smithers was letting him have twelve free copies of the published version of *The Ballad*. 'Of course you are to have a presentation

that I happened to be with Wilde at the time he finished writing this fine poem (far the best thing he ever did in poetry), for otherwise he would certainly have succumbed to some of Ross's inept attacks on his best phrases. "The Black dock's dreadful pen" he defends against Ross, and he kept it in spite of Ross's efforts to make him change it. It is a fine phrase': Douglas, *Autobiography* (2nd ed.), 157.

[1] *After Berneval*, 16–18. Cf. Douglas, *loc. cit., supra*. 'The fact is that Ross was a poor critic, and if he had had his way he would have spoiled *The Ballad of Reading Gaol* which is the one entirely fine and sincere poem Wilde wrote, forgetting his "art for art's sake" heresies which Ross encouraged. It was I again who influenced him here. If the poem had ended at the point suggested by Ross it would have been a heavy loss to literature.'

copy, and Robbie and More. The rest are for the Governor, Chaplain, warders and prisoners of Reading Gaol.'

Two days later he told Turner that Smithers had sent the £20 he had asked for. 'With it we go to Capri for three days. I want to lay a few simple flowers on the grave of Tiberius. As the tomb is of someone else really, I shall do it with the deeper emotion.'[1]

2

While Wilde was waiting for proofs of his poem, there were various technical questions in connexion with the publication which had to be settled. These included the title, dedication, price, the number of copies to be printed in the first edition, the prospect of the poem being accepted in America, whether the work should appear with Wilde's name as the author, and the possibility of publishing first in a newspaper or periodical. The choice of the title, *The Ballad of Reading Gaol*, came from Robert Ross. The poem was dedicated to the memory of the executed soldier: an additional dedication to Ross was cancelled at Smithers's suggestion.[2] It was agreed that Wilde's cell number at Reading—C.3.3—and not his name should appear on the title page as that of the author. At one time Smithers wanted the price to be 3*s*. 6*d*., but Wilde thought this too high. 'As regards the ultimate shape', he wrote to Smithers, 'do consider seriously the impossibility of asking 3/6 for a meagre pamphlet. I think no one, except a damned and chosen few, would buy it. They would be content with reviews and pirated quotations.'[3] Smithers then talked of an edition of 600 copies at 2*s*. 6*d*. 'If the thing goes at all it should certainly sell 1,500 copies at that price', remarked the author. 'If, on the other hand, 500 is the probable sale, it should be five shillings. Smithers knows all about bad wine and bad women, but on books he is sadly to seek.'[4] Eventually the price was fixed at half-a-crown for the ordinary edition, of which Smithers undertook to print 800 copies. In addition, there was to be a small limited printing of thirty copies on Japanese vellum, price one guinea.

[1] Wilde to Turner, October 14, 16, 19: Turner MSS; H–D, 656, 658, 662.

[2] This read: 'When I came out of prison some met me with garments, and with spices and others with wise counsel. You met me with love.' See Mason, *Bibliography*, at p. 408.

[3] *Kern Sale Catalogue*, II, 461.

[4] *After Berneval*, 25.

As Smithers intimated that he had no objection to *The Ballad* first appearing in journal form, Wilde considered this idea as a means of raising more money. 'I now think it would be a mistake after all to publish the poem in a [daily] paper', he wrote to Smithers. 'It is too long for the *Chronicle*. . . . Frank Harris has been so offensive to me and about me that I do not think negotiations possible with him. . . . My idea is *Reynolds's*. . . . It circulates widely among the criminal classes—to which I now belong—so I shall be read by my peers—a new experience for me.'[1] He also thought of the *Sunday Sun*. 'Do you think T. P. O'Connor would publish it?' he asked Turner. 'If he did it would be a great thing—better, of course, then *Reynolds's*.'[2] Wilde put the matter in the hands of a well-known literary agent in London, whom he hoped could get him at least £300. But the agent had no success.

Wilde had also sent a copy to Miss Elizabeth Marbury, who in the days of his success had acted as his theatrical agent in America. Here again the initial outcome of this inquiry was not encouraging. 'I had no idea there were such barriers between me and publication in America', Wilde wrote to Ross on November 16. 'I thought it would romp in and secure me a good lump sum. It is curious how vanity helps the successful man and wrecks the failure. In old days half my strength was my vanity.'[3] On the same day he wrote to Smithers, to whom he had already applied for a further advance.[4]

Villa Giudice, Posilippo. Tuesday, 16th [November]. Do remember that what is comedy to you may be the reverse of comic to others.

Since I received your letter, in which you said 'I expect that before the arrival of this letter you will have received the £10,' I have been down twice *a day* to Naples to Cook's office, and have just returned from a third visit now—5.30. Of course there was nothing, and I am really so ashamed of my endless enquiries about a sum of £10 to be telegraphed from London.

Perhaps you only wrote what you did to give me hope. But, my dear fellow, hope constantly disappointed makes one's bread bitter —especially as I have just heard from *my own* solicitor to say that,

[1] *Glaenzer Sale Catalogue*, 24; Mason, 412; H–D, 663.
[2] Wilde to Turner, October 19: Turner MSS; H–D, 662. [3] *After Berneval*, 23.
[4] *The Yale University Library Gazette*, vol. 28, No. 2 (October, 1953), pp. 82, 84; H–D, 675. The originals of this letter and that of December 8, 1897, also quoted here, are in the Katherine S. Dreier Collection at Yale.

as I am in Naples with Alfred Douglas, he is going to give his decision that I am leading an infamous life, and so deprive me of my sole income, £38 a quarter! For one's own solicitor this seems a little strong. Unluckily he has it in his power to stop my wretched allowance, and he is going to do so. And as I see my poem is a very unsaleable affair, I simply have starvation or suicide before me—the latter, as I dislike pain, from choice. Alfred Douglas has no money—not enough for his own wants—and cannot do anything, even temporarily for me.

I am anxious however to correct my proofs before retiring from a world of injustice, worry and annoyance. So do let me have them. You said you would send them last Wednesday—as yet, no sign of them. I should not like to die without seeing my poem as good as I can make a poem, whose subject is all wrong, and whose treatment is too personal. I hope to receive the proofs this week. As regards the cover, do what you like—the simpler the better.

I won't write any more about America. I have no hope; but I do trust you will copyright it in the States. There is a *chance*—just a chance—of a big sale.

The weather is entrancing, but in my heart there is no sun.

A few days later he received a letter from the publisher, announcing the dispatch of the proofs and criticising certain passages about the prison doctor. To this Wilde replied by return.[1]

Posilippo Friday 19*th* [*November*]. Your letter announcing proofs just received. I expect the latter this afternoon.

With regard to the description of the prison doctor: the passage in which it occurs does not refer to a particular execution, but to executions in general. I was not present at the Reading execution, nor do I know anything about it. I am describing the general scene with general types.

The Governor of Reading, for instance, was a 'mulberry faced Dictator', a great red-faced, bloated Jew, who always looked as if he drank, and did so. His name was Isaacson. He did not, could not have had a yellow face of Doom or anything else. Brandy was the flaming message of his pulpy face.

By 'Caiaphas' I do not mean the present Chaplain of Reading. He is a good-natured fool, one of the silliest of God's sheep, a typical clergyman in fact. I mean any priest of God who assists at the unjust and cruel punishments of man.

I will change one word so as to avoid being misunderstood. I will put 'While some coarse-mouthed Doctor' etc. That fitly

[1] Communicated by the late Mr Frederick Peters; H–D, 676.

describes the type of prison doctor in England. As a class they are brutes and excessively cruel. The Chiswick Press is idiotic.[1]

I hope you sent Miss Marbury the poem. Otherwise she cannot get offers. If you have not, perhaps better wait till the proofs arrive. But I suppose America is a foolish dream as far as buying my poem goes.

I still go to Cook's every day to inquire if there is a telegram of £20 for me. For four days I have had no cigarettes, no money to buy them or note paper. I wish you would make an effort.

The proofs duly arrived by the afternoon post on the same day. At first sight Wilde was unfavourably impressed.

In the first place the paper did not please him. 'In old days of power and personality', he wrote to Smithers later that evening, 'I always insisted that my proofs should be sent to me on the paper to be ultimately used. Otherwise I would not have been able to judge of the look of a page. Of course the paper of these proofs is awful and the whole thing looks to me mean in consequence. . . . The public is largely influenced by the *look* of a book. So are we all. It is the only artistic thing about the public.' Then the author had intended that wherever there was a break in the poem a new page should begin. This had not been done. Otherwise he felt it would be better to print the text on alternate leaves. 'You say this will necessitate a cloth binding. Well, let us have one. A plain olive-green, or cinnamon cloth, with a white back gold-lettered. The colours, nowadays, in cloths are lovely.' Nor were these the only blemishes in the proofs. The title page did not please him at all. Here the author's pseudonym—'C.3.3.'—was too small, while the publisher's name was too large. Also the type used for the dedication he found 'revolting' to his taste. 'It is like a bad brass by Gilbert Scott. There need be no suggestion of a Pugin tomb-stone about it. Joy and assertion are its notes.' To the style of the dedication itself he gave the most careful consideration.[2]

'The poem as printed looks like a sixpenny pamphlet', he

[1] The Chiswick Press, which printed the book, evidently had some difficulty in deciphering Wilde's MS corrections in the proofs. For instance, Wilde complained to Smithers that the lines about the doctor in the thirteenth stanza of Part I were corrected by the printers to read 'While some coarse mouthed doctor straddles by with a flattened bulldog nose': see *Catalogue of the Oscar Wilde Collection of John B. Stetson Jr.* (New York, 1920), at p. 63.

[2] See H–D, 676, for the complete text of this interesting letter with its considered comments on the make-up of the poem.

wrote to Ross the same evening. 'I have written to Smithers to say that if he wishes to ask 3s 6d, he should make it look as a book to be worth at least ninepence. This can be done by different pagination.' Some of Smithers's manuscript corrections puzzled him. 'By the way, is there any difference between "grey" and "gray"? I believe there is, but I don't know what it is. In one place in the poem Smithers suggests "gray". In others he leaves "grey". Perhaps he is seeing red.'[1] To Smithers he wrote: 'Is there any rule about it? I only know that *Dorian Gray* is a classic and deservedly.' Meanwhile Wilde continued to press the publisher for more money. 'I have been seven times to Cook's and also went at 7 o'clock after their Bank closes and woke them up', he wrote to him on November 23. 'Of course nothing at all had arrived—so I have had no dinner. I hope you had a better one.'[2] Eventually Smithers sent £5, with a promise of a further £5 in the following week. Against this unsatisfactory financial background Wilde put the last finishing touches to *The Ballad*. 'I think after Christmas would be better for publication', he wrote to Ross. 'I am hardly a Christmas present.'[3]

As we have seen, Wilde's solicitor, Hansell, had decided as arbiter under the terms of the Deed of Arrangement that Wilde had forfeited his allowance by setting up house with Alfred Douglas, and on his wife's instructions the allowance had accordingly ceased to be paid. This had added to Wilde's financial troubles. ('Women are so petty—and Constance has no imagination.'[4])

Wilde wrote to Smithers when he had received confirmation of this action:

> I wish you would start a Society for the Defence of Oppressed Personalities. At present there is a gross European concert headed by brutes and solicitors against us. It is really ridiculous that after my entire life has been wrecked by Society, people should still propose to exercise social tyranny over me, and try to force me to live in solitude—the one thing I can't stand. I lived in silence and solitude for two years in prison. I did not think that on my release, my wife, my trustees, the guardians of my children, my few friends, such as they are, and my myriad enemies would combine to force me by starvation to live in silence and solitude again. . . .

[1] *After Berneval*, 27. [2] Clark MSS. [3] *After Berneval*, 30.
[4] Wilde to Ross, October 3, 1897: Clark MSS; H–D, 653.

> The scheme is put forward on moral grounds! It is proposed to leave me to die of starvation, or to blow my brains out in a Naples urinal. I never came across anyone in whom the moral sense was dominant who was not heartless, cruel, vindictive, log-stupid and entirely lacking in the smallest sense of humanity. Moral people, as they are termed are simply beasts. I would sooner have fifty unnatural vices than one unnatural virtue.[1]

'At present I don't know what to do', he wrote to More Adey on November 29. 'Bosie will probably go back to Paris. I see nothing to do but to stay on here, and try to get literary work. Of course I am depressed by the difficulty of reaching an audience. The adventures of my American poem have been a terrible blow to my ambition, my vanity and my hopes.'[2] Douglas now made up his mind to leave. 'I do not know if, now that we are going to separate, there is any likelihood of my income being restored to me', Wilde wrote to Smithers. 'I unluckily have no one to plead my cause aright. I have alienated all my friends, partly thro' my own fault and partly thro' theirs. The Paris *Journal* has a sympathetic paragraph to say I am starving at Naples—but French people subscribe nothing but sonnets when one is alive and statues when one is not.' Wilde's nervous condition was as bad as his financial state. 'My handwriting once Greek and gracious is now illegible', he told Smithers. 'I am very sorry, but I really am a wreck of nerves. I don't eat or sleep. I live on cigarettes.'[3]

Early in December Douglas departed for Paris, leaving Wilde alone in the villa. In a letter which he sent shortly afterwards to Ross, Wilde explained what had happened between them. 'The facts of Naples are very bald and brief', he wrote. 'Bosie for four months, by endless letters, offered me a home. He offered me love affection and care, and promised that I should never want for anything. After four months I accepted his offer, but when we met at Aix on our way to Naples, I found he had no money, no plans, and had forgotten all his promises. His one idea was that I should raise money for us both; I did so to the extent of £120. On this Bosie lived quite happily. When it came to his having to repay his own *share*, he became terribly unkind and penurious, except where his own pleasures

[1] A. C. Dennison and H. Post. *Some Letters from Oscar Wilde to Alfred Douglas* (1924), xvii; H–D, 686.
[2] Clark MSS; H–D, 687.
[3] H–D, 689.

were concerned, and when my allowance ceased, he left . . . the bald fact is that I accepted the offer of the home, and found that I was expected to provide the money, and when I could no longer do so I was left to my own devices. It is, of course, the most bitter experience of a bitter life. It is a blow quite awful and paralysing. But it had to come, and I know it is better that I should never see him again. I don't want to, he fills me with horror.'[1]

It must be admitted that, when he wrote this letter, Wilde did considerably less than justice to his friend. In fact, what happened was this. Douglas's mother, Lady Queensberry, who was making an allowance of about £8 a week to her son, had threatened to cut this off, if he continued to live with Wilde. Douglas consequently agreed to separate and furthermore undertook never to sleep again under the same roof as Wilde, if his mother would pay Wilde the 'debt of honour' which Wilde considered was due to him from the Queensberry family.[2] Lady Queensberry could not apparently manage the whole sum, but she promised to let Wilde have £200. This she sent Wilde in two instalments through More Adey.[3] About the same time she also sent her son some money, with which he was to settle the hotel bill in Naples which had remained unpaid when he and Wilde moved into the villa, and also to pay three months' rent of the villa in advance for Wilde before he left. There would appear, therefore, to be some justification for Douglas describing Wilde's letter about him as 'one of the most astonishing products that the history of literature has ever recorded'.[4] Indeed, Wilde's conduct seems to be a good illustration of the line about all men killing the thing they love, which occurs so frequently in *The Ballad*. Incidentally, when they were together in Naples, Douglas asked Wilde what exactly he meant by this line. Wilde replied: 'It's a mistake to ask a poet what he means by any obscure phrase in a poem, because he may mean one thing or several things. The answer

[1] Wilde to Ross, March 23, 1898: Clark MSS; H–D, 709.

[2] See above, p. 15.

[3] That Lady Queensberry's action was prompted by her son is clear from a letter written by him to her dated December 7, 1897: 'It was for you to force me to go, and to give me the means of going by accepting my terms. This you have done, and you *must* fulfil them to the letter. You must pay this £200 *at once*. . . . Also if you possibly can pay him the rest of the £500': Douglas, *Without Apology*, 304.

[4] Douglas. *Autobiography* (2nd ed.), 159.

is that it means just what it says in the poem.' On another occasion, Douglas repeated the question, and this time Wilde said: '*You* should know.' This reply gave Douglas the clue he wanted, namely that if one loves anyone very much, one creates an image of the beloved in one's mind and then is apt gradually and inevitably to destroy it.[1]

To encourage Wilde and show him what fine work he was capable of producing, Smithers now sent him the second volume of Vincent O'Sullivan's poems which he was publishing.[2] At the same time he told him that the revised proofs of his own book would follow shortly. By now Wilde had to some extent recovered his customary good spirits, due in part no doubt to the receipt of the first instalment of Lady Queensberry's £200.

> *Posilippo, Monday* [*December* 8]. I am very glad you have heard from Miss Marbury, but do send her the poem. Her suggestion of *illustration* is of course out of the question. Pray tell her from me that I feel it would entirely spoil any beauty the poem has, and not add anything to its psychological revelations. The horror of prison life is the contrast between the grotesqueness of one's aspect and the tragedy in one's soul. Illustrations would emphasise the former, and conceal the latter. Of course I refer to realistic illustrations.
>
> I received today Vincent O'Sullivan's poems. They are beautifully bound and printed. I like the format of the book intensely, and I think the poems better than the former ones—more concentrated in motive, better thought out, more fully realised. But in what a midnight his soul seems to walk! And what maladies he draws from the moon! When I have read them more carefully, I am going to write to him. . . .
>
> I await the revise, and promise you not to make my quietus with a bare bodkin till I have returned them. After that, I think of retiring. But first, I would like to dine with you here. To leave life as one leaves a feast is not merely philosophy but romance.[3]

Wilde did not remain for long in the villa after Douglas had left. About the middle of December he accepted an invitation from an elderly Russian ('He is very cultivated and of advanced years'), whom he had met in Italy, to spend a week or two as

[1] Douglas. *Without Apology*, 46–8. Douglas points out that Wilde took the phrase 'All men kill the thing they love' from Shakespeare, but he characteristically inverted the meaning. The reference is to the trial scene in *The Merchant of Venice* (Act IV, Scene 1) when Bassanio asks Shylock 'Do all men kill the things they do not love?'

[2] *The House of Sin*. Smithers had published his *Poems* in the previous year.

[3] See above, p. 166; partly quoted in Mason, 512–13; H–D, 691.

his guest at Taormina. Unfortunately, during his absence the servant, whom he left in charge at the villa, stole all his clothes and some other belongings, including a portrait which William Rothenstein had painted of him, and also it seems probably the MS of the first draft of *The Ballad*. On his return to Naples at the beginning of the New Year, Wilde found a long letter from Smithers dealing with various printer's corrections to *The Ballad* and enclosing a further proof of the title page, with which Wilde had been dissatisfied on the ground that the publisher's name appeared too large. 'I trust the "Leonard Smithers" is now small enough to satisfactorily show that I am not the author of the poem, but only that humble person, its introducer to the public', wrote the publisher. 'It has been a somewhat awkward title page to set with satisfaction, and even now, owing to the lightness of the impression of the "C.3.3." it does not look perfectly satisfactory. But this will be set quite right when the sheet is properly made ready for the press, which is a matter which takes several hours coaxing of the type to accomplish properly.'[1]

The revised proofs had now reached Wilde, and he told Smithers to go ahead and begin printing without waiting for them to come back.[2] By this time he had returned to Naples, but he did not stay in the villa again, although the rent had been paid until the end of February.

51, *Santa Lucia, Naples. January* 9, 1898. The revise has never arrived and I have waited from day to day for it. To wait longer would be foolish. I am sure it is all right.

As regards your suggestion, or request, that I should revert to 'in God's sweet world again' instead of 'for weal or woe again'—(Canto II somewhere)—certainly! Pray make the correction yourself. Second thoughts in art are always, or often, worst. . . .

The cover etc. I leave to you. The post here is impossible, so pray bring it out as soon as possible—without further consultation. I, as all poets, am safe in your hands.

As regards America, I think it would be better to publish there *without* my name. I see that it is my *name* that terrifies. I hope an edition of some kind will appear. I cannot advise what should be done, but it seems to me that the withdrawal of my name is essential in America as elsewhere, and the public likes an open secret. Half the success of Marie Corelli is due to the no doubt unfounded

[1] Mason, 413. [2] Mason, 414; H–D, 698.

> rumour that she is a woman. In other respects pray do as you like about America, but do see that there is some edition.
>
> I have had misfortune since I wrote to you: influenza, the robbery during my absence in Sicily, of *all* my clothes, etc. by a servant whom I left in the villa, ill-health, loneliness, and general *ennui*, with a tragi-comedy of an existence. But I want to see my poem out. . . .

The only newspaper in America which showed any interest in the poem was a Sunday publication, the *New York Journal*. For this reason Smithers arranged with the agent, Miss Marbury, that publication should take place simultaneously in London and New York on February 13, which was a Sunday. Unfortunately the best offer which Miss Marbury could persuade the *New York Journal* to make was only $100.[1] This offer was refused and Smithers contented himself with asking Miss Marbury to secure the American copyright, while adhering to February 13 as the date of publication in England. Meanwhile, Wilde had left Naples for Paris, where he put up in the Hotel de Nice, a small hotel in the Rue des Beaux Arts, the street in the Latin Quarter where he was to die not quite two years later. From here he continued to bombard the publisher with anxious and at times pathetic letters. 'Is the book out?' he asked Smithers. 'Tell me and send me a few copies. Give my address to B[osie] and beseech him to write to me, for I simply long to hear from my old friends. I am so lonely and poor. What is the end to be?'[2]

To this appeal Smithers replied, stating that *The Ballad* was with the binder, and sending Wilde samples of the binding together with twenty copies of the title sheet. He requested Wilde to inscribe them to those to whom he wished author's presentation copies to be sent, and to return the sheets to be bound up with the rest of the text. 'I would send you a sample copy of the book, which I have received today from the binder', Smithers added, 'but as it is not yet in a complete state, with its white and cinnamon back on it, I must remember the old proverb, which says that children should never see things half finished. So I will hold it back until it has got its binding on it.'[3]

Apart from what he considered one blemish, Wilde was delighted with the appearance of *The Ballad*, when he received the first bound copy. 'I am really charmed with the book', he wrote to Smithers. 'It is quite right, except for the final signa-

[1] Mason, 415. [2] Clark MSS. [3] Mason, 416.

ture of C.3.3. (page 31). That is awful—it should have been cut. . . . The cover is very nice and the paper excellent. The title page is a masterpiece, one of the best I have ever seen.'[1] But he was disappointed with the sales methods adopted by his unorthodox publisher. 'Smithers is absurd', he wrote to Ross, 'only printing 400 copies to begin with, and not advertising. I fear he has missed a popular "rush". He is so fond of "suppressed" books that he suppresses his own.'[2]

3

The date of publication of *The Ballad*, originally fixed to coincide with its appearance in New York, which never materialised, was February 13, 1898. Since this was a Sunday, it was not until the following day that copies were on sale to the English public. Despite the previous lack of advertising and the fact that very few review copies had been sent out, there was an immediate rush to buy the book, such as Wilde had indeed anticipated. Fifty copies were sold at one bookshop the morning after it was published, and by the end of the week the whole of the first edition, including most of the *de luxe* copies printed on Japanese vellum, was sold out. Among its purchasers was Wilde's defender at the Old Bailey, Sir Edward Clarke, who is said to have taken a dozen copies. Smithers was completely taken by surprise at this unexpected demand. Some delay in reprinting was inevitable, and although the publisher announced on the Saturday following publication that a second edition would be 'ready next week', the delay proved damaging.

Nor could the Press notices be regarded as satisfactory. 'I fear that the Press will boycott the work', Wilde wrote apprehensively to Ross on publication day. 'It is very bitter and unfair, and I have not much hope of recognition.'[3] His fears were to a great extent justified, but as much by reason of the small review list as by any personal animus towards the anonymous author, whose identity was soon generally recognised. The first review appeared in the London evening newspaper,

[1] *Kern Sale Catalogue*, II, 460. The final 'C.3.3' to which Wilde objected was corrected in the second edition.

[2] *After Berneval*, 39. Apart from the thirty copies on Japanese vellum, 400 copies were printed on January 24, 1898, and the remaining 400, to complete the first edition, on February 8: Mason, 408.

[3] *After Berneval*, 40.

the *Echo*, on February 19. It occupied a column and a half, under the heading of 'A Book of the Week', and it was an extremely good notice. More Adey immediately posted off a copy of that paper to Wilde in Paris. 'Many sincere thanks', replied the author. 'It is a capital review, but of course I want the literary papers to criticise it. It is not altogether a *pamphlet* on prison reform.'[1] Another Liberal organ, the *Morning Leader*, gave it a distinctly partial notice. 'It is a heavy judicial charge', Wilde wrote to Smithers, who had sent him a copy of the newspaper. 'People don't understand that criticism is prejudice, because to understand one must love, and to love one must have passion. It is only the unimaginative who are ever fair. But I am glad they noted it.'[2] The only national 'daily' to notice it was the *Daily Telegraph*, which described the poem as 'a moving piece of work, without doubt, despite its tone' and as having 'already had a certain vogue, not merely for the reason that it is a strikingly vivid and realistic description of prison life, but also because everyone is ready with a suggestion as to whom the anonymous author really is.'[3]

The poet and critic, W. E. Henley, who had always disliked Wilde, wrote a bitter unsigned review in *The Outlook* in much the same style as he had castigated *The Picture of Dorian Gray* when it was first published. 'I have read Henley', commented Wilde. 'It is very coarse and vulgar—so entirely lacking in literary or gentlemanly instinct.' To some extent this was offset by a friendly appreciation by Arthur Symons, whom Frank Harris got to review it for the *Saturday Review*.[4] 'I was greatly pleased with Symons article', Wilde wrote to Smithers. 'It is admirably written and most artistic in its mode of approval. . . . I don't think I should answer Henley. I think it would be quite vulgar—what does it matter? He is simply jealous. He made his scrofula into "vers libre", and is furious because I have

[1] Wilde to Adey, February 21, 1898: Clark MSS.

[2] Wilde to Smithers, March 7, 1898: Harold Hartley, *Eighty-Eight Not Out* (1939), p. 250.

[3] *Daily Telegraph*, February 27, 1898. On the subject of this review Wilde wrote to Smithers next day: 'The D.T. by the influence of Reggie Turner has been forced to notice the book, but grudgingly and badly': Mason, 428.

[4] Arthur Symons (1865–1945), poet and essayist. Early in February 1898, he wrote to Smithers: 'I see by your advertisement in *The Athenaeum* that you are publishing Wilde's poem. I need scarcely say that if I could do anything that would be of service to Wilde, now that he is making his first attempt to return to literature, I should be only too glad to do it': *Stetson Sale Catalogue*, 70. Symons expanded his review in the critical appreciation which he subsequently wrote of Wilde as a writer: see *A Study of Oscar Wilde* (1930), pp. 25–52.

made a sonnet out of "skilly". Besides, there are only two forms of writers in England, the unread and the unreadable. Henley belongs to the former class. (You can send this aphorism to the *Sunday Special.*)'[1] Wilde who had a considerable respect for Henley's strength of will, which impelled him to struggle successfully against a crippling bodily infirmity, had already written a character sketch of Henley which he proposed sending to the unfriendly critic. It is doubtful, however, if he ever sent it to Henley. 'My little reply is a very slight affair', he told Vincent O'Sullivan. 'I was at Compiègne. I wrote it as I was getting into a cab to go to the station.'[2]

Like most authors Wilde was peculiarly sensitive to praise and blame, where his literary work was concerned. He was also disappointed by the lack of immediate acknowledgement on the part of those who had received the first presentation copies. 'Except you and Reggie [Turner]', he wrote to Ross on the day of publication, 'none of the people to whom I sent copies has written to me. The lack of recognition in people is astonishing.' He did, however, receive 'a charming letter' from a fellow-poet, who like him had done a spell in prison—R. B. Cunninghame Graham—he had managed somehow to see an advance copy, as he does not seem to have been on the presentation list.[3] The author was naturally anxious to know the opinions of the recipients of presentation copies. 'I wonder', he wrote, 'what that good kind fellow Major Nelson thinks of

[1] Mason, 428. The reference to Henley's verse is, of course, to the *In Hospital* poems, of which the best known begins 'Out of the night that covered me'.

[2] After meeting William Rothenstein at Dieppe in the summer of 1897, Wilde had written the character sketch of Henley for the artist's *English Portraits*, which Rothenstein had been reluctantly obliged to reject: 'He founded a school and has survived all his disciples. He has always thought too much about himself, which is wise; and written too much about others, which is foolish. His prose is the beautiful prose of a poet, and his poetry the beautiful poetry of a prose-writer. His personality is insistent. To converse with him is a physical no less than a mental recreation. He is never forgotten by his enemies, and often forgiven by his friends. He has added several new words to the English language, and his style is an open secret. He has fought a good fight and has had to face every difficulty except popularity': Rothenstein, *Men and Memories*, I, 312.

[3] *After Berneval*, 40. Cunninghame Graham had been imprisoned in Pentonville for his part in the Trafalgar Square Riots in 1887: see his account of his imprisonment quoted by A. F. Tchiffely in *Don Roberto* (1937), at p. 226 *et seq.* In a letter to William Rothenstein, in which he repeated the reference to the staple prison diet, which he had used in writing to Smithers, Wilde remarked: 'Cunninghame Graham will explain to you what "skilly" is. You must never know my personal experience.' Rothenstein had written praising the poem, and Wilde told him that his letter had given him 'more pleasure, more pride, than anything has done since the poem appeared': Rothenstein, *op. cit.*, I, 316.

it.'[1] (Nelson's copy had been inscribed—'from the author, in recognition of many acts of kindness and gentleness.') Perhaps it was as well for him that he did not know, since the Governor of Reading shared Ross's feelings about the poem. 'Although thinking some stanzas very fine,' Nelson had written to Ross, '[I] am of opinion that the work is not worthy of the writer's best effort. It is a terrible mixture of good and bad and indifferent.'[2] A more favourable view was expressed by Wilde's wife, to whom at his request Smithers had sent a copy, and to whom, in spite of his behaviour with Alfred Douglas, she still felt not unkindly. 'If you do see him', she wrote to a mutual friend, Carlos Blacker, 'tell him that I think *The Ballad* exquisite, and I hope that the great success it has had in London, at all events, will urge him on to write more.'[3]

The second edition of 1,000 copies was on sale towards the end of February. It contained twenty alterations to the text as well as the resetting in fresh type of the final 'C.3.3.', to which Wilde had objected.[4] Four further impressions appeared during the next six weeks. Although they were designated as separate editions, they were identical in collation with the text of the second edition, which except for one word has remained unchanged.[5] In spite of the delay in bringing out the second edition, some 3,000 copies were sold in three weeks. 'Such is the public', was Henley's uncharitable comment, when he heard this news.[6] Smithers put what Wilde called 'a flaming advertisement' of these sales figures into *The Athenaeum*. 'When I read it', said Wilde, 'I feel like Lipton's tea.'[7] After this the demand gradually fell off, although the book continued to sell slowly and most of a further 2,000 copies were disposed of during the succeeding twelve months. In particular, there was a limited edition of ninety-nine copies numbered and signed by

[1] Wilde to Adey, February 21: Clark MSS.

[2] Margery Ross. *Robert Ross*, 50.

[3] H–D, 714 note. *The Happy Prince* was dedicated to Carlos Blacker.

[4] See Mason, 417–19, for these textual alterations.

[5] Mason, 423.

[6] John Connell. *W. E. Henley* (1949), p. 335. On April 1, 1898, Wilde wrote to Ross: 'The reviews you sent me are excellent, and really the Press has behaved very well, and Henley's hysterical personalities have done no harm—but rather the contrary. I am quite obliged to him for playing the *rôle* of *advocatus diaboli* so well: without it my beatification as a saint would have been impossible. But I shall now live as the infamous St. Oscar of Oxford, Poet and Martyr': *After Berneval*, 49.

[7] Wilde to George Ives, March 21, 1898: Louis Marlow. *Seven Friends* (1953), at p. 20.

the author, and specially bound in purple and white. This so-called third edition or 'Author's Edition', as Wilde described it, was also distinguished by a leaf design embossed in gilt on the front, which was the work of Charles Ricketts.[1] The possibility of bringing out a popular sixpenny edition, with 'a prison reform preface' by Michael Davitt or John Burns, was also discussed, but nothing came of this idea.[2] On March 15, 1899, Smithers wrote to Wilde that he was proposing to print some more copies and asked him whether he had any objection to his name appearing on the title page, underneath the 'C.3.3.' in a parenthesis. 'I think the time has now come when you should own *The Ballad*', he added. Wilde had no objection, and accordingly 2,000 copies were printed of this new edition, with the author's name on the title page. This was the last English edition to appear in Wilde's lifetime.[3]

Wilde had distributed a few copies among his French literary friends, such as Henri Bauer and Octave Mirbeau. ('A poem gives one *droit de cité*, and shows that one was still an artist.')[4] Then the leading Paris bookshops, such as Brentano's and Galignani's, sold a fair number of copies.[5] One copy reached the publishing offices of the *Mercure de France*, where it was reviewed appreciatively by Henry Davray.[6] This prompted Wilde to write to the reviewer, asking him to undertake a French translation for publication either in periodical or book form, '*car aucun homme de lettres français ne sait rendre l'anglais comme vous*'.[7] After speaking to the editor of the *Mercure de France*, who agreed, Davray set to work, and quickly produced a draft. When Davray showed it to the author, Wilde who was

[1] Mason, 420.

[2] *After Berneval*, 54. Davitt had spent seven years in prison for political offences and had published accounts of his experiences. Burns was convicted, along with Cunninghame Graham, for his part in the Trafalgar Square riots in 1887 (see above, p. 177, note 3). All three were M.P.s. Wilde had written to Davitt about the flogging of Prince at Reading: H–D, 586.

[3] After Wilde's death, Smithers, who claimed to have purchased the copyright from Wilde, brought out a number of unauthorised editions. These pirated editions are easily distinguishable from the authorised version by the fact that the publisher's address does not appear on the title page; the printing of 'C.3.3' is also different (see Mason, 408). After Smithers's death in 1907 his heirs attempted without success to claim the copyright, when about 1,000 'pirated' copies were seized by the authority of Wilde's literary executor.

[4] *After Berneval*, 40. [5] H–D, 719.

[6] Henry-D. Davray (1873–1944) edited the 'Collection of Foreign Authors' for the *Mercure de France*. Besides Wilde, he translated Meredith, Kipling, Conrad and other English writers into French. He later described his association with Wilde in *Oscar Wilde. La Tragédie finale* (1928).

[7] Davray, *op. cit.*, 104.

himself a fine French scholar, felt he had perhaps been over-generous in his estimation of Davray's capabilities as a translator. 'I saw Davray's translation of *Reading Gaol* yesterday, and went over some part of it with him', he wrote to Ross on March 30, 1898. 'It is a very difficult thing to translate, as, unfortunately and oddly, Davray has never been in prison, so knows nothing of prison terms.' For instance, 'We banged the tins' appeared as '*On battait le fer blanc*'. 'I shall have to work for days over it', Wilde added.[1]

Davray's translation was in prose, since both men considered it impossible to render the sense in verse. According to Davray, Wilde took immense pains with the translation, going over it line by line and word by word, and for Davray, as he admitted, the length of these sessions was compensated by the details he learned of English prison life.[2]

The poem appeared in its French garb in the May issue of the *Mercure de France*. For the book version the editor suggested that the English text should be published alongside Davray's translation. This proposal alarmed Smithers, who thought that the appearance of the poem in this form would injure the English sales. But Wilde successfully overcame his objections. 'As regards the French translation with the English original of *The Ballad*', he wrote to Smithers on May 20, 'there will be no sale for it in London except a few copies for bibliophiles. No one wants a poem with a French translation except French people. . . . The book will be brought out here at 2 francs. It will be . . . unattractive in form except its ordinary Jonquil paper cover . . . Send me, if you can, four pounds, or even three. I am now trying to leave my Hotel and get rooms where I can breakfast, and so stay in during the morning. Going out for breakfast is fatal to work.'[3]

But Wilde had a foreboding at the time that his poem would be his last work, which he would live to complete. 'It is my *chant de cygne*', he told Carlos Blacker, 'and I am sorry to leave with a cry of pain, a cry of Marsyas, not a song of Apollo. But Life that I have loved so much—too much—has torn me like a tiger. So when you come and see me, you will see the ruin and wreck of what once was wonderful and brilliant . . . I don't

[1] *After Berneval*, 48. In the final version 'We banged the tins' appeared as '*On heurtait les gamelles*'.

[2] Davray, *op. cit.*, 108.

[3] *Glaenzer Sale Catalogue*, 35; H–D, 741.

think I shall ever write again: *la joie de vivre* is gone and that, with will-power, is the basis of art.'[1] He felt the same throughout the spring and summer of 1898, and indeed until his death, just over two years later. 'Something is killed in me', he wrote to Ross in August. 'I feel no desire to write—I am unconscious of power. Of course my first year in prison destroyed me body and soul. It could not be otherwise.'[2]

This is not the place to narrate the tragedy of the last phase of Wilde's life, since the present book is principally concerned with his prison experiences and his writings, which were the outcome of those experiences. Amongst his literary plans never carried out was a work on prison life and penal reform. 'I have no doubt we shall win', he told the criminologist, George Ives, shortly after the publication of *The Ballad*, 'but the road is long, and red with monstrous martyrdoms. Nothing but the repeal of the Criminal Law Amendment Act would do any good. That is the essential. It is not so much public opinion, as public officials that need educating.'[3] He collected some books and pamphlets on the subject of prisons, including John Howard's celebrated treatise, and these were found among his few effects after his death. But apart from the two letters to the *Daily Chronicle* on the case of Warder Martin and the Prisons Bill of 1898, he completed nothing on this, or indeed any other subject, after the publication of *The Ballad*. Judging by the *Daily Chronicle* letters, it is a pity that he did not do so. Many of his friends considered he should make the attempt, and even his wife thought so after she had read the second letter in the *Daily Chronicle*. 'I think that Oscar had better write a book on the present prison system, which I am sure would sell', she wrote to Carlos Blacker, 'as people know exceedingly little about it and they always want to know those sort of things.'[4] Incidentally, the letter in which Constance Wilde expressed this opinion, was one of the last she wrote.

A day or two later she entered a nursing home in Genoa, where she died very shortly afterwards from the effects of an operation to correct a spinal injury. Wilde was over-

[1] Wilde to Blacker: March 9, 1898; H–D, 715.

[2] Wilde to Ross, August 16, 1898: Clark MSS; H–D, 760.

[3] Louis Marlow. *Seven Friends*, 20. George Ives (1867–1950) was the author of a *History of Penal Methods* and other works on penology.

[4] Constance Wilde to Carlos Blacker, March 30, 1898. Communicated by Mr Vyvyan Holland.

whelmed by the news which he had not in the least expected. 'It is awful,' he wrote to Blacker. 'I don't know what to do. If we had only met once and kissed each other. It is too late. How awful life is.'[1]

Although he completed no other work, Wilde had several ideas for plays, and the scenario of one of them he sold several times to different people.[2] Smithers was concerned in these negotiations. Unfortunately for Wilde he was to be involved even more deeply in Wilde's affairs, since Wilde gave him an authority to receive moneys owing on his behalf in London. These included a long outstanding debt from Ernest Leverson, which had worried Wilde so much during his last months in Reading. Smithers also published *The Importance of Being Earnest* and *An Ideal Husband*, for which there had been no time to find a publisher before Wilde's arrest and trials. They both came out in 1899 each being described on the title page as being 'By the Author of Lady Windermere's Fan'. They passed practically unnoticed in the Press, which disappointed Wilde, particularly for the sake of the publisher, whom he considered had displayed great pluck in bringing them out at all. ('However I hope some of the faithful and all the elect will buy copies.'[3]) Smithers was usually glad of an excuse to slip over to Paris, and on one occasion Wilde tried to persuade Mrs Smithers to come down to the Riviera, when he was staying with Frank Harris. 'Leonard must be quite exhausted with neglecting his business', Wilde wrote, 'and the rest would do him good.'[4] There was more truth in this jest than Wilde realised

[1] Mrs Wilde died on April 7, 1898. Her death certificate from the British Consulate in Genoa, in which her age appears as forty, is reproduced in Sherard, *Life of Oscar Wilde*, at p. 375. She was buried in Genoa, where in the following year Wilde visited her grave: 'I went to Genoa to see Constance's grave. It is very pretty, a marble cross with dark ivy leaves inlaid in a good pattern. The cemetery is a garden at the foot of the lovely hills that climb into the mountains that girdle Genoa. It was very tragic seeing her name carved on a tomb, her surname—my name not mentioned, of course—just "Constance Mary, daughter of Horace Lloyd, Q.C." and a verse from Revelations. I bought some flowers. I was deeply affected, with a sense, also, of the uselessness of all regrets. Nothing could have been otherwise, and life is a very terrible thing.' Wilde to Ross, February, 1899: *Dulau Sale Catalogue*, 59; H–D, 783.

[2] Among them was Frank Harris, who based his play *Mr and Mrs Daventry* on this scenario. The play was produced at the Royalty Theatre, London, on October 25, 1900, with Mrs Patrick Campbell in the leading role and ran for 121 performances. For further details in which Wilde felt he had been cheated by Harris, see the present writer's Introduction to the first published edition of the play (1956).

[3] Wilde to Ross, February 25, 1899: *Dulau Sale Catalogue*, 58; H–D, 782.

[4] December 18, 1898: *Glaenzer Sale Catalogue*, 37; H–D, 773.

at the time. About the middle of 1900 Smithers went bankrupt, and his failure added to the already heavy burden of financial worry which marked the last months of Wilde's life. Yet his defection did not interfere with the habits of this extraordinary publisher, who continued his Paris visits. 'Smithers appeared here with his new mistress', wrote Wilde in June, 1900. 'She is quite clean, and charmingly dressed.'[1]

Wilde's death took place in Paris on November 30, 1900. Soon afterwards the irrepressible Smithers started up in business again, and proceeded to bring out several unauthorised editions of *The Ballad*, purporting to be the owner of the copyright. Pirated editions had also appeared in both North and South America. Besides French and Spanish the poem was quickly translated into German, Italian, Greek and Russian, and was published in the countries of those languages within a few years of Wilde's death. A Yiddish version also appeared in America at this period.[2] It was not until *The Ballad* was republished in the first collected edition of Wilde's works in London in 1908 that its inclusion in the Wilde literary estate ceased to be disputed.

In spite of its success and wide emotional appeal, opinions about the merits of *The Ballad of Reading Gaol* must remain divided, as they did in the author's lifetime. While Frank Harris, for instance, described it as incomparably the greatest ballad in all English poetry, Robert Ross, as we have seen, regarded it as considerably inferior to most of Wilde's other poetic writings. It has, however, been warmly praised by such diverse authors and critics as Laurence Housman, John Cowper Powys, Arthur Ransome, Lord Alfred Douglas and André Maurois. On the other hand, in so-called 'highbrow' literary circles, it has become fashionable to decry *The Ballad*, where it has been described as 'the book of Wilde's best suited to the great reading public, which responds to the same kind of art

[1] *Dulau Sale Catalogue*, 79; H–D, 830.

[2] For details see Mason, *A Bibliography of the Poems of Oscar Wilde* (1907); also Abraham Horodisch, *Oscar Wilde's Ballad of Reading Gaol. A Bibliographical Study* (New York, 1954), which contains interesting particulars of the various European and American editions. Although Smithers had asked the American agent, Miss Marbury, to secure U.S. copyright, the formalities were not complied with, and the book was consequently unprotected in the United States. Editions have also appeared in Bulgarian, Czech, Danish, Dutch, Finnish, Hebrew, Hungarian, Japanese, Polish, Portuguese, Serbo-Croat, Swedish and White Russian.

as the great theatre and film public'.[1] However that may be, few will deny that there is a grim realism about *The Ballad of Reading Gaol,* which renders it perhaps the most moving denunciation of the inhumanity of capital punishment ever written in poetic form.

[1] O'Sullivan. *Aspects of Wilde,* 97.

CHAPTER VIII

'De Profundis'

1

WHEN Wilde handed over to Ross in Dieppe the MS of the long letter, which he had written from Reading to Lord Alfred Douglas but had not been allowed to send, that was virtually the last he had to do with it. Ross, who was later to give the MS the celebrated title of *De Profundis*, under which carefully selected portions were first published in 1905, took the document with him when he returned to London. There he had it copied in accordance with the detailed instructions he had received when Wilde was in Reading.[1] That Wilde was anxious about the progress of the copying, and when the document would be ready for dispatch to Douglas, is evident from the postcard which he sent Ross about a fortnight after Ross had left Berneval. On June 15, 1897, Wilde wrote: 'You have never told me anything about the type-writer,[2] or my letter: pray let there be no further conspiracies. I feel apprehensive. It is only by people writing to me the worst that I can know the best.'[3] Ross's assurances seem to have satisfied Wilde. Apart from a reference, in the following month, to how a second copy might best be made, Wilde never alluded to the matter again in the long correspondence which he carried on until his death with his closest friend and future literary executor, although no doubt they discussed it when Ross again came over to Dieppe. Nor is there any mention of it in any of the letters which Wilde wrote to Douglas after his release from Reading.

The work took some time to complete, since Ross would not let the MS out of his hands. First, he dictated the whole to a typist, who made a single copy. He then marked those parts which Wilde had asked should be specially copied and sent to a few close friends, such as Miss Adela Schuster, and which he

[1] See above, p. 90. [2] i.e., typist. [3] *Dulau Sale Catalogue*, 33; H–D, 609.

considered should form the basis of an eventual general publication, at Ross's discretion, and additional copies were made of the marked passages. When they had been checked with the MS, the parts copied were dispatched to their intended recipients. A second complete copy then seems to have been made from the original typescript at Mrs Marshall's typewriting agency. 'Better to have it done in London', wrote Wilde to Ross on July 20, 'scratching out Bosie's name, mine at the close, and the address. Mrs. Marshall can be relied on.'[1] According to Ross, one of the typed copies was sent to Douglas on August 9, 1897, and its receipt was acknowledged by him.[2] This is important, in view of Douglas's subsequent denial that he had ever seen it until a copy was supplied to his solicitors and shown to him during the interlocutory proceedings of an action for libel which he brought against Mr Arthur Ransome and the Time's Book Club in 1913. Douglas had already been warned by More Adey, before Wilde's release, to expect the letter, and the text of Douglas's reply to Adey is extant. 'I look forward without much excitement to Oscar's letter', he wrote on February 8, 1897, '. . . if he is going to abuse me I would rather not see it. . . . Please let me know if possible by return when exactly I may expect his letter.'[3]

That Wilde was under the impression that his friend had read it, at the time Ross states that he dispatched it, appears from an incident which took place between Wilde and Douglas after their reunion. Douglas was reproaching Wilde about something and Wilde replied: 'Surely you are not bringing up against me what I wrote in prison when I was starving and half mad? You must know that I didn't mean a word of what I said.'[4] But why Ross should have sent Douglas one of the two typed copies instead of the original letter, which Wilde had asked him to do in the first instance, is not clear. It can only be assumed that, while he was at Berneval, Wilde changed his mind and asked his literary executor designate to send Douglas the typescript and to keep the original MS along with the other typed copy.

What seems to have happened then is that Douglas read a few pages at the beginning of the typescript, which contain the

[1] H–D, 624.

[2] See statement by Ross quoted in *The Library of William Andrews Clark, Jr.* (San Francisco, 1922), II, 70.

[3] Clark MSS. [4] Douglas, *Autobiography* (2nd ed.), 135.

most bitter and scathing denunciation of his alleged conduct towards Wilde. He felt annoyed and put down the typescript. After a while he took it up again and read some more pages. They were in a similarly vituperative strain, as indeed is almost the whole of the first half of the complete version. In a fit of irritation he then destroyed the offensive document. This hypothesis is to some extent confirmed by Douglas himself, who states that, when he was staying at Nogent-sur-Marne, he received a long letter from Ross, which may have contained extracts from Wilde's *De Profundis* letter. He admits to reading a few pages and then tearing up the whole letter in a rage and throwing the fragments into the River Marne.[1] It is clear that, when he did so, he had not read as far as any of the subsequently published portions, since he would unquestionably have recognised them when the first published version appeared. Nor is it conceivable that he would have reviewed the work, as he did at the time of publication, as 'this interesting posthumous book', if he had known that the 'unnamed friend', to whom Ross had stated in his preface that its contents were addressed, was himself.[2] In fact he was under the impression that the friend was Ross and this seems to have been fairly generally assumed at the time. In publishing the severely expurgated version in the form that he did, Ross was subsequently accused of perpetrating a great literary hoax, when the facts about the MS became publicly known at the time of the *Douglas* v. *Ransome* libel action in 1913. But, however one may look at Ross's action, there is no evidence that, either in the matter of the dispatch of the typed copy to Douglas or in the matter of the partial publication which he arranged, Ross did not faithfully abide by the author's wishes.

How publication came to take place at all is noteworthy. It was not Ross's intention that *De Profundis*, even in an expurgated version, should be published in England, at least not so soon after the author's death as a little more than four years.

[1] Douglas, *Autobiography* (2nd ed.), 135. In a letter to More Adey written from Nogent-sur-Marne on June 30, 1897, now in the Clark Library in the University of California, Los Angeles, Douglas declared that he had just received an 'enormous envelope' from Ross, which turned out to be a 'typewritten statement' to which Ross had referred in a previous letter. This may well have been the copy of the *De Profundis* letter, although Ross has stated that it was not sent to Douglas until some weeks later.

[2] Douglas's review, signed 'A', appeared in the *Motorist and Traveller*, March 1, 1905. See below, Appendix D.

In Ross's words, 'Wilde's name unfortunately did not bring very agreeable memories to English ears: his literary position, hardly recognised even in the zenith of his successful dramatic career, had come to be ignored by Mr. Ruskin's countrymen, unable to separate the man and the artist.' The position on the Continent was considerably different. There Wilde's works had come to be judged independently of his career. In France, as we have seen, *Salomé*, which had been prohibited from being publicly performed in England by the Lord Chamberlain, was actually produced while the author was in prison. And in Germany this and his other plays, as well as his prose writings and poetry, were all translated in the early years of the new century, and they had an immense success. While his books were virtually unobtainable in England and his plays were banned in the London theatres—they were occasionally performed in the provinces without his name—the German public took to them eagerly. *Salomé*, in particular, had a remarkable success in that country, so that it was no surprise when the distinguished German composer Richard Strauss announced that he was working on an opera, for which the play should form the libretto. One of the remarkable facts about Wilde, which emerges strongly from a reading of *De Profundis*, and which Ross pointed out at the time of the original publication, is that he should have exaggerated his lost contemporary position in England whilst showing no idea of his future European reputation.

It came to be known in Germany, as well as elsewhere, that Wilde had been engaged on a literary work in prison. This prompted Dr Max Meyerfeld, who used to visit London from time to time, to ask Robert Ross whether he could not be allowed to translate it for the benefit of German readers. Ross explained that some day he hoped to issue portions of it 'in accordance with the writer's wishes', though he thought it would be premature to do so at the moment. But the German was not to be put off. He continued to press Ross, and eventually Ross rather reluctantly consented, promising, 'at a leisured opportunity, to extract such portions of the work as might be considered of general public interest'. Ross was in no hurry to carry out his promise and it was only as the result of Meyerfeld's repeated entreaties in a series of personal visits and letters, 'of which frankly I began to hate the sight' said Ross afterwards, that the task of selection was eventually accomplished.[1] The result was handed over to Meyerfeld, together with extracts from four of Wilde's prison letters to Ross, including the instructions for the copying of the MS. Meyerfeld himself undertook the translation and wrote an introduction; he also arranged that it should appear in the Berlin journal, *Die Neue Rundschau*, in January and February, 1905, under the short title *De Profundis*. It did in fact so appear under this title, which, as we have seen, had been Ross's suggestion.[2]

Having dispatched the translation copy to Meyerfeld, it now occurred to Ross that an approximately simultaneous publication of the English text 'might gratify Wilde's English friends and admirers who had expressed curiosity on the subject'. This decision was not reached without some misgiving for the reason already given above. Anticipating refusal, Ross sent the text to Messrs Methuen, the only publishers to whom he submitted it. Somewhat to his surprise, it was accepted, this action being taken on the advice of the well known critic and man of letters, E. V. Lucas, who acted as the firm's reader. However, Lucas urged, in view of the uncertainty of the book's reception, that certain passages should be deleted. To this Ross readily assented, with the result that a rather shorter version than the first German edition appeared in England. The English edition, from which were also omitted the extracts from Wilde's prison letters, was published with a brief introduction by Ross, on February, 23 1905.[3] Its reception was on the whole favourable and very gratifying to Ross and the publishers, who had naturally incurred some risk in bringing it out at that date. 'The book is going very well', wrote Mr Algernon Methuen to Ross on the day after publication, 'and we shall have to print a second edition at once.' Next day Mr Laurence Housman, who was later to recapture something of the brilliance of Wilde's conversation in his *L'Echo de Paris*, wrote to Ross, 'Its reception seems to me remarkable—unprophesiable five or six years ago. Perhaps before we die a tablet will be put up in Tite Street on the house where he used to live. . . .' (Mr

[1] See Preface by Robert Ross to the edition published in the *Collected Works of Oscar Wilde* in 1908.

[2] The sub-title was *Aufzeichnungen und Briefe aus dem Zuchthause in Reading*. The work was published in book form later the same year by Verlag S. Fischer, Berlin, with Meyerfeld's introduction.

[3] Mason, 442.

Housman, though not Ross, was to live to see his words come true almost exactly half a century later, and also to send an appropriate message for the occasion.)[1]

The Press notices of *De Profundis* were very different, both in quantity and quality, from those which had greeted the appearance of *The Ballad of Reading Gaol* seven years before. The book was reviewed in over thirty national newspapers and periodicals, and, although there were a few exceptions, generally speaking the critics showed themselves, in Ross's words, 'ready to estimate the writer, whether favourably or unfavourably, without emphasising their natural prejudice against his later career, even in reference to this book where the two things occasion synchronous comment'. Those who wrote sympathetic reviews under their own names or easily recognisable initials included H. Hamilton Fyfe,[2] James Douglas,[3] H. L. W. Massingham,[4] 'John Oliver Hobbes',[5] Max Beerbohm,[6] R. B. Cunninghame Graham,[7] Professor R. Y. Tyrell,[8] William Archer[9] and G. Lowes Dickinson.[10] Perhaps the most humane and charitable opinion was expressed in an unsigned review in the *Westminster Gazette*, which was no doubt the work of the editor, J. A. Spender. 'We will not moralise over this tragedy', the reviewer remarked. 'What had to be said was said and done with years ago. In the slightly fanciful but touchingly written pages on the character of the Christ which are to be found in this book, the writer finds comfort, as thousands before him, in His divine pity for the outcast and sinner. Society has vindicated itself towards this sinner and can afford to be Christian to his memory.'[11]

It was natural that the critics should regard the prison back-

[1] Ross. *Robert Ross. Friend of Friends*, 99, 100. A plaque was erected by the London County Council and unveiled by Sir Compton Mackenzie on the centenary of Wilde's birth, October 16, 1954. On this occasion Mr Laurence Housman sent the following message, which was read out at the unveiling ceremony: 'I am very glad that this memorial meeting is being held for so good a purpose. Oscar Wilde was incomparably the best talker I have ever met. But he was not only the best talker, he was also the most courteous and the most charming. His unhapppy fate has done the world a signal service in defeating the blind obscurantists: he has made people think. Far more people of intelligence think differently today because of him. And when he wrote his *Ballad of Reading Gaol* he not only gave the world a beautiful poem but a much needed lesson in good will, pity, pardon and understanding for the down-and-out': *The Times*, October 18, 1954.

[2] *Daily Mail*, February 23, 1905.

[3] *Star*, id.

[4] *Eastern Daily News*, February 24.

[5] *Morning Leader*, February 24.

[6] *Vanity Fair*, March 2.

[7] *Saturday Review*, March 4.

[8] *Speaker*, March 4.

[9] *Morning Leader*, March 11.

[10] *Independent Review*, April.

[11] *Westminster Gazette*, February 23.

ground of *De Profundis* as tragic. 'We see him here as the spectator of his own tragedy', wrote Max Beerbohm. 'His tragedy was great. It is one of the tragedies that will live always in romantic history.'[1] Only one critic, and a fellow-countryman of Wilde's who had unsuccessfully tried to get up a petition for his release, could not accept this conventional view. This was Bernard Shaw. 'It is really an extraordinary book', he wrote in a private letter to Ross at the time, 'quite exhilarating and amusing as to Wilde himself and quite disgraceful and shameful to his stupid tormentors. There is pain in it, inconvenience, annoyance, but no real tragedy, all comedy. The unquenchable spirit of the man is magnificent: he maintains his position and puts society squalidly in the wrong—rubs into them every insult and humiliation he endured—comes out the same man he went in—with stupendous success. The little aside in which, after writing several pages with undisguised artistic enjoyment and detachment, he remarks that they have been feeding him satisfactorily of late, is irresistible. It annoys me to have people degrading the whole affair to the level of sentimental tragedy.'[2]

Although the MS had been shown to both the English and German publishers, doubts were expressed in certain quarters as to its genuineness. Among others a well-known French writer openly hinted that it was a forgery by Ross or at least a synthesis of letters written by Wilde to his friend at various times. To remove these doubts, therefore, Ross had a facsimile reproduction made of part of one folio and after he had shown the original for purposes of comparison to Hamilton Fyfe, the editor of the *Daily Mirror*, the reproduction was published in that newspaper.[3]

The strongest criticism of the publishers for bringing out *De Profundis* came from clergy of the Church of England, since Messrs Metheun had published a good deal of religious literature and the idea that anything by Wilde should appear in the same list as their own works came as a shock to them. Dr W. Lock, the Warden of Keble College, Oxford, who was editing a theological book for Methuen, was strongly pressed to withdraw from the editorship, but to his credit refused to do so.

[1] See below, Appendix C. [2] Ross. *Robert Ross. Friend of Friends*, 111.
[3] March 13, 1905. Also reproduced in Mason, 448–9. The reproduction was of the first page of folio 14.

Another of Methuen's authors, and a contemporary of Algernon Methuen at Oxford, the Rev H. C. Beeching, Canon of Westminster, went so far as to denounce *De Profundis* as containing 'a doctrine of devils' in a sermon which he preached in Westminster Abbey. When he heard that Methuen was now contemplating the further publication of a collected edition of Wilde's works, likewise to be edited by Ross, the Canon was horrified and admonished the publisher in the strongest language to 'think better' of it. Methuen's answer to this remonstrance was apt. 'It is quite clear that the spirit of the Spanish Inquisition is not yet defunct', he told Canon Beeching. 'I am not sure', this Christian clergyman rejoined, 'that the Spanish Inquisition would not have been well occupied in burning O[scar] W[ilde]. He would have made a good blaze.'[1]

Before finally making up his mind, the publisher took the advice of J. A. Spender, whom he regarded as a cool-headed man 'of excellent taste and great caution'. Methuen first informed this editor of the qualitative test which he proposed to apply. Spender answered as follows:

The Westminster Gazette,
Tudor Street, E.C.
May 5, 1905.

Dear Mr. Methuen,

Your own method of deciding the question seems to me perfectly sound—not to publish anything that you think indecent, but not to be prevented by any clamour from publishing what you think sound and fine.

If Oscar Wilde had been dead a hundred years instead of seven years, no one would dream of objecting to the publication of good work which he had done because of the scandal of his life. Literature has its rights in these matters, and if a man has done ill in one way, he may at least be allowed to make amends in another, e.g. by giving us good literature. Canon Beeching's objection would go hard with some of the ancients and Elizabethans whom he loves, but I cannot think he will press his point. There seems to me to be a kind of cruelty in bottling up the good things that a man did because we judge him to have been a sinner in other respects.

I understand the objection of the Christian preacher to certain pages in *De Profundis,* though I cannot think the total effect of that book other than quite wholesome, but I confess I don't under-

[1] Original correspondence in the possession of Methuen & Co. Ltd.

stand the objection to publishing what is, *ex hypothesi*, good and sound.

Yours sincerely,
J. A. SPENDER

Fortunately Spender's sensible advice was acted upon by the publisher. Meanwhile *De Profundis* continued to sell well, five further editions being printed in the same year. With its inclusion in the First Collected Edition of Wilde's works, published in 1908, Ross restored those passages which had been omitted from his original draft, but which had appeared in the German edition of Max Meyerfeld, together with a selection of Wilde's prison letters. It is clear, however, from the prefatory dedication to Dr Meyerfeld which Ross wrote for this new edition, that he had no intention of publishing the remainder, much of which he rightly pointed out was taken up with business and private matters 'of no interest whatever' to the public. On one point he was able to give a specific assurance about the unpublished portion. 'Contrary to a general impression,' he stated, 'it contains nothing scandalous.'

In November, 1909 Robert Ross presented the MS of *De Profundis* to the British Museum on the understanding that it should be kept sealed up and not shown to the public for fifty years, at the end of which period he considered that there would be no objection to inspection or publication of the whole, since presumably everyone mentioned in it would be dead. The gift was accepted by the Trustees subject to this condition.

2

The MS might well have lain undisturbed safely under lock and key in the British Museum until 1960, without the public having any inkling of the contents of the unpublished parts, had not the accident of a libel action suddenly necessitated the production of the MS in court within a few years of Ross's handing it over to the Museum authorities. It came about in this way. Mr Arthur Ransome, who was then a young author, wrote a book on Wilde, mainly from the literary point of view, which he called *Oscar Wilde: A Critical Study*. This work was published in 1912. In its composition the author received considerable information from Robert Ross, to whom the book was dedicated. In his preface to the edition of *De Profundis*, which appeared in the First Collected Edition of Wilde's works in 1908, Ross had revealed that the friend to whom the book had been cast in the form of a letter was not himself, as had been generally assumed when the first edition appeared three years previously, but he gave no clue as to the friend's identity. It remained for Mr Ransome to reveal the secret four years later. The letter, he observed, was addressed to 'a man to whom Wilde felt that he owed some, at least, of the circumstances of his public disgrace. It was begun as a rebuke to this friend, whose actions, even subsequent to the trials, had been such as to cause Wilde considerable pain.'[1] Although Mr Ransome did not refer to the friend anywhere in the book by name, his reference to him, particularly in connexion with their reunion in Naples, left no doubt in the mind of many readers that the individual in question was Lord Alfred Douglas.

Douglas promptly issued writs for libel against the author, publisher and printer, and likewise against The Times Book Club, which had circulated the book amongst its subscribers. Before the action came to trial, the publisher, who apologised and withdrew the book from circulation, and the printer, who also apologised, dropped out of the case. But the other two defendants considered that they had a good defence. Here we are only concerned with the author. Mr Ransome pleaded justification, that is to say that the statements complained of were true in substance and in fact. In support of this plea he largely relied on Wilde's statements about Douglas's behaviour in the unpublished parts of *De Profundis*, which Ross now caused the British Museum authorities to produce. An authenticated copy of the complete MS was supplied to the plaintiff for the purposes of the trial, and he was subsequently shown the original in court, which he admitted to be in Wilde's handwriting, but added that he had never received a copy of it before the present trial.

The main interest in the trial, which began before Mr Justice Darling and a special jury in the King's Bench Division of the High Court of Justice on April 17, 1913, consisted in the reading by Mr Ransome's counsel of passages from the MS, for the purpose of putting them to Douglas in cross-examination. These passages, which were published more or less in full by *The Times* in its report of the trial, amounted to a considerable

[1] Ransome, *op. cit.*, 157.

portion, although not the whole, of the unpublished parts.[1] However, there is no doubt that, consisting as they did of a devastating attack on Douglas's character and conduct in his relations with Wilde, they created a strong impression in the minds of the jury and were largely responsible for their returning a verdict in favour of Mr Ransome, the jury finding that the words complained of constituted a libel but moreover were true.[2] The MS was thereupon returned to the British Museum.

Shortly before he lost this action, Douglas had begun to write a book, giving his own version of his friendship with Wilde, which he proposed to call *Oscar Wilde and Myself* and which in fact eventually appeared under that title. He now let it be known that he intended to include in it the unpublished portions of *De Profundis* with his personal comments. Since the unpublished as well as the published parts were protected under British copyright law, Ross had no difficulty in obtaining an injunction against Douglas's English publishers. The situation was otherwise in America, where the unpublished parts were unprotected. Unless they could first be registered in that country, Douglas would be free to publish there and indeed to secure the American copyright for himself. To be effective, registration with the U.S. Library of Congress involved prior printing and publication. Fortunately Ross knew an American publisher, Mr Paul R. Reynolds of New York, who agreed to co-operate. The sole remaining typed copy, which had been made in 1897, was still in Ross's possession and this he sent over to New York by the first boat. From this typescript fifteen copies were hurriedly printed and bound, and the book was ready within ten days. So great was the hurry to prevent Douglas being able to secure the copyright that there was no time to send the proofs to Ross for correction, and the book consequently appeared with some errors and omissions. However, it served its purpose, and registration with the Congressional Library was duly effected by Reynolds on Ross's behalf.

The publisher then sent twelve of the copies to Ross in England, two having been deposited in the Library of Congress. The fifteenth copy he was obliged to exhibit for sale in his showroom to satisfy American copyright requirements. Hoping to

[1] *The Times*, April 18, 19, 22, 23, 1913.

[2] A detailed account of this trial has been given by the present writer in *Cases that Changed the Law* (1951), pp. 164–76.

discourage possible purchasers, he put a price of $500 on the volume which he considered prohibitive. To his surprise, however, a member of the public, whose identity remains unknown, walked into the showroom, paid the price and thus acquired this unique copy. Ross distributed the twelve copies which were sent to him, as gifts among a few intimate friends under pledge of secrecy and they are now regarded as collector's rarities.[1] He explained his action in a letter to Sir Edmund Gosse, a close friend, to whom he had given one of the twelve copies.[2] 'Apart from my natural wish to preserve the rights for the Wilde literary estate', he wrote to Gosse, 'I am obliged to consider the risk however small of the Queensberry family bringing an action against me for libel, as they could and might do, so I am informed. That is the only reason for any present secrecy. There is nothing in *De Profundis* that I do not want the whole world to know now.'

After Robert Ross's death in 1918, the typed copy of the original manuscript, which had been returned by the American publisher, came into the possession of Wilde's only surviving son, Mr Vyvyan Holland. It had previously been shown by Ross to Dr Max Meyerfeld, who published a German translation of the complete text in 1925.[3] A French translation by Henry Davray followed a year later.[4] In 1936, it was proposed to publish the complete version in English, and to this Lord Alfred Douglas agreed. But he later withdrew his consent, and the project had to be abandoned. Douglas's death in 1945 removed the final objection, and four years later the complete *De Profundis* at last appeared in generally accessible form in

[1] *The Suppressed Portion of 'De Profundis'. Now for the first time published by his Literary Executor Robert Ross* (Paul R. Reynolds, New York, 1913). Eleven copies, of which the present writer possesses one, were given by Ross to the following: Viscount Haldane, Sir Edmund Gosse, A. L. Humphreys, John Lane, More Adey, Algernon Methuen, G. E. Webster, Sir George Lewis, Stuart Mason, Martin Holman, and Vyvyan Holland. The twelfth copy, which Ross retained for himself, eventually passed after his death to the Clark Collection in the University of California, Los Angeles.

[2] This letter, dated October 21, 1913, which contains further interesting details of the American publication, together with Gosse's copy of the book, were subsequently acquired by the late Mr Walter Ledger for his unique collection of Wilde's works. Under his will, the collection, now known as the Robert Ross Memorial Collection, became the property of University College, Oxford. It is at present preserved in the Bodleian Library.

[3] Oscar Wilde. *Epistola in Carcere et Vinculis. Deutsch von Max Meyerfeld* (S. Fischer Verlag, Berlin, 1925).

[4] Oscar Wilde, *De Profundis. Precédé de lettres écrites de la prison par Oscar Wilde à Robert Ross. Traduits par Henry—D. Davray* (*Mercure de France*, Paris, 1926).

England, although there were still some omissions as well as a number of errors.[1] In introducing it to the general public Mr Holland observed that its author hoped that posterity, and even his enemies, might find some sympathy for him. 'In this tragic document he has, as he himself says, tried to explain his conduct without defending it. Let it rest at that.'[2]

3

In accordance with the terms of Robert Ross's bequest to the British Museum, the MS of *De Profundis* was officially opened to the public on January 1, 1960. This date fell on a Friday, and accordingly at nine o'clock in the morning of that day I presented myself at the Department of Manuscripts, where the twenty folios comprising the whole were placed in my hands. I was thus the first member of the public to be allowed to see the interesting and controversial document. In the following Sunday's edition of the London *Sunday Times*, I gave an account of the MS and the circumstances in which it was written and subsequently kept sealed up for half a century.[3]

It had been generally assumed that Mr Vyvyan Holland's edited version, published in 1949, was the complete text, as indeed it was so described in the title. However, examination of the original MS revealed that this version was neither complete nor wholly accurate. On the contrary, about a thousand words had been omitted by Ross from the typed copy on which the 1949 version was based; the latter was also seen to contain several hundred errors, which appear to have been occasioned by Ross's dictating from the original to a typist rather than letting her take a direct copy. Several passages were also inexplicably transposed in the typescript.

The omissions consisted almost entirely of those parts which might be considered particularly offensive to the Queensberry family. A typical example occurs in Wilde's description of Lord Queensberry's appearance in court during the trials.[4]

> I used to feel bitterly the irony and ignominy of my position when in the course of my three trials, beginning at the Police Court, I

[1] Oscar Wilde. *De Profundis. The Complete Text.* Edited, with an Introduction by Vyvyan Holland (London, 1949).
[2] *Op. cit.*, 12.
[3] *Sunday Times*, January 3, 1960. ('The De Profundis Affair')
[4] H–D, 492. This passage is on the second page of folio 15.

used to see your father bustling in and out in the hopes of attracting public attention, as if anyone could fail to note or remember the stableman's gait and dress, the bowed legs, the twitching hands, the hanging lower lip, the bestial and half-witted grin. Even when he was not there, or was out of sight, I used to feel conscious of his presence, and the blank dreary walls of the great Court-room, the very air itself, seemed to me at times to be hung with multitudinous masks of that apelike face.

As has already been noticed, in the composition of *De Profundis*, Wilde was supposed to have been issued with one folio sheet of prison writing paper at a time, which was removed from his cell at locking up for inspection by the prison Governor. But the sympathetic Major Nelson seems to have interpreted the Prison Commission's orders on this point with considerable latitude, since it would appear that each folio was subsequently returned to the prisoner for purposes of revision and continuity. Four of the folios (1, 2, 13 and 17) have every appearance of being fair copies, since unlike the rest they are almost entirely free from interlineations and corrections. Also, only two out of the twenty folios (apart from the last) finish at the end of a sentence. Furthermore, in his letter to Robert Ross, dated April 1, 1897, in which he gives directions for the copying of the MS, Wilde is so specific in his references to individual folios and in his quotations that, although he claims to be quoting 'from memory', it is difficult to credit such a claim, since the details are so literally accurate.

At all events, the so-called 'complete text', which appeared in 1949, has now been superseded by the authentic version, which Mr Rupert Hart-Davis verified from the MS in the British Museum and included in his definitive edition of *The Letters of Oscar Wilde*, first published in 1962.[1]

Thus concludes the epilogue to the long-drawn-out Wilde story. Any fresh assessment may well begin with Wilde's advice to Lord Alfred Douglas in the final paragraph of *De Profundis*.

Do not be afraid of the past. If people tell you it is irrevocable, do not believe them. The past, the present and the future are but one moment in the sight of God, in whose sight we should try to live. Time and space, succession and extension, are merely accidental

[1] H–D, 423–511.

conditions of Thought. The Imagination can transcend them, and move in a free sphere of ideal existences. Things, also, are in their essence what we choose to make them. A thing *is*, according to the mode in which one looks at it. 'Where others', says Blake, 'see but the Dawn coming over the hill, I see the sons of God shouting for joy.' What seemed to the world and to myself my future I lost irretrievably when I let myself be taunted into taking action against your father: had, I dare say, lost it really long before that. What lies before me is my past. I have got to make myself look on that with different eyes, to make the world look on it with different eyes, to make God look on it with different eyes. This I cannot do by ignoring it, or slighting it, or praising it, or denying it. It is only to be done by fully accepting it as an inevitable part of the evolution of my life and character: by bowing my head to everything that I have suffered.

APPENDIX A

PRISON REGULATIONS CONCERNING LETTERS AND VISITS[1]

The following regulations as to communication, by Visit or Letter, between Prisoners and their friends, are notified for the information of their correspondence.

The permission to write and receive Letters is given to Prisoners for the purpose of enabling them to keep up a connection with their respectable friends and not that they may be kept informed of public events.

All letters are read by the Prison Authorities. They must be legibly written, and not crossed. Any which are of an objectionable tendency, either to or from Prisoners, or containing slang, or improper expressions, will be suppressed.

Prisoners are permitted to receive and to write a Letter at intervals, which depend on the rules of the class they attain by industry and good conduct; but matters of special importance to a Prisoner may be communicated at any time by Letter (prepaid) to the Governor who will inform the Prisoner thereof, if expedient.

In case of misconduct, the privilege of receiving and writing a Letter may be forfeited for a time.

Money, Books, Postage Stamps, Food, Tobacco, Clothes etc., should not be sent to Prisoners, for their use in Prison, as nothing is allowed to be received at the Prison for that purpose.

Persons attempting to clandestinely communicate with, or to introduce any article to or for Prisoners, are liable to fine or imprisonment, and any Prisoner concerned in such practices is liable to be severely punished.

Prisoners' friends are sometimes applied to, by unauthorised persons to send Money, &c., to them privately, under pretence that they can apply it for the benefit of the Prisoners, and under such fraudulent pretence, such persons endeavour to obtain money for themselves.

[1] These regulations, which were in force during the period of Wilde's imprisonment, had been drawn up by the Prison Commissioners in 1887.

Any letter containing such an application, received by the friends of a Prisoner should be, at once, forwarded by them to the Governor.

Prisoners are allowed to receive Visits from their friends, according to rules at intervals, which depend on their class.

When visits are due to Prisoners, notification will be sent to the friends whom they desire to visit them.

APPENDIX B

PETITION OF LORD ALFRED DOUGLAS TO QUEEN VICTORIA[1]

Hotel de la Poste,
Rouen.
25th June, 1895.

Your Majesty,

In daring thus personally to address you, I will remind you that I am making use of an appeal which in former days your illustrious ancestors did not deny to the meanest of their subjects. I appeal to you to exercise your power of pardon in the case of Oscar Wilde, the poet essayist and dramatist who now lies in prison, unjustly convicted by the force of prejudice; a victim not to the righteous indignation of abstract Justice but rather to the spite and unscrupulous cunning of another man, the Marquis of Queensberry, whose son I have the misfortune to be. Your Majesty cannot be ignorant of the true character of this man, for he has not scrupled to speak of you in letters, which have been read in open court, in terms which not many years ago would have cost him his head or at least his liberty. Your Majesty will not have been deceived, as were the ignorant public, by his pretension to righteous motives, but will have seen that his sole object in attacking his son's friend was to dishonour that son and to add yet more misery, shame and sorrow to the load which he had already heaped on the head of the gentle unfortunate lady who was his wife.

Most gracious lady, your heart is kind and tender, and even in these latter days the arm of the Queen is strong. Will you not save this man, who even if he be guilty has already been punished more, a thousand times more cruelly than he deserves, seeing that in addition to the ruin of his life, the destruction of his art and the loss of every worldly possession, he has been condemned to a sentence which the highest authorities have declared to be equivalent to a sentence of 'death or madness', and which has been unanimously condemned as

[1] Home Office Papers. On June 29, 1895, the Queen's Private Secretary, Mr Arthur Bigge (later Lord Stamfordham) wrote to the Home Secretary's Private Secretary from Windsor Castle: 'I have opened this letter which Her Majesty has *not* seen, and forward it to be dealt with as the Secretary of State may direct.' The Home Secretary, Sir Mathew Ridley, saw the Petition on July 3, and next day a formal letter of rejection was sent on his instructions to Lord Alfred Douglas.

inhuman by the Prison Commission which has just recently laid its report before Your Majesty's Court?

In the hope that Your Majesty, remembering how my ancestors have served your ancestors on many fields and in many councils, will not utterly scorn my humble petition and will pardon the boldness and presumption which have led me in my extreme despair to address you, I am Your Majesty's most loyal and most humble servant,

ALFRED BRUCE DOUGLAS

APPENDIX C

'A LORD OF LANGUAGE'

By (Sir) MAX BEERBOHM[1]

There was a coincidence last week in London. An exhibition of Whistler's paintings was opened, and a book by Oscar Wilde was published; and all the critics are writing, and the gossips gossiping, very glibly, about the greatness of Whistler, and about the greatness of Oscar Wilde. Whistler during the 'seventies and 'eighties, and Oscar Wilde during the 'eighties and early 'nineties, cut very prominent figures in London; and both were by the critics and the gossips regarded merely as clever *farceurs*. Both, apart from their prominence, were doing serious work; but neither was taken at all seriously. Neither was thanked. Whistler got a farthing damages, Oscar Wilde two years' hard labour. None of the critics or gossips took exception to either verdict. Time has rolled on. Both men are dead. A subtly apocalyptic thing, for critics and gossips (especially in England), is the tomb; and praises are by envious humanity sung the more easily when there is no chance that they will gratify the subjects of them. And so, very glibly, very blandly, we are all magnifying the two men whom we so lately belittled. M. Rodin was brought over to open the Whistler exhibition. Perhaps the nation will now commission him to do a statue of Oscar Wilde. *Il ne manque que ça.*

Some of the critics, wishing to reconcile present enthusiasm with past indifference, or with past obloquy, have been suggesting that 'De Profundis' is quite unlike any previous work of Oscar Wilde—a quite sudden and unrelated phenomenon. Oscar Wilde, according to them, was gloriously transformed by incarceration. Their theory comprises two fallacies. The first fallacy is that Oscar Wilde had been mainly remarkable for his wit. In point of fact, wit was the least important of his gifts. Primarily, he was a poet, with a life-long passion for beauty; and a philosopher, with a life-long passion for thought. His wit, and his humour (which was of an even finer quality than his wit), sprang from a very solid basis of seriousness, as all good wit or humour must. They were not essential to his genius; and, had they happened not to have been there at all, possibly his genius would, even while he himself was flourishing, have been recognised in Eng-

[1] From *Vanity Fair*, March 2, 1905. Not hitherto republished.

land, where wisdom's passport is dullness, and gaiety of manner damns. The right way of depreciating Oscar Wilde would have been to say that, beautiful and profound though his ideas were, he never was a real person in contact with realities. He created his poetry, created his philosophy: neither sprang from his own soul, or from his own experience. His ideas were for the sake of ideas, his emotions for the sake of emotions. This, I take it, is just what Mr. Robert Ross means, when, in his admirable introduction to 'De Profundis' he speaks of Oscar Wilde as a man of 'highly intellectual and artificial nature'. Herein, too, I find the key to an old mystery: why Oscar Wilde so saliently original a man, was so much influenced by the work of other writers; and why he, than whom none was more fertile in invention, did sometimes stoop to plagiarism. If an idea was beautiful or profound, he cared not what it was, nor whether it was his or another's. In 'De Profundis' was he, at length, expressing something that he really and truly felt? Is the book indeed a heart-cry? It is pronounced so by the aforesaid critics. There we have the second fallacy.

I think no discerning reader can but regard the book as essentially the artistic essay of an artist. Nothing seemed more likely than that Oscar Wilde, smitten down from his rosy-clouded pinnacle, and dragged through the mire, and cast among the flints, would be *diablement changé en route*. Yet lo! he was unchanged. He was still precisely himself. He was still playing with ideas, playing with emotions. 'There is only one thing left for me now,' he writes, 'absolute humility.' And about humility he writes many beautiful and true things. And, doubtless, while he wrote them, he had the sensation of humility. Humble he was not. Emotion was not seeking outlet: emotion came through its own expression. The artist spoke, and the man obeyed. The attitude was struck, and the heart pulsated to it. Perhaps a Cardinal Archbishop, when he kneels to wash the feet of the beggars, is filled with humility, and revels in the experience. Such was Oscar Wilde's humility. It was the luxurious complement of pride. In 'De Profundis', for the most part, he is frankly proud—proud with the natural pride of a man so richly endowed as he, and arrogant with all his old peculiar arrogance. Even 'from the depths' he condescended. Not merely for mankind was he condescending. He enjoyed the greater luxury of condescending to himself. Sometimes the condescension was from his present self to his old self: sometimes from his old self to his present self. Referring to the death of his mother, 'I, once a lord of language,' he says, 'have no words in which to express my anguish and my shame'. Straightway, he proceeds to revel in the survival of that lordship, and refutes in a fine passage his own dramatic plea of impotence. 'She and my father had bequeathed to me a name they had made noble and honoured. . . . I had disgraced that name eternally. I had made it a low byword among low people.

I had given it to brutes that they might make it brutal, and to fools that they might turn it into folly. What I suffered then, and still then, is not for pen to write or paper to record.' Yet pen wrote it, and paper recorded it, even so. And sorrow was turned to joy by the 'lord of language'.

'A lord of language.' Certainly that was no idle boast. Fine as are the ideas and emotions in 'De Profundis', it is the actual writing—the mastery of prose—that most delights me. Except Ruskin in his prime, no modern writer has achieved through prose the limpid and lyrical effects that were achieved by Oscar Wilde. One does not seem to be reading a written thing. The words sing. There is nothing of that formality, that hard and cunning precision, which marks so much of the prose that we admire, and rightly admire. The meaning is artificial, but the expression is always magically natural and beautiful. The simple words seem to grow together like flowers. In his use of rhyme and metre, Oscar Wilde was academic—never at all decadent, by the way, as one critic has suggested. But the prose of 'Intentions' and of his plays, and of his fairy-stories, was perfect in its lively and unstudied grace. It is a joy to find in this last prose of his the old power, all unmarred by the physical and mental torments that he had suffered.

Oscar Wilde was immutable. The fineness of the book as a personal document is in the revelation of a character so strong that no force of circumstance could change it, or even modify it. In prison Oscar Wilde was still himself—still with the same artistry in words, still with the same detachment from life. We see him here as the spectator of his own tragedy. His tragedy was great. It is one of the tragedies that will live always in romantic history. And the protagonist had an artist's joy in it. Be sure that in the dock of the Old Bailey, in his cell at Reading, on 'the centre platform of Clapham Junction', where he stood 'in convict dress, and handcuffed, for the world to look at', even while he suffered he was consoled by the realisation of his sufferings and of the magnitude of his tragedy. Looking joyously forward to his release, 'I hope', he says, 'to be able to recreate my creative faculty'. It is a grim loss to our literature that the creative faculty, which prison-life had not yet extinguished in him, did not long survive his liberation. But, broken as he was thereafter, and powerless, and aimless, the invincible artist in him must have had pleasure in contemplation of himself draining the last bitter dregs of the cup that Fate had thrust on him.

APPENDIX D

'DE PROFUNDIS'

By 'A' (LORD ALFRED DOUGLAS)[1]

In a painful passage in this interesting posthumous book (it takes the form of a letter to an unnamed friend), Oscar Wilde relates how, on November the 13th, 1895, he stood for half an hour on the platform of Clapham Junction, handcuffed and in convict dress, surrounded by an amused and jeering mob. 'For a year after that was done to me,' he writes, 'I wept every day at the same hour and for the same space of time.' That was before he had discovered or thought he had discovered that his terrible experiences in prison, his degradation and shame were a part, and a necessary part, of his artistic life, a completion of his incomplete soul. After he had learnt humility in the bitterest school that 'man's inhumanity to man' provides for unwilling scholars, after he had drained the cup of sorrow to the dregs, after his spirit was broken—he wrote this book in which he tried to persuade himself and others that he had learnt by suffering and despair what life and pleasure had never taught him.

If Oscar Wilde's spirit, returning to this world in a malicious mood, had wished to devise a pleasant and insinuating trap for some of his old enemies of the press, he could scarcely have hit on a better one than this book. I am convinced it was written in passionate sincerity at the time, and yet it represents a mere mood and an unimportant one of the man who wrote it, a mood too which does not even last through the 250 pages of the book. 'The English are very fond of a man who admits he has been wrong,' he makes one of his characters in 'An Ideal Husband' say, and elsewhere in this book he compares the advantages of pedestals and pillories in their relation to the public's attitude towards himself. Well here he is in the pillory, and here also is Mr. Courtney in the 'Daily Telegraph' getting quite fond of him for the very first time. Here is Oscar Wilde, 'a genius', 'incontestably one of the greatest dramatists of modern times' as he is now graciously allowed to be, turning up unexpectedly with an admission that he was in the wrong, and telling us that his life and his art would have been incomplete without his imprisonment, that he has learnt humility and found a new mode of expression in suffering. He

[1] From the *Motorist and Traveller*, March 1, 1905.

is 'purged by grief,' 'chastened by suffering,' and everything, in short, that he should be, and Mr. Courtney is touched and pleased. What Mr. Courtney and others have failed to realise, and what Wilde himself did realise very soon after he wrote this interesting but rather pathetically ineffective book, is that the mood which produced it was no other than the first sympton of that mental and physical disease generated by suffering and confinement which culminated in the death of its gifted and unfortunate author a few years later. As long as the spirit of revolt was left in Oscar Wilde, so long as left the fire of creative genius. When the spirit of revolt died, the flame began to subside, and continued to subside gradually with spasmodic flickers till its ultimate extinction. 'I have got to make everything that has happened good for me.' He writes, 'The plank bed, the loathsome food, the hard rope shredded into oakum till one's finger tips grow dull with pain, the menial offices with which each day begins, the harsh orders that routine seems to necessitate, the dreadful dress that makes sorrow grotesque to look at, the silence, the solitude, the shame—each and all these things I have to transform into a spiritual experience. There is not a single degradation of the body which I must not try and make into a spiritualising of the soul.' But, alas! plank beds, loathsome food, menial offices, and oakum picking do not spiritualise the soul; at any rate, they did not spiritualise Oscar Wilde's soul. The only effect they had was to destroy his magnificent intellect, and even, as some passages in this book show to temporarily cloud his superb sense of humour. The return of freedom gave him back the sense of humour, and the wreck of his magnificent intellect served him so well to the end of his life that, although he had hopelessly lost the power of concentration necessary to the production of literary work, he remained to the day of his death the most brilliant and the most intellectual talker in Europe.

It must not be supposed, however, that this book is not a remarkable book and one which is not worth careful reading. There are fine prose passages in it, and occasional felicities of phrase which recall the Oscar Wilde of 'The House of Pomegranates' and the 'Prose-Poems', and here and there rather unexpectedly comes an epigram like this for example: 'There were Christians before Christ. For that we should be grateful. The unfortunate thing is that there have been none since.' True, he spoils the epigram by adding, 'I make one exception, St. Francis of Assisi.' A concession to the tyranny of facts and the relative importance of sincerity to type, which is most uncharacteristic of the 'old Oscar'. Nevertheless, the trace of the master hand is still visible, and the book contains much that is profound and subtle on the philosophy of Christ as conceived by this modern evangelist of the gospel of Life and Literature. One does not travel further than the 33rd page of the book before finding glaring and startling inconsistencies in the mental attitude of the writer towards his fate, for whereas on page 18 in a rather rhetorical passage he speaks of the 'eternal disgrace' he had brought on the 'noble and honoured name' bequeathed him by his father and mother, on page 33 'Reason' tells him 'that the laws under which he was convicted are wrong and unjust laws, and the system under which he has suffered a wrong and unjust system'. But this is the spirit of revolt not quite crushed. He says that if he had been released a year sooner, as in fact he very nearly was, he would have left his prison full of rage and bitterness, and without the treasure of his new-found 'Humility'. I am unregenerate enough to wish that he had brought his rage and bitterness with him out of prison. True, he would never have written this book if he had come out of prison a year sooner, but he would almost certainly have written several more incomparable comedies, and we who reverenced him as a great artist in words, and mourned his downfall as an irreparable blow to English Literature would have been spared the rather painful experience of reading the posthumous praise now at last so lavishly given to what certainly cannot rank within measurable distance of his best work.

APPENDIX E

LETTERS FROM WARDER MARTIN TO ROBERT SHERARD[1]

R. H. Sherard dedicated his *Life of Oscar Wilde,* which appeared in 1906 and was the first of many biographies of Wilde, to 'T. M.', as having, 'in the extreme of adversity, proved himself the true friend of an unhappy man'. These initials concealed the identity of the former Warder Thomas Martin of Reading Gaol, who had Wilde under his charge towards the end of his sentence and who was subsequently dismissed from the prison service in the circumstances described above.[2] To this work Martin also contributed anonymously the remarkable chapter entitled 'The Poet in Prison'. Shortly afterwards Martin lost touch with Sherard and remained out of touch wth him for over 25 years. They resumed their correspondence in 1933. The following extracts are from the letters Martin wrote to Sherard in his last years. He died in 1939.[3]

Norwich,
January 23, 1937.

. . . I notice that on one page you assume that I may have posted a letter for Oscar.[4] This I never did. In the first place he never asked me, and if he had I certainly should have refused. It is always dangerous to post letters for prisoners, as their friends, when writing back, are likely to mention something or other which the prisoner had said in his letter which was posted surreptitiously. And as official copies are always taken of prisoners' letters, this would soon be discovered.

No, if anybody posted letters for Oscar, it was Major Nelson himself. I am certain that he received letters, addressed to himself, for Oscar and these he would deliver personally and wait in the cell until they were read, then bring the letters away with him, but sometimes forgetting the envelope.

Oscar, when short of paper, would sometimes use one of these envelopes to write one of his notes on, which he passed under the door to me. I sent Ross several of them.[5]

[1] In the possession of Mrs A. M. Sherard.
[2] See above, p. 116. [3] See above, p. 151, note 1.
[4] The reference is to a statement to this effect in his *Bernard Shaw, Frank Harris and Oscar Wilde* (1937), at p. 221.
[5] See above, p. 107, and note.

I know for a positive fact that the Governor infringed the rules of the prison (in regard to Oscar) quite as much as I did—who got the sack! Only last year a presentation copy of *The Ballad of Reading Gaol*, with Major Nelson's name inscribed, was sold at Sotheby's and fetched over £70.[1]

Wilde, during the last few weeks of his imprisonment, received several letters and visits from his solicitors. His solicitors were Stoker and Hansell of Lincoln's Inn. I cannot recall seeing their names in any of your books.

Aug. 25, 1938.

. . . I can say without fear of contradiction that there were no female nurses in male prisons at that period. In convict establishments there were a few (but only a few) male nurses. They were assisted by orderlies (convicts), who were usually doctors by profession. In the local prisons (especially the smaller ones, such as Reading) a warder was detailed off for the purpose of watching over them [i.e. sick prisoners] in the hospital, which was only a small room. He had a prisoner with him (a trusty) who did the necessary work.

Oscar's experience of picking up crumbs (and he soon became an adept at the job) was due entirely to my severe admonitions. A single crumb of contraband food found in a cell would have transformed the whole prison staff into Sherlock Holmes's.

The note which he asked me to deliver to the young prisoner, who was located in another block, and which I tore up, was merely a request from him to call at the Post Office and ask for a letter, and he would find a little money in it which would help him. I told the youth verbally what Oscar had said in the note and several months afterwards I was glancing through the pages of a new penny weekly journal (I have forgotten its name) when I noticed a headline entitled: 'Curious Letters from Oscar Wilde'. On reading through I learned that the two letters quoted were written from Berneval to this youth, who wanted to sell them. The contents, though not compromising, were indiscreet, and I wrote to Oscar immediately and advised him to be more careful. [2]

[1] Martin is inaccurate here. This copy was sold, together with the MS letter to Major Nelson quoted above at p. 149, at Sotheby's, on December 17, 1929. The price for the two items as one lot was £175.

[2] In a letter dated May 31, 1937, to A. J. A. Symons, who was collecting material for a book on Wilde, Sherard remarked: 'If you have got into touch with Martin, find out about the prisoners in Reading, whom O. W. admired and with whom he carried on a surreptitious correspondence, getting Martin to "shove" notes under the doors of their cells.' (Communicated by Mr G. F. Sims.) Sherard's inference was mistaken: see following letter.

Sept. 12th, 1938.

. . . In regard to the other subject of your letter, I may say that I have no knowledge whatever of Oscar having indulged in any such [homosexual] practices as you mention.

I am well aware that in convict prisons especially this vice is prevalent. When I was at Dartmoor, I heard the warders speak about it. In fact these sexual problems presented a never-ceasing worry to the officials and necessitated constant vigilance. For instance, two prisoners were never allowed to be left alone together. It was a sure 'half-sheet' for the warder in charge and a subsequent heavy fine, if a principal warder made the discovery. The food restrictions, in a great measure, are due to reasons of sexual psychology.

In regard to Oscar, I never heard his name mentioned in connection with anything of the sort. And the subject never once entered my mind until I read your letter this morning. Of course, it would be absolutely impossible for me to state definitely and emphatically that he did not. I never did night-duty in the prison. Oscar was generally sound asleep at six a.m. when I opened his cell door; and from that time until I went off duty in the evening he spent the day reading or writing in his cell, exercising in the yard or pacing his cell—which he generally did in the evenings. About once or twice a week (I cannot now recall how frequently) I would be on duty until eight o'clock in the evening. On these occasions I noticed that Oscar was pacing the cell. He was allowed the privilege of having the gas burning and I know he remained up as late as possible.

No, if I were you I should taboo this subject altogether.[1] Nothing of a downright, convincing unassailable declaration could be made either way; and I am sure Oscar would feel annoyed at this kind of publicity. You see I write as a Spiritualist, who believes that those who have passed over know what is going on in the world they have left. . . .

Sept. 16th, 1938.

. . . In regard to Frank Harris's stuff, it is on the whole well written from a literary point of view.[2] But the portions relating to Oscar's prison experiences are to me incomprehensible. Of course, everyone will agree that to one of Oscar's temperament and upbringing confinement in a prison—or indeed in any institution—would be the more heart-breaking than it would be to the average individual. That goes without saying. Had he enlisted in the Army

[1] Sherard proposed to deal with this in a book he was writing by way of reply to the Preface, which Bernard Shaw had contributed to the English edition of Frank Harris's biography of Wilde. The book, which he entitled *Ultima Verba*, was never published. The original typescript is now in my possession.

[2] The English edition of *Oscar Wilde*, by Frank Harris, with a Preface by Bernard Shaw, was published in 1938.

on leaving Oxford, he would have found military life quite as unendurable. Had he been sent down a Welsh coal mine, he would have committed suicide at the first opportunity.

But apart from the well-known and recognized sufferings which prison life involves, I cannot altogether accept as Gospel some of the awful stories told by Frank Harris. For instance, I cannot conceive of a warder bringing a prisoner out of his cell for the mere sake of changing his shoes! It is ridiculous. Warders at that period hadn't got the time to spare to double their work in any such silly way. Besides, to have left a prisoner unattended in a corridor would have invoked a severe reprimand from the powers that be. No warder would have risked it.

Then there is the story of Oscar falling off his bed when he was dressing! As the 'beds' were on the floor, he would not have far to fall! Then there is the attitude of the doctor. Now can anyone imagine a medical man speaking to anyone, whether a prisoner or a pauper, in the manner described? It is too ridiculous for words. In short, if I were to wade through these prison stories one by one, the word 'ridiculous' would be worn threadbare.

Next, we are given the story of that unprecedented interview with Oscar in the prison, where Frank Harris has *carte-blanche* rights (bestowed on him by the Home Secretary) to enter the prison, see a prisoner (without a warder being present) and ask what questions he likes! During this poignant interview the tears literally roll down Oscar's cheeks—a man close on forty years of age or perhaps a little over. It may be true, but for the life of me I cannot visualise it.

Next, the question of Oscar's release comes up. Now, if the Home Secretary had been in any way anxious over this matter, a hint to the prison doctor would have done the trick, and no embarrassing questions could have ensued.

My opportunities of conversing with Oscar at any length seldom occurred, which accounts for my being unable to furnish any information regarding his prison life before I met him. But I will say this. He never struck me as being any more depressed than one would naturally expect.

As I have indicated in previous correspondence to you, our talks were mainly confined to general subjects. Seldom, indeed, did he ever border on the personal. But I remember just about a week or so before his sentence expired he was anxious to know to what address he could write to me; at the same time he gave me, on a piece of paper, his new name, also the names and address of his solicitors.

'Mr Wilde,' I said, 'I hope you will not mar our friendship by sending me any money?'

'My dear man,' he replied, 'I haven't got any money, and if I had it would have to be so considerable that I could endow you with sufficient to justify you in throwing up your depressing job. You are far too intelligent for a prison warder. But if I cannot do what I would like in that way, let me give you some valuable advice. Read more, study more. Read Emerson, Carlyle, Meredith. And if you ever think of writing—first study the poets.'

'I suppose you will go to some of your friends?' I ventured.

'Yes,' he returned, 'but only because I have nowhere else to go. I should like to be able to go into a nice house, but failing that I should like to get away from everybody and live with you. But I know how impossible that is. When one has been unfortunate, everything which is good is so remote—so impossible.'

And so saying, he turned his head away.

Index